Information and Democracy

Around the world, there are increasing concerns about the accuracy of media coverage. It is vital in representative democracies that citizens have access to reliable information about what is happening in government policy so that they can form meaningful preferences and hold politicians accountable. Yet much research and conventional wisdom questions whether the necessary information is available, consumed, and understood. This study is the first large-scale empirical investigation into the frequency and reliability of media coverage in five policy domains, and it provides tools that can be exported to other areas, in the United States and elsewhere. Examining decades of government spending, media coverage, and public opinion in the United States, this book assesses the accuracy of media coverage and measures its direct impact on citizens' preferences for policy. This innovative study has far-reaching implications for those studying and teaching politics as well as for reporters and citizens.

Stuart N. Soroka is Professor of Communication at the University of California, Los Angeles, and Adjunct Research Professor in the Center for Political Studies at the University of Michigan.

Christopher Wlezien is Hogg Professor of Government, Department of Government, University of Texas at Austin.

Editor

W. Lance Bennett, University of Washington
Founding Co-Editor, Emeritus
Robert M. Entman, The George Washington University

Politics and relations among individuals in societies across the world are being transformed by new technologies for targeting individuals and sophisticated methods for shaping personalized messages. The new technologies challenge boundaries of many kinds – between news, information, entertainment, and advertising; between media, with the arrival of the World Wide Web; and even between nations. Communication, Society and Politics probes the political and social impacts of these new communication systems in national, comparative, and global perspective.

Other Books in the Series

Erik Albæk, Arjen van Dalen, Nael Jebril, and Claes de Vreese, *Political Journalism in Comparative Perspective*

Eva Anduiza, Michael James Jensen, and Laia Jorba, eds., *Digital Media and Political Engagement Worldwide: A Comparative Study*

C. Edwin Baker, *Media Concentration and Democracy: Why Ownership Matters*

C. Edwin Baker, *Media, Markets, and Democracy*

W. Lance Bennett and Robert M. Entman, eds., *Mediated Politics: Communication in the Future of Democracy*

Rodney Benson, *Shaping Immigration News: A French-American Comparison*

Bruce Bimber, *Information and American Democracy: Technology in the Evolution of Political Power*

Bruce Bimber, Andrew Flanagin, and Cynthia Stohl, *Collective Action in Organizations: Interaction and Engagement in an Era of Technological Change*

Clifford G. Christians, *Media Ethics and Global Justice in the Digital Age*

Lynn S. Clark and Regina Marchi, *Young People and the Future of News*

Peter Dahlgren, *Media and Political Engagement, Citizens, Communication and Democracy*

Murray Edelman, *The Politics of Misinformation*

Frank Esser and Barbara Pfetsch, eds., *Comparing Political Communication: Theories, Cases, and Challenges*

(continued after the Index)

Information and Democracy

Public Policy in the News

STUART N. SOROKA

University of California, Los Angeles

CHRISTOPHER WLEZIEN

University of Texas at Austin

CAMBRIDGE
UNIVERSITY PRESS

CAMBRIDGE
UNIVERSITY PRESS

University Printing House, Cambridge CB2 8BS, United Kingdom

One Liberty Plaza, 20th Floor, New York, NY 10006, USA

477 Williamstown Road, Port Melbourne, VIC 3207, Australia

314–321, 3rd Floor, Plot 3, Splendor Forum, Jasola District Centre,
New Delhi – 110025, India

103 Penang Road, #05–06/07, Visioncrest Commercial, Singapore 238467

Cambridge University Press is part of the University of Cambridge.

It furthers the University's mission by disseminating knowledge in the pursuit of
education, learning, and research at the highest international levels of excellence.

www.cambridge.org
Information on this title: www.cambridge.org/9781108491341
DOI: 10.1017/9781108868242

First published 2022

A catalogue record for this publication is available from the British Library.

ISBN 978-1-108-49134-1 Hardback
ISBN 978-1-108-81189-7 Paperback

Contents

Figures

Tables

Preface

Media are critical to representative democracy. This is well known and acknowledged throughout modern political history, from the founding of democratic republics to the present day. Information about government policy and performance is central to effective accountability and control. Indeed, it is difficult to imagine how large-scale democracy would work without reasonably accurate media coverage of current affairs.

It is of some significance, then, that we are in the midst of both public and scholarly debate about the nature and quality of media coverage in the United States and elsewhere. The current academic debate is fueled by several factors. There is a growing body of work on journalists' misrepresentation – and the public's corresponding misunderstanding – of scientific issues such as global warming and vaccinations. There is a burgeoning literature on selective exposure and motivated reasoning suggesting that even were media coverage to portray issues accurately, exposure and interpretation of that information would be subject to a range of preexisting biases, and that this is enhanced in an increasing high-choice media environment. There also are concerns about an increasingly polarized electorate, which may enhance the likely impact of selective exposure and the systematically biased media coverage that may accompany it (bearing in mind that producers of the latter have an incentive to cater to the former).

Consternation over the accuracy of American media news reached a fevered pitch in the wake of the 2016 US presidential election, the loose interpretation of facts by the Trump administration including contestation of the 2020 election results, and ongoing claims of and concerns about "fake news." There have been few moments since the rise of modern media during which information about current affairs was so suspect, not just by the public but by media professionals and academics as well.

The current climate in the United States is in some ways relatively unique. The availability of inaccurate information is *not* one of those ways, however. There have of course been other periods of heightened concern about media accuracy, during the Vietnam and Gulf Wars, for instance. There are long-standing concerns about media accuracy on a broad range of policy issues as well, including climate change, health care, and taxes. There *always* has been variation in the quality and accuracy of media coverage across issues and media outlets and over time, and there has *always* been accurate and inaccurate information about public policy. There is accordingly a rich body of work, with well-developed theories and models, that can help us examine instances in which media have facilitated or inhibited representative democracy.

This observation is the starting point for the work that follows. Our intention is partly to respond to very current concerns about the state of public affairs, especially the role that mass and social media currently play in connecting public preferences and policymaking in representative democracies. However, we also take seriously the possibility that while there are times that media content is inaccurate, there are times when it is accurate. Our aim is to leverage existing theories, and over forty years of data on public policy and media coverage across six policy domains in the United States, to better measure and understand both the successes and failures of mass media in modern representative democracy.

Ascertaining the quantity and quality of media content is a defining feature of the book, but we also want to know how well this content informs the public about the actions of government. For this, we need to assess whether the public actually receives (and accepts) that information, which leads us to public perceptions and preferences themselves. Indeed, this was the motivation for our research on media coverage of policy and it occupies a good deal of our attention in the pages that follow.

The book has roots dating back to our time at Nuffield College, Oxford, where we met in 2001 and began research on the dynamics of public opinion and policy, which led to a stream of articles and a book, *Degrees of Democracy*. Much of that work showed that spending policy in the United States, the United Kingdom, and Canada follows the ebb and flow of public opinion, and also that the public tends to respond, adjusting its preferences for more policy thermostatically in response to policy change. The mechanisms of public responsiveness to government policy actually were on our minds as we wrote *Degrees*, and the mass media were our primary suspects; indeed, they seemingly had to be a large part of the story. We nevertheless were not sure how to go about addressing this empirically, as we had little idea how to conceptualize coverage of government policy, let alone measure it. We were spurred on, however, by reactions to our work, perhaps most notably by Jason Barabas and Armen Hakhverdian, both of whom pushed us in reviews of our book to account for the mechanism(s) of public responsiveness. Others encouraged us more informally to undertake such research, including our current and former colleagues and coauthors Kevin Arceneaux, Peter Enns, and Patrick Fournier. We are thankful for this.

When we decided to move forward years later, we started not with policy but with something seemingly more tractable – the economy. Though it took some time, the methodology we developed with Dominik Stecula worked, neatly capturing the tone of mass media coverage of real economic ebbs and flows, first when applied in the United States and then in Canada and the United Kingdom. Having done this, we trained our sights on policy, beginning with what struck us as the most self-contained domain and a highly salient one as well – US spending on defense. We produced two journal articles, one on measuring media coverage of policy change published in *Policy Studies Journal* and the other more comprehensive analysis of policy, coverage, and public opinion, with Fabian Neuner, for the *International Journal of Press/Politics*, both published in 2019. With the financial support of National Science Foundation (NSF) grants (SES-1728792 and SES-1728558), we were able to build on our proof of concept and undertake a comprehensive data collection in various spending and non-spending domains, involving millions of newspaper articles and television news broadcasts as well as (many) millions more Facebook posts and tweets. It led to a methodological paper with Lindsay Dun that assesses dictionary and supervised learning methods for measuring media coverage of government policy, which was published in *Political Communication*. The grants also funded the much more expanded data collection and analysis in this book.

We were fortunate to have had excellent research support along the way. Lauren Guggenheim of the Center for Political Studies at the University of Michigan helped with grant preparation, data management, and crowdsourced human coding. Sarah Fioroni helped with manuscript revisions. Stuart Tendler and Katie Beth Willis at the University of Texas provided management of the grant expenditure, particularly research assistance. There were a number of research assistants at the University of Michigan and University of Texas at Austin: Lindsay Dun, Connor Dye, Sydney Foy, Amanda Hampton, Daniel Hiaeshutter-Rice, Andrew Segal, and Dominic Valentino. We also relied on numerous undergraduate student coders in Austin: Alec Carden, Gabrielle Chavez, Hannah Cobb, Evita Escobedo, Rahul Gupta, Macy Jackson, Alex Montellano, Amanda Quintanilla, David Trevino, and Alfredo Valenzuela. Last but not at all least, the resources and support staff at the Texas Advanced Computing Center (TACC) literally were indispensable to the research, and we want to single out Charlie Dey and especially Anna Dabrowski.

Many people provided useful comments, including Bethany Albertson, Carolyn Barnes, Neal Beck, Daniel Beland, Matthew Bergman, Luca Bernardi, Amber Boydstun, Nate Breznau, Keith Dowding, Johanna Dunaway, Patrick English, Peter Enns, Laurenz Ennser-Jedenastik, Richard Fording, David Fortunato, Jane Gingrich, Kirby Goidel, Kristin Goss, Lauren Guggenheim, Rod Hart, Sol Hart, Ariel Hasell, Marc Hooghe, Simon Jackman, John Jackson, Bryan Jones, Wiebke Junk, Orit Kedar, Matthew Kerby, Ann-Kristin Kölln, Ken Kollman, Heike Klüver, Tse-Min Lin, Sofie Marien, Wolfgang Müller, Fabian Neuner, Diana O'Brien, Alex Pacek, Josh Pasek, Julia Partheymüller, Carolina Plescia, Anne Rasmussen, Jochen Rehmert, Jeroen Romeijn, Deondra Rose, Edella Schlager, Ann Schneider, Gijs Schumacher, Tamir Sheafer, Christopher Skovron, Talia Stroud, Raanan Sulitzeanu-Kenan, Dimiter Toshkov, Nicholas Valentino, Stephen van Hauwaert, Rens Vliegenthart, Markus Wagner, Stefaan Walgrave, Daniel Weitzel, Bernhard Weßels, Guy Whitten, Christopher Williams, and Fiona Yap.

We benefited from the many other attendees at presentations of the research. Papers related to the book were presented at the University of Amsterdam, University of Antwerp, University of Arizona, Australian National University, Campus den Haag, Leiden University, UCLA, CIDE (Mexico City), University of Copenhagen, Hebrew University, Humboldt University, University of Leuven, University of Liverpool, University of Michigan, University of Sydney, University of Texas at Austin, Texas A&M University, and the University of Vienna. We benefited from several opportunities to present ideas at the Political Communication Working Group at the University of Michigan. Papers also were presented to panels at conferences in Austin, Chicago, Houston, New Orleans, San Juan, San Francisco, Toronto, Tucson, and Washington, DC. Finally, we also thank our colleagues at the University of Michigan and the University of Texas at Austin for providing supportive research environments.

The book itself would not have happened without people at Cambridge University Press, beginning with Robert Dreesen for showing early interest in the work, and then Lance Bennett, Sara Doskow, Claire Sissen, and Jadyn Fauconier-Herry for carrying things forward and providing guidance and comments along the way.

Media in Representative Democracy

This book is about the role of media in representative democracy. Specifically, we want to know how well media inform the public about the actions of government. Our work is motivated primarily by the following questions: How consistently does media content convey accurate information about what policymakers do? To what degree (or in which instances) do media help the public understand and respond to government action?

That the public responds to mediated information about public policy may seem far-fetched to some, given long-standing concerns about public ignorance alongside recent increases in both misinformation and misperceptions. However, the admittedly optimistic starting point for our investigation is the expectation that even as there are failures in media and public responsiveness, there are successes. In some ways, at some times, media coverage is accurate and the public responds. Put in terms of the quantities that will concern us for the next seven chapters: even as there are inaccuracies in both media coverage and public perceptions, there are nevertheless instances in which media content reflects reality and the public react to changes in both the state of the world and US budgetary policy.

We will review the theoretical (and practical) significance of accurate media and public responsiveness in some detail later in the text. We will also review the likely impediments to that responsiveness, highlighting especially the burgeoning literatures on public misperceptions and misinformation. But we begin here with some basic empirics: brief accounts of two policy domains in which we see evidence of public responsiveness to policy change, fueled (we suspect) by media coverage.

Consider first the US public's reaction to President Ronald Reagan's defense build-up in 1981 and 1982. Reagan entered office early in 1981 in the wake of the Iranian hostage crisis and the Soviet invasion of Afghanistan.[1] Seemingly in response to these events, public support for defense spending rose dramatically in 1980: preferences for more defense spending went from below 30 percent at the end of 1978 to above 60 percent at the beginning of 1980. The upward shift is clearly evident in Figure 1.1, which plots the percentage of respondents in the General Social Survey (GSS) supporting more defense spending since the early 1970s.

Reagan's predecessor, Jimmy Carter, proposed substantial increases in defense spending for fiscal year (FY) 1980 and then again for 1981. Reagan supplemented the increases to the latter and then proposed an even bigger budget for 1982. Indeed, from 1978 to 1982 appropriations for defense nearly doubled, increasing by 100 billion dollars,[2] and the public seemed to notice. By the end of 1981, only 37 percent of the public

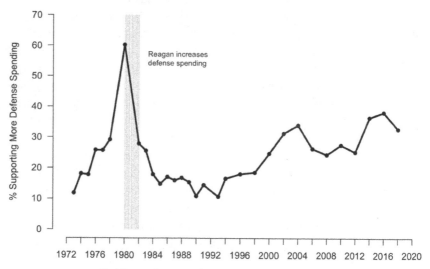

FIGURE 1.1 Public preferences for more defense spending, 1972–2019

[1] The former involved the 1979 takeover of the US Embassy in Tehran, ending just as Reagan was inaugurated; the latter began in 1979 but continued throughout Reagan's two terms, until February 1989.
[2] They reached 217 billion dollars in 1982, compared to 117 billion dollars in 1978, though budget authority continued to increase in the ensuing years up to 295 billion dollars in 1985.

favored more defense spending, and quarterly Trendex public opinion polls during the year showed decreases in each quarter.[3] GSS data in Figure 1.1 show the same precipitous drop in support for more spending. To be clear, as defense spending *increased*, preferences for more defense spending *decreased*.

Some commentators (and even scholars) might bemoan a fickle US public, massively supportive of defense spending increases one year and then unsupportive just a year or two later. This public reaction nevertheless makes a lot of sense. Yes, the threat – and "need" for high levels of defense spending – may not have changed much during the period, particularly as regards the Soviet Union. Spending had changed, however, and really quite dramatically. A substantial drop in support for more spending was thus a sign not of a fickle public but an informed one. Citizens recognized a need for more spending and once it was met, they adjusted their preferences for additional appropriations accordingly.[4]

The early 1980s was not the only moment when the US public responded sensibly to changes in the real-world environment and defense policy. Other moments of public responsiveness are not highlighted in Figure 1.1, but note that the trend in preferences suggests increasing public support for more spending corresponding with (and in likely reaction to) cuts in spending during the Clinton years (between 1993 and 2000). It also indicates an increase in support for more spending following 9/11, and then decreasing demand as spending was increased by Bush (2004–2008). A similar dynamic is evident during Obama's second term (2013–2016), where the public grew supportive of more spending as spending was cut.

There is evidence of public responsiveness outside the defense domain as well. Consider another well-known policy change: the Bush tax cuts of 2001 and 2003 (the Economic Growth and Tax Relief Reconciliation Act, and the Jobs and Growth Tax Relief Reconciliation Act, respectively). These tax cuts are notable here not just because they produced a decrease in the marginal tax rates for nearly all US taxpayers but because this period has been held up as an illustration of the ignorance of public

---

[3] In the Trendex quarterly survey data throughout the time period, support for more spending shot up from 39.3 percent in the fourth quarter of 1979 to 71.9 percent in the first quarter of 1980, remaining in the 60s for another year, and then declined steadily over the course of 1981 and into 1982.

[4] Note that this pattern also comports with Richard Fenno's detailed qualitative account of events in his examination of Budget Chairman Pete Domenici role in passing of Reagan's budget (1991: 57–59).

preferences. Bartels' (2005) "Homer Gets a Tax Cut" paper highlights a blind spot in public preferences, to be sure. Even as most Americans observed increasing inequality, and regarded it as problematic, they supported tax cuts that would be beneficial mainly to the wealthy. Bartels suggests that respondents' preferences were affected in part, irrationally, by their own tax burdens. Citizens seemed to misunderstand the nature of the tax cuts they supported, namely, that the cuts would increase rather than decrease income inequality.[5]

Even as the public response to the Bush tax cuts may have reflected some confusion, there was sensible responsiveness as well. Following the cuts, there was a steady decrease in the percentage of Americans who felt their taxes were too high. This is readily evident in Figure 1.2, which shows the proportion of GSS respondents who believe that their taxes are too high. The sample is divided in each year into income terciles, in order to identify the perceptions of high-, middle-, and low-income Americans. All groups tend to feel that their taxes are too high; higher-income groups feel this more than lower-income groups, which is not surprising given the distribution of the federal tax burden. However, the Bush tax cuts produce an especially large decline in the series for high- (and middle-) income

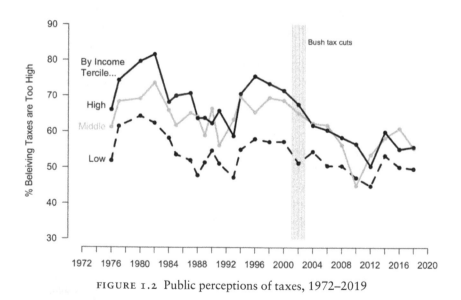

FIGURE 1.2 Public perceptions of taxes, 1972–2019

[5] Of course, they may have noticed that inequality would increase but really did not want to do anything about it.

respondents between 2000 and 2004. To be clear, following tax cuts that most benefited wealthier Americans, they revised downward their opinions that they were being taxed too much. By contrast, the preferences of the middle and especially the poor, whose taxes were cut to a lesser degree, changed comparatively little during the period.

Note that this is not the only instance of what appears to be informed public responsiveness to changes in taxes. Figure 1.2 also shows sharp upward shifts in response to Clinton's tax increases in 1993 and Obama's – as a consequence of the Affordable Care Act – in 2013. We also see that when taxes are more progressive (at the start of the series), the gap in perceptions across income groups is larger; when taxes are least progressive (toward the end of the series), the gap in perceptions across income groups narrows.

Figures 1.1 and 1.2 offer evidence that the US public can and sometimes does respond sensibly to policy change. These findings are also in line with past work, including Page and Shapiro's (1992) well-known book *The Rational Public*. That volume offers multiple instances of "rational" public responsiveness to conditions, including policy change. Perhaps more importantly, it reveals parallel publics, where various groups respond in similar ways across a wide range of policy domains. This implies that basic policy information is widely available and also received and readily accepted.

The significance of this kind of public responsiveness to policy is, we believe, fairly obvious. In democracies around the world, citizens are regularly asked to vote for candidates based on what those candidates have done or say they will do on a range of public policies. Policies are not the only things citizens take into account when voting, to be sure, but they often matter. The match between candidate and citizen preferences can be relevant to voting decisions and to representation between election years as well. At any time in the electoral cycle, representatives may look to citizens for approval or disapproval of policy proposals, and citizens may shift their support for representatives based on the degree to which policies are in line with their preferences. These are the basics of effective representative democracy. Sometimes they appear to work relatively well, at other times less so.

That the public acquires information about policies is thus of fundamental importance. The aforementioned examples suggest that the public sometimes does learn about policy. *But how?* Citizens do not experience most policies directly.[6] We could not tell you from direct experience what

---

[6] This is of some significance given that past works find that experience matters; see, for example, Mettler (2018).

the government is doing for national security, for instance, or the environment, or many other areas that are not consumed privately. Even in those areas where we might, it is difficult to tell based on our own experience just how well it reflects what policymakers have done.

Indeed, just as we do not directly experience most policies, we do not have firsthand knowledge of most policy-relevant information. We have little independent knowledge of whether the water quality in Flint, Michigan, is increasing or decreasing, whether there are children being held in cages at the US border, what exactly the US military is doing in the South China Sea, or whether more Americans have access to health care now than five years ago. To the extent that we are aware of these things, we typically have learned them second hand, that is, from a source other than the government itself. Representative democracy nevertheless regularly requires that we get this kind of information. That information, we believe, most of the time, comes from media.

Effective mediation between government actions and the public is critical to the functioning of modern democracy for at least two reasons. First, without reasonably accurate information it is difficult, if not impossible, for people to hold governing authorities accountable for what they actually do. Second, without this information, it is also difficult for the public to communicate meaningful signals about preferred policy changes to elected officials, as those preferences would be disconnected from what policymakers have already done. There would be little incentive for politicians to represent public opinion and little basis for doing so among those interested in representing the public for other, non-electoral reasons. Representative democracy depends on a reasonably well-informed public, which in turn depends on informative media content.

This is a long-recognized fact, and it has led to a good deal of hand-wringing among democratic theorists, social-scientific researchers of media and democracy, and popular commentators alike. The most common concern is that the media do not reliably reflect what government does. Even putting aside relatively recent claims of "fake news" and the like, there are long-standing concerns about the focus of the news. There are claims that news-producing organizations concentrate on politics instead of policy when reporting on governance, much as they report on the horse race of elections more than the substance of the politicians' positions. At the root of much of this concern are the interests of organizations, particularly commercial ones motivated by profit. Of course, even noncommercial organizations depend on funding, and publicly funded ones often (need to) pay attention to ratings. Regardless of the source of funding, then, there are concerns about money or audiences, or both. And past work discussed later in this chapter and the next suggests that these concerns can lead media coverage to focus on things that are more attention-grabbing than the details of public policy.

Audience-seeking pressures on media also may be increasing rather than decreasing. While many scholars and commentators still acknowledge the importance of the traditional (or "legacy") news media, these outlets appear to be in decline. The growth of broadcast and then cable television posed the first challenges to news outlets like newspapers and radio, and the explosion of the Internet has hastened their disappearance. What remains is subject to increasing corporate consolidation. One concern is that there is more and more competition for audiences, and thus less and less news about governance. The coverage that exists may be getting both narrower in content and thinner in substance.

The extent to which this is true is as yet unclear, and there are reasons to believe that technological change may lead to improvements in the availability of policy-relevant information. Consider first that there is much more choice available to people now than a few decades ago, among both news outlets and the countless non-news alternatives. This presents both disadvantages and advantages. On the one hand, in contrast with the period of broadcast television, people can more readily opt out of news coverage entirely – a fact first explored by Markus Prior (2007) and then a stream of other scholars. On the other hand, even as people are increasingly able to avoid political news, they also have access to (much) more political information than was previously available. This allows interested citizens to become real experts, and one consequence is increased variation in public knowledge. Indeed, even those who consume political news increasingly choose what they get, which also has consequences for the quality of information they receive (see especially Stroud 2008; Arceneaux and Johnson 2013; Levendusky 2013). The role of the media clearly has changed, and in ways that may well compromise effective accountability, but also in ways that might improve it.

What we find most striking about the current environment is not the significance of communication media to representative democracy – this we view as a long-established fact. What we find striking is the ongoing lack of research that empirically tests whether media coverage – considered over extended periods of time and across multiple policy domains – meets the basic requirements of representative democracy. Has there been much coverage of policy decisions historically? Has that coverage reflected whether and how policy changed? How does coverage relate to public preferences? How has coverage evolved over time? There is very good work focused on attentiveness to different policy issues in media coverage, and there are long-standing literatures on the ways in which policy issues can be framed in media coverage. We consider this work in more detail in Chapter 2. But much of this work is case-specific, limited in time and/or topic. This literature has unquestionably added to what we know about media and democracy. However, it cannot address directly what we see as *the* central issue where media content and democracy are concerned: Is there a sufficient amount of accurate media coverage of public policy to allow citizens to have meaningful policy preferences and hold their representatives accountable?

It would not be uncommon to react to that question by claiming that most citizens barely pay attention and know very little about politics regardless of the content of media. This is why we began with the two examples earlier. They illustrate what a considerable body of literature has found – that citizens can, and often do, respond in understandable ways to changes in the real-world environment and public policy. Perhaps most notable is prior research demonstrating that people respond *thermostatically* to policy change, adjusting their preferences for more policy downward when policy increases (Durr 1993; Wlezien 1995; Erikson et al. 2002; Soroka and Wlezien 2004, 2005; Enns and Kellstedt 2008; Jennings 2009; Soroka and Wlezien 2010; Bartle et al. 2011, 2019; Ellis and Faricy 2011; Ura and Ellis 2012). This is exactly what we have seen in Figures 1.1 and 1.2. It requires that people, collectively at least, have an accurate sense of the direction and magnitude of policy change, as they otherwise could not adjust their preferences accordingly. There is not always such public responsiveness, of course – just as there is variation in policy representation across issues, time, and space (Monroe 1998; Soroka and Wlezien 2010), there is variation in public responsiveness – and in some domains (and contexts) there is no responsiveness at all (Wlezien 1995; Soroka and Wlezien 2010). As we have seen, however, there are domains in which people can and do adjust their preferences for more (or less) or less policy in response to actual policy.

How can we reconcile evidence of systematic public responsiveness to policy with evidence of seemingly uninformed publics? We regard this as a crucial and largely unanswered question in current research on representative democracy. It is interesting and important unto itself but also because of the considerable body of work showing that, in some domains at least, public preferences drive policy change (see, e.g., Bartels 1991; Stimson et al. 1995; Wlezien 1996, 2004; Erikson, MacKuen, and Stimson

2002; Eichenberg and Stoll 2003; Soroka and Wlezien 2010; Wlezien and Soroka 2012). That is, preferences appear to matter for what policymakers do, at least to some degree.

The apparent gap in the literature has also been on the minds of scholars of opinion-policy relationships. Consider Barabas' (2011: 194) review of *Degrees of Democracy*, which develops and tests the thermostatic model in the United States, Canada, and the United Kingdom: "At a more microlevel, there is an assumption throughout the book that people get the signal on policy change and then update their preferences accordingly. However, there is no direct examination of media messages or other ways of documenting these linkages." Also consider Hakhverdian's (2012) assessment of the same book: "The public has to possess knowledge on whether appropriations in defense and domestic domains have gone up or down. Legacy and new media assumedly play a large mediating role in conveying this message, and with spending data one can perhaps picture people adjusting their preferences for 'more' or 'less' spending based on media information they receive." "Assumedly" and "perhaps" are accurate reflections of the state of knowledge about the mechanisms of public responsiveness; although previous research is suggestive, it does not provide real evidence.

How exactly does the public learn about public policy? We think that the media play a central role. We make our case later in the text. We draw first on rich literatures in political science on representation and political behavior to make the argument that public responsiveness is not a pipe dream but an objective fact (at least some of the time). We then turn to work in political communication and journalism to both (1) consider what exactly the "media" is given technological change and (2) argue for the value of media content, namely, for the possibility that, even as media coverage may include a fair amount of "noise," it also may include a "signal" about where policy is headed.

1.1 PUBLIC RESPONSIVENESS

Our account begins with the following supposition: public responsiveness to policy does not require a high level of information. It may only require that people have a sense for the direction of policy change – whether policy has gone up or down and *perhaps* the general magnitude – whether it has gone up by a little or a lot. These are rather basic pieces of information that can easily be accessible through simple cues available in the media environment (see, e.g., Lupia and McCubbins 1998). Public responsiveness need not depend on citizens knowing what exactly is happening in a policy domain.

Note that this argument conflicts directly with some of the early work on media and public opinion in democracy. Most forceful among the critics may be journalist Walter Lippmann. His book *Public Opinion* (1922) considered the role of the public in representative democracy, and Lippmann sees public opinion as largely inchoate, dependent on opinion leadership and the "manufacture of consent."[7] His follow-up treatise, *The Phantom Public* (1925), provides even sharper relief, in which he distinguishes between "agents" and "bystanders," where the latter form a "bewildered herd," largely inattentive to and uninformed about politics and policy.[8] To Lippmann, theories of democratic account-ability and control depend on a "false philosophy" in which the public is positioned to guide elected officials. The people have other things to do, and about all they can be expected to provide to the elites is an electoral sanction from time to time; in between elections, elites have nearly free reign, entirely unsupervised by the "phantom" public.

This view may be back in fashion. Consider Achen and Bartels' (2016) popular *Democracy for Realists*, in which the authors posit that even elections do not work to guide politicians. They argue that the "folk theory" of democracy, where voters have policy preferences and choose their parties and politicians based on those preferences, simply does not apply. To Achen and Bartels, most voters do not have informed opinions; those who do vote on the basis of group attachments and policy views not only do not drive their votes but are driven by them instead. Election outcomes end up turning on random events. This is a provocative account to be sure and has much in common with Lippmann's. We regard it as a caricature both of democratic theory and of the research on voting and elections, however.

Take the theoretical literature on representative democracy. Here scholars emphasize a principal–agent relationship in which elections are important because they allow voters, the principals, to choose the parties and/or candidates, or agents, to represent them. Voters can decide on the basis of various considerations, from the sublime to the ridiculous, the range of which often is reflected in popular coverage of (and some

---

[7] The terminology was later picked up by Chomsky and Edwards in *Manufacturing Consent*, in which they highlight the media's propaganda function.

[8] Lippmann's distinction echoes Machiavelli's between the "great" and the "people," though he was seemingly (much) more optimistic than Lippmann about the latter.

scholarly writing about) voters and their motivations. Of obvious importance then is what voters want from their elected officials and, of course,
what they ultimately get.

Many theorists have posited – or assumed – that policy evaluations play
a role in this principal–agent interaction. Policy assessments may be based
on voters' interests and/or preferences.[9] Scholars often also suggest the
importance of accountability, where voters choose on the basis of politicians' policy promises and then evaluate politicians based on whether they
delivered (Naurin 2011). Mansbridge (2003) refers to this as "promis-
sory" representation, and it has much in common with the (older) more
empirical literature on the "responsible party model" (see Ranney 1951;
Schattschneider 1960).[10]

Some are less sanguine, including Schumpeter (1954), who sees
democracy as merely a method for selecting political decision-
makers. In his "realistic" theory, there is no real collective "will" for
representatives to deliver and no basis for effective accountability,
even if elections do incentivize politicians. Riker (1982) echoes this
theme, highlighting how even if individuals in society have rational
preferences, it does not ensure a rational *public* preference. Of critical
importance is theory demonstrating "cycling" of aggregate preferences
for policy, where Option A is preferred to B and Option B is preferred
to C, and yet Option C is preferred to A. Owing to this intransitivity,
there is not a single publicly preferred policy; what ultimately matters
is politics among the elected officials. This is pretty damning, according to Riker, as it implies even a minimally populist view of democracy just does not make any sense – it's just not clear what the public
wants.

Other scholars push back, including Mackie (2003) in *Democracy
Defended*. He points to research showing that cycling among policies is
not that common and even where it exists, it usually is confined to
a small subset of similar options. He also highlights research showing
that other potential problems with representative institutions are

---

[9] Note that interests and preferences may not be one and the same, at least as typically
conceived. For instance, it may be that voters would benefit materially from a policy but
still oppose it, such as tax cuts for the rich.

[10] It may be that voters' preferences change in between elections, perhaps owing to circumstances themselves (and even policies and their effects); elected officials may respond to
this change, perhaps in anticipation of accountability at the next election, where the threat
of electoral sanction serves as an incentive. This is what Mansbridge calls "anticipatory"
representation, which also has roots in the empirical literature.

overstated.[11] That said, even as Mackie provides good news for representative democracy, his work still is not a full-blown defense of the quality of democratic representation that Achen and Bartels challenge: Are elections in practice not at all about policy preferences? Are they really just all about groups, or the consequence of random events?

It seems very likely, based on the available evidence, that the truth is somewhere in between what some see as the democratic ideal and the view that "the sky is falling." We thus do not see either a perfectly responsive public or a complete lack of accountability. To begin with, it is important to keep in mind that for effective accountability, people need not vote entirely on the basis of policy positions. Consider our own statement on the subject in *Degrees of Democracy*, published in 2010:

It is not necessary for people to really vote on the basis of their preferences and government action, rewarding and punishing politicians at each and every turn. It is necessary only that there is a reasonable probability that they will on any particular decision. That is, politicians must have a reason to think that they will pay a price for their behavior, i.e., that there is some level of risk for defying the public will. (Soroka and Wlezien 2010: 36)

Notice that this characterization does not require policy voting, just the possibility of it, and we were careful to point out that "politicians also must value that risk." Ours is not a singular view – numerous scholars expect politicians to care about what the public wants and deliver on it. Perhaps the strongest – and most complete – statement comes from Robert Erikson, Michael MacKuen, and James Stimson in their classic *The Macro Polity* (2002). While recognizing the importance of *performance*, following Fiorina (1981), and candidate *affect*, following Campbell et al. (1960) and Stokes (1963), they highlight the prominent role of *policy*, building on Anthony Downs' (1957) pioneering essay on the subject and the research it spawned. Erikson et al. invoke "rational expectations" from economics and portray elected officials as "keen to pick up the faintest of signals in their political environment. Like antelope in an open field, they cock their ears and focus their full attention on the slightest hint of danger."

The burgeoning literature on electoral behavior traditionally has emphasized the role of groups and their relevance for political judgments. This has roots back in the Columbia School models of the vote (Berelson, Lazarsfeld, and McPhee 1954), which saw *membership* in groups as primary determinants of interests, preferences, and vote choice (also see

---

[11] It still may be that different election rules produce different outcomes, but this is most common when public preferences are divided or unclear.

Campbell et al. 1960). Later work emphasized *identification* with groups, among both members (Gurin, Miller, and Gurin 1980; Conover 1984; Lau 1989) and nonmembers (Koch 1993). It is important to keep in mind that, as Leonie Huddy (2018) has articulated forcefully, those identifications are not mindless and blind to interests and policy preferences. Social scientists have known for a long time that groups play important roles in political decision-making.[12]

Policy positions do as well. Following Downs (1957), scholars have hypothesized and found evidence of proximity voting, where citizens choose politicians whose policy positions are closest to them (see, e.g., Enelow and Hinich 1984; Jessee 2012). Others have argued that proximity matters less than directionality, that is, whether and the degree to which politicians are on the "right" side of the issue (Rabinowitz and MacDonald 1989; MacDonald et al. 1991). Still others find evidence of both the proximity and directional models (e.g., Iversen 1994; also see Adams et al. 2005). Most importantly, *all* of this research highlights the importance of policy issues in voters' decision-making.

Some scholars are skeptical, to be sure: Following a growing literature on the endogeneity of survey responses to partisanship and electoral preferences (see, e.g., Wlezien et al. 1997; Bartels 2002; Evans and Andersen 2006), some argue that people's positions do not cause political judgments (such as vote choice) but rather are caused by those judgments themselves (Lenz 2012). To be clear, we may not be Democrats due to our attitudes on health care; we may instead have views on health care that are determined by our Democratic partisanship or support. We regard this as a fair criticism of at least some of the existing literature on issue voting. That said, we see additional evidence in support of policy responsiveness in research on aggregate election outcomes – research that largely eschews concerns about endogeneity in analyses of cross-sectional voting behavior (Erikson et al. 2002; Bolstad 2012; Wlezien 2017a). In this work, scholars assess whether and how objective policy and the vote relate and reveal a referendum effect whereby voters punish governments that push policy too far off to the left or right. The tendency actually may help explain the

---

[12] Also see, e.g., Converse 1964; Brady and Sniderman 1985; Miller et al. 1991. Note that the difference between *membership* and *identification* is important – the literature shows that people may not identify with groups to which they belong, and some may identify with groups to which they do not belong, that latter of which is what Herbert Hyman saw as the defining feature of "reference group" theory (Hyman and Singer 1968). Note also that, as Huddy (2018) makes clear, group influences are neither separate nor disconnected from political issues and conflict (also see Wlezien and Miller 1997).

recurring cost-of-ruling effect in elections in the United States and around the world, where the incumbent government vote share(s) tend to decline the longer they remain in power (Stokes and Iverson 1966; Paldam 1986; Nannestad and Paldam 2002; Cuzan 2015). There is evidence that the effect does partly reflect the increasing policy drift that is apparent the longer parties control government (see Wlezien 2017a). But again, the most important point for our purposes is that policy has a direct causal impact on election outcomes: As policy moves further away from public preferences, support for governing parties declines.[13]

In sum, even as other things matter on Election Day, we have seen that policy positions and outputs do as well, which means that people must know something about what government has done. As we have also seen, substantial bodies of research demonstrate that these actions inform public preferences for policy themselves and that those preferences in turn guide policymakers. Most people presumably do not have very detailed information, which is as we would expect, given the very large literature documenting the limits of public knowledge (Luskin 1990; Page and Shapiro 1992; Lupia 1994; Popkin 1994; Delli Carpini and Keeter 1996; Delli Carpini 2005). And while some have a lot of information, many apparently have some idea about what governments actually have done, that is, more than knowledge of which party is in power and what we might expect them to do. This is enough to motivate and guide policy-makers, at least in a general way on certain important issues in certain institutional contexts.

1.2 MEDIA CONTENT

The information the public has about policy needs to come from some-where, and there are good reasons to expect that at least some policy information is transmitted by the media.

We define "the media" here as comprising both (a) "mass" or "legacy" media such as newspapers and television and (b) "new" or "digital" media.[14]

---

[13] Of course, policy is not everything on Election Day. Group membership and identification matters, as we have seen; and economic performance does as well. This may have little to do with government policy, and yet other things that politicians do not control can matter for candidate evaluations, though it now seems clear that some of those worries, e.g., the seeming effects of shark attacks on the presidential vote, are not well-founded (see Fowler and Hall 2018).

[14] The two are not mutually exclusive: newspapers distribute information both on paper and digitally, for instance, and increasingly have digital-only content in addition to their

Our empirical tests, and much of our theoretical motivation, focus primarily on newspapers and television. This emphasis is necessary given that we track media coverage back to 1980, well before digital media existed. It is of course reasonable to question whether our results hold in an increasingly complex digital media ecology. Recent work emphasizes the "hybridity" of the evolving media system, in which legacy and new media are interconnected and both audiences and information flow across multiple media platforms (Chadwick 2017). A related literature suggests that technological change has not just introduced new digital media but has also fundamentally altered the content of (or biases in) legacy media (see, e.g., Benkler et al. 2018; Bennet and Livingston 2020). These are just two ways in which the nature of "the media" may be changing. In later chapters we consider whether declines in legacy media matter and provide analyses of Facebook data in order to better assess what media content might look like going forward. Regardless, acknowledging changes in technology and content does not minimize the critical role that the media – legacy, new, and whatever comes next – play in representative democracy.

Moreover, even as concerns about the content of new media are especially salient at present, there is a long history of worry about the quality of media coverage. Focusing on the legacy media of twenty years ago, for instance, the prospect that media were providing the information critical for public responsiveness may seem to be at odds with well-established critiques of media content. There is a considerable body of work detailing a range of biases in legacy media content, and a good deal of research lamenting variability in, or a total lack of, policy content specifically (e.g., Lawrence 2000; Dunaway 2011), alongside research identifying inadequate and sometimes misleading coverage of policy issues (e.g., Bennett 1988; Friedman et al. 1999; Schudson 2003; Stocking and Holstein 2009). Consider also the vast body of work on sensationalism and/or negativity in news content (e.g., Sabato 1991; Patterson 1994; Lichter and Noyes 1995; Altheide 1997; Cappella and Jamieson 1997; Soroka 2012); and studies focused on the importance – and potentially misleading impact – of framing in media coverage of public policy (e.g., Iyengar 1991; Neuman et al. 1992; Entman 1993; Lee et al. 2008).

These are just some of the literatures concerned with problems of both the frequency and accuracy of legacy media coverage, of course. They are illustrative of broader – and also very current – concerns that media

printed coverage. Some exclusively digital sources also primarily redistribute content from legacy outlets.

content offers a systematically biased of the world, and political issues in particular. In some cases, concerns are focused mainly on a *lack of information*. There are some policy domains that just do not reliably find their way into media coverage. In these cases, public responsiveness seems very unlikely – there simply is no (or little) available information that people can use.

In other cases, media coverage is regarded as a source of *misinformation*, and consequently *misperceptions*. Note that we might regard all inaccurate information about policy as misinformation, whether it is purposeful or inadvertent, whether it is expressly false or simply misleading. Misinformation is in our view a lack of correspondence between what media content suggests is happening and what is actually happening. Viewed in this way, misinformation is not a peculiar consequence of a social-media-fueled and politically polarized information environment. It is and has been a regular feature of mass media coverage since the dawn of mass media. But concerns about misinformation (and disinformation), particularly in social media, have reached a fevered pitch in the time since the 2016 presidential election, including the COVID-19 pandemic (Fleming 2020; Motta et al. 2020).

Note that our definition of misinformation is in line with recent work by Lazer et al. (2018: 1094), who distinguish between fake news ("fabricated information that mimics news media content in form but not in organizational process or intent"), disinformation ("false information that is purposely spread to deceive people"), and misinformation ("false or misleading information"). Fake news and disinformation are in this view subsets of the overarching category of misinformation. There are reasons to believe that new media have contributed to a marked increase in the flow of both fake news and disinformation. And, as noted earlier, there are reasons to believe that the modern media ecology has led to increased misinformation in legacy media as well. These trends have led to a burgeoning and fascinating body of work focused on misinformation and misperceptions. (There is a lot of terrific work in this area, but see, e.g., Nyhan and Reifler 2010; Bode and Vraga 2015; Southwell and Thorson 2015; Weeks 2015; Pasek et al. 2015; Del Vicario et al. 2016; Garrett et al. 2016; Thorson 2016; Allcott and Gentzkow 2017; Flynn et al. 2017; Bennett and Livingston 2018; Tandoc et al. 2018; Scheufele and Krause 2019.) Increasing political polarization, perhaps also fueled in part by changes in media technology (see, e.g., Trussler 2020), likely contributes to the ready spread of pro-in-partisan/anti-out-partisan fake news and disinformation. And this nexus of technological development, partisan polarization, and biased news consumption – misinformation or otherwise – is central to the large and growing literatures on motivated reasoning (e.g., Slothuus and de Vreese 2009; Druckman and Bolson 2011), selective exposure (e.g., Stroud 2008, 2010; Garrett 2009), "echo chambers," and "filter bubbles" (e.g., Flaxman et al. 2016).

There is, in short, a lot of concern about the magnitude and consequences of inaccurate information in media, legacy, and otherwise. These concerns are justified and important. There nevertheless are reasons to think that media content sometimes provides the basic information that citizens need to assess the direction of policy change, at least in very salient policy areas that attract a lot of attention. Put differently, even as media can be inefficient and biased and provide inaccurate information, there also can be a signal of actual policy change amidst this noise.

We can imagine several different possibilities. First, there is both accurate and inaccurate information about policy, but the volume of accurate coverage outweighs the volume of inaccurate coverage. Second, there is both accurate and inaccurate information about policy, but the inaccuracies are random rather than systematic, so the accurate "signal" is evident even among the "noise." Third, there are some policies for which reporting is largely (or at least sufficiently) accurate but others in which systematic inaccuracies predominate – due to the varying complexity of issues or the politicization (or polarization) of different policy proposals. These are not mutually exclusive accounts, of course, and there may be others. Taken separately or together, each allows for the possibility that there can be misinformation and misperceptions about the details of, say, Obamacare even as there are relatively accurate signals about – and perceptions of – whether or not health policy is increasing or decreasing, and whether by a little or a lot.

Each of these possibilities also helps account for the considerable body of work suggesting that media reflect government and elite sources (e.g., Bennett 1990; Entman 2003; Walgrave and Van Aelst 2006; Vliegenthart and Walgrave 2008), which should lead to some correspondence between policy change and media content, at least insofar as all elites are not purposefully obfuscating what actually is happening with policy. (Purposeful obfuscation may sometimes be the case, of course.) They also help account for research that finds evidence of learning about policy from news content, albeit with some heterogeneity across individuals (e.g., Eveland 2001, 2002). Following work on cues (e.g., Zaller 1992; Lupia and McCubbins 1998), we suggest that news coverage contains informational heuristics that allow citizens to discern the direction and magnitude of spending changes without necessarily increasing specific knowledge about policy. This aligns with work in the framing tradition showing that frames can act as heuristics that in some cases helpfully simplify news content for readers (see, e.g., Entman 1993; de Vreese 2005; Hänggli and Kriesi 2010).

This view of media coverage – as providing not a perfect, detailed portrait of policy, but at least some of the most important pieces of policy-relevant information – also fits nicely with research on political knowledge and political learning. A good amount of work suggests that people can and do learn from the mass media, after all (e.g., Druckman 2005; Jerit et al. 2006). There is research showing that coverage reflects real-world conditions, at least to some degree (see, e.g., Sanders et al. 1993; Goidel and Langley 1995; Vliegenthart and Boomgarden 2007; Soroka et al. 2015; Enns 2016; Hopkins, et al 2017), and people also appear to pick up the signal (also see Behr and Iyengar 1985). Recent scholarship in the area highlights the importance of focusing on more than just citizens' ability to recall and learn static political facts. For instance, scholars have shown how learning from media coverage is particularly pronounced for policy-specific knowledge and surveillance knowledge (Barabas and Jerit 2009; Barabas et al. 2014).

There are, we suspect, two different kinds of objections to what we propose to do in the chapters that follow. The first is that we already know that media cover public policy and that this coverage matters to public perceptions of policy. This, however, is not the case.

There exists an important literature on mass media and policy, to be sure. The largest body of work here examines media coverage of issues in order to understand the sources of public *priorities*. Here, media attention is a source or indicator of the salience of issues, where the greater the attention, the greater the salience. There is a long history of this type of scholarship, beginning with McCombs and Shaw's (1972) classic research, and then a vast body of literature on public and policy "agenda-setting." Baumgartner and Jones' work (1993, 2005) has been especially influential here. In this tradition, the media play an especially prominent role in Boydstun's (2013) *Making the News*, where the amount of coverage is central to establishing the salience of an issue, which in turn conditions policy representation itself – *whether* policymakers respond to public preferences for policy in different domains (see, e.g., Soroka and Wlezien, 2010).

Other research by Boydstun and coauthors (e.g., Card et al. 2015) shifts from the volume of coverage to its substance, specifically, what they call "policy frames." This work draws on a vast literature on policy framing or "issue definition" in media coverage (e.g., Iyengar 1991), where scholars argue either for the impact that frames have on citizens' policy preferences or for the impact frames have on *how* policymakers respond to the public. (These two things presumably are related.) This research is focused not just on whether there is policy action but also on the substance of that action.

The extant literature has however focused on mass media's role as an *input* into the policymaking process, not as a provider of information about policy *output*. To be clear, measures of media coverage have not concentrated on whether and how content reflects what policymakers actually do. Given our interest in public responsiveness to policy, this is the focus of the research in this book. What follows is to our knowledge one of the first efforts to expressly examine the possibilities that (a) media content contains an adequate number of cues about the ongoing state of public policy, and (b) people respond to those cues.

The other possible objection to our work is quite the opposite. That is, given pervasive flaws in media coverage, there is no reason to expect it to facilitate public responsiveness to policy. As noted in the preceding section, there is a large body of work detailing the failures of modern media coverage. Whether these entirely preclude the kind of content that is required for effective public responsiveness has however not been directly addressed.

We want to make clear that we are not arguing that media are the only means by which citizens learn about policy or that media coverage is necessarily accurate. Regarding the former, there clearly are various ways in which people might learn about policy change.[15] Regarding the accuracy of media coverage, we readily acknowledge that even as accurate media reports may facilitate responsiveness, inaccurate reports may produce reactions that are not in line with actual policy change. As we shall see, our approach to measuring the media policy signal not only captures accurate information about policy change but also reveals seeming misinformation. We do not begin with the supposition that all media content is fundamentally flawed, nor do we begin with the assumption that it is wholly accurate.

---

[15] Some citizens will have direct experience with certain policies, some may learn about policy change through social networks, and some may have a sense for policy change not through any observation about policy itself but through the partisan control of government. For instance, if Republicans are in office one might simply assume that social welfare spending is decreasing, but see Wlezien (1995) and also Branham (2018).

There is a middle ground; in that middle ground, it seems possible for media to play a useful role in facilitating public responsiveness to policy change. The extent to which this is true can – and should – be settled empirically.

1.3 THEORETICAL EXPECTATIONS

Let us set out, succinctly, our expectations for the research that follows. If the media play a central role in public responsiveness, we should observe three patterns.

First, there should be a sufficient amount of coverage of public policy. This is a simple question of volume: there should be enough coverage of policy that media consumers can reasonably expect to learn, at least minimally, about policy change.

Second, coverage will reflect what is actually happening to policy. At minimum, we will observe a positive correlation between policy changes and the "signal" in media content. In the hypothetical extreme, there will be perfect congruence between the two. There must be at a minimum *some* positive relationship between media coverage and policy, and exploring this possibility is a central goal of this project.

Third, if media content is driving public responsiveness, public opinion should reflect the media's policy signal. Examining this hypothesis is the other goal of our project. Determining this is more complicated, particularly if there is a close match between policy and the media signal over time. But there is likely to be some degree of mismatch between policy and the media coverage; and the difference between policy and media coverage should give us some leverage over questions about what exactly the public is responding to. In short, we should be able to determine both (a) when coverage deviates from policy and (b) when the public is reacting to coverage or policy (presumably mediated in other ways), or both. To do this, we need to observe disjunctures between media coverage and policy, and then assess whether the public follows the (measured) media signal or policy itself.

There will of course be variation in the accuracy of coverage, and in the nature of public responsiveness, across domains and perhaps also over time. We more fully address these possibilities in the course of our investigation.

1.4 SYNOPSIS AND PROGNOSIS

These are the ideas that guide our research in the chapters that follow. Chapter 2 develops a theoretical model relating policy, the media, and the public that guides our empirical analysis. Chapter 3 implements our basic dictionary measures of media coverage, requiring a technical (but hopefully accessible) dive given the "big" data involved and the central importance of it to the book. Chapter 4 explores these measures of the "media signal" and considers alternative approaches, including the use of machine learning. Chapter 5 then explicitly assesses the accuracy of the signals for numerous newspapers and television outlets, most importantly, how they relate to policy itself. Chapter 6 connects policy, the media signal(s), and the public to establish whether coverage effectively mediates between the former and latter. Chapter 7 probes the results in preceding chapters, particularly issues in the "mediation" between policy and the public, including the declining reliance on traditional news media and the causal relationships between policy and media coverage, and public opinion as well. Our closing Chapter 8 reviews what we have learned and what remains and considers our results in light of the changing media ecology, and whether and how those results travel to other policy domains and countries.

2

Public Responsiveness to Media

Is there any reason to expect citizens to understand and respond to policy change? Is there any reason to think that media coverage would help rather than hinder reasoned public responsiveness to policy? As we have discussed in Chapter 1, popular treatment of these topics might suggest that the answer to both questions is "no." Some academic research also supports this position.

Indeed, there is a long history of research documenting that individual citizens – in the United States and around the world – have at best a thin understanding of politics and policy (e.g., Berelson et al. 1954; Converse 1964; Page and Shapiro 1992; Delli Carpini and Keeter 1996; Popkin and Dimock 1999). Many citizens do not know the name of their representatives; still more barely understand the constitution or monitor major political events from one week to the next. We frequently get the facts wrong. Our ignorance is a standard trope in political behavior research and a regular feature of on-the-street interviews on late night talk shows as well.

That said, as Chapter 1 has outlined, there is a considerable body of scholarly work suggesting that citizens can and often notice and respond to changes in the "real world" environment. People do not have a detailed encyclopedic knowledge of the actions of government to be sure, but they evidently do have a sense of the tenor of government policy. Knowledge also appears to extend beyond an undifferentiated sense of what "government" is doing, as people regularly notice trends in different policy domains, at least those highly salient ones, which also tend to be those on which we spend the most money. Are we doing more on defense? On welfare? On health? People seem to know what is going on in these areas, at least very generally, and it's not only the highly educated or politically interested. Much as Page and Shapiro (1992) showed decades ago on a range of issues, public opinion moves largely in parallel, that is, responsiveness to policy change often is evident regardless of education, income, and even party identification (Soroka and Wlezien 2008, 2010; Enns and Kellstedt 2008; also see Enns and Wlezien 2011).

To reconcile evidence of public responsiveness with evidence of uninformed publics, some previous work has concentrated on the advantages of aggregation (see especially Page and Shapiro 1992). The argument for the "miracle" of aggregation is roughly as follows: if individuals regularly make errors, so long as those errors are approximately random they will cancel out in the aggregate. Even if individual citizens are error-prone, therefore, a *public* can be rational. This depends on error being more or less random and not systematic, of course; see Althaus (2003) for a critique of this assumption, and also Weissberg's (1978) earlier explication of the advantages of "collective" representation, which depends on that assumption.

Even if there is a miracle of aggregation, it alone cannot account for public responsiveness, as the latter involves change over time, not stability. A change in public preferences for more or less defense spending, or more or less environmental regulation, means that people are adjusting their demand; and change that is responsive to policy means that they are adjusting based in part on policy. The fact that there is pervasive responsiveness – across groups – means that many *different* people are doing so as well. And this all leads us to the central question of the book: *How do people learn about policy change?*

As we have discussed in Chapter 1, there is good reason to think that media coverage is critical here, and previous work already points in that direction. The empirical evidence is nevertheless incomplete. To redress this imbalance, we have proposed a simple media-centered account based on the following theoretical propositions: (a) public responsiveness to policy requires only basic levels of knowledge about policy, (b) this basic information is readily available in media content, and (c) citizens can recognize and respond to these informational media cues. We will argue each point in more detail later. To begin, we outline the basics of thermostatic responsiveness. The section that follows draws in part on *Degrees of Democracy*, and on the papers that preceded it as well (e.g., Wlezien 1995, 1996, 2004; Soroka and Wlezien 2004, 2005). It is necessary here to set the stage for our *media-centered account of public responsiveness*.

2.1 PUBLIC POLICY AND THE PUBLIC

That policy can "feed back" on the public is well known. This can find numerous expressions, including interest in politics, political participation, and system support, among other things. Each is an instance in which policy action by governments leads to a change in public attitudes or behavior. We are interested here in public opinion about policy, and we are especially interested in whether and how the public adjusts its preference "inputs" based on policy "outputs." This feedback can be either "negative" or "positive." In what follows, we set out this negative and positive feedback formally, that is, using equations. Doing so has the advantage of clarifying our theory and establishing the basis for the statistical models that will be central to our tests of public responsiveness in Chapters 5 through 7.

With *negative feedback*, the public adjusts its preferences thermostatically based on policy (Wlezien 1995; Soroka and Wlezien 2010). This means that as policy moves upward (downward), public preferences for more policy shift downward (upward). Drawn from engineering, this expectation has deep roots in political science research, stretching back to the classic Eastonian (1965) depiction of a political system and Deutsch's (1963) models of communication and control. In theory, the public's preference for more policy – its relative preference – represents the difference between the public's preferred level of policy and the level it actually gets. We can depict the relationship formally for any particular policy area, as follows:

$$R_t = P_t^* - P_t, \tag{2.1}$$

where R is the public's relative preference, P^* the public's preferred level of policy, P policy itself, and t represents time. In this model, relative preferences change if either the preferred level of policy *or* policy itself changes; indeed, R can go up even if P^* goes down, provided that P goes down by a greater amount.[1]

Such negative feedback of policy on preferences is the fundamental feature of the thermostatic model. It is what distinguishes a reasonably

---

[1] Unlike the thermostat that governs the heating (and/or air conditioning) units in our homes, which sends a dichotomous (directional) signal, R captures both direction and magnitude. Also note that while we have characterized public responsiveness across time, an identical model applies across spatial contexts as well, that is, we can replace the subscripted "t"s in Equation 2.1 with "i"s to represent different places. Indeed, we can incorporate both time and space into an analysis.

informed public – one that knows something about what policymakers actually do – from an uninformed public – one with preferences that are unaffected by changes in policy. Observing negative feedback means that the people are responding to policy, adjusting their preferences for policy based on what governments do. It also means that the signal people send to policymakers contains useful information, which makes possible effective accountability and control.[2]

That said, the public may not respond thermostatically to policy change, and it even may be that policy feeds back *positively* on preferences – an increase in spending could lead people to want more spending in that domain. In Equation 2.1, this feedback is indirect, through P^*, where the public's preferred levels of policy are conceived to be a function of policy itself:

$$P_t^* = f\{P_t\}, \tag{2.2}$$

in which the relationship between P^* and P is positive. Notice that this highlights the importance of explicitly accounting for P^* in analyses of relative preferences, per Equation 2.1 (Wlezien 1995; Soroka and Wlezien 2010).[3] In theory, then, the thermostatic model encompasses both negative and positive feedback.

It is important to make clear that this characterization of feedback as negative and positive contrasts with others in the policy literature (see Mettler and Soss 2004, Beland 2010, and Campbell 2012 for comprehensive and cogent reviews). Schneider and Ingram's (1993) classic treatise posits that policy design influences "social constructions of target

---

[2] As we have discussed in our previous research (Soroka and Wlezien 2010), there is reason to think that policy (P) and the public's preferred level of policy (P^*) are *integrated* time series, ones that do not revert to a fixed mean but wander over time. The theoretical model represented in Equation 2.1 thus implies that the two models are cointegrated, whereby they wander together, with P following P^*; if so, their linear combination, which is reflected in the public's relative preferences (R), would be *stationary*. Based on this theoretical model, the equation is "balanced" (Enns and Wlezien 2017; Enns et al. forthcoming), where both sides are stationary, which is important when we turn to estimation in Chapter 6.

[3] Not doing so would conceal thermostatic feedback where policy positively influences the amount people want, as the effect of P would capture the net effect of the two types of feedback. It also may be that policy feeds back negatively on the preferred level in Equation 2.2, say, if increased spending makes things worse (see Soroka and Wlezien 2010:115–119). Some refer to this alternative type of negative feedback as "undermining" (Jacobs and Weaver 2014; also see Beland et al. 2019). Measures of – or proxies for – P^* thus allow us to differentiate between thermostatic responsiveness and undermining feedback (also see Wlezien and Soroka 2021).

populations," which can influence politics and future policy itself. Some research shows that policy can have self-reinforcing effects, increasing public support for a particular policy (Campbell 2003). Other related research demonstrates implications for citizenship and civic participation (Mettler 2005). Policy also can influence support for elected officials (Wlezien 2017a; Fording and Patton 2019).

This work differs from ours partly because the focus often is not on policy preferences per se but on other attitudes (or behavior) affected by policy change. The research also conceives of individuals as responsive to their own personal consumption of policy, rather than the collective policy (e.g., Soss and Schram 2007). This is of relevance to our own representation of positive feedback, as we might observe that individuals' P^*_{it} reflect the micro-level (individually experienced) P_{it} instead of the macro P_t. Of course, individuals (i) could respond to both the micro and macro levels, as follows:

$$P^*_{it} = f\{P_{it}, P_t\}. \tag{2.3}$$

For example, people may observe an increase in policy that works and favors more, which may be most common when government is entering a new area, for example, the US policy response to the Great Depression or even Obamacare. That feedback may reflect the beneficial outcomes that the policies produce, for both those who participate in government programs and the broader society.[4]

What is critical about the foregoing Equations 2.1–2.3 is that policy can influence relative preferences in different ways, both directly and indirectly, through P^*. The relationships can vary across domains (and institutions) and across time as well; and our expectation is that a functioning representative democracy requires a reasonable degree of thermostatic responsiveness, as borne out in the research discussed earlier.

That research does not perfectly follow these equations, in large part because we rarely observe P^* directly. Survey organizations do not ask people how much policy they want, presumably because those producing the questionnaires do not expect people to have specific preferred levels of

---

[4] As discussed in footnote 3 in this chapter, policies can undermine support as well, perhaps because it makes conditions worse. On the surface, this can look like thermostatic feedback, in that increased policy leads to decreased support, but there is a critical difference: while undermining feedback is mediated by P^*, thermostatic responsiveness is direct. Also see Wlezien (2017b) and Wlezien and Soroka (2021).

policy in mind.[5] They more commonly ask about relative preferences, whether we are spending "too little," whether spending should "be increased," or whether the government should "do more." Using survey questions like this, public preferences are necessarily relative.[6]

Because we do not directly measure the public's preferred level of policy (P*), we have to rely on proxies (O). Equation 2.4 presents an empirically tractable version of Equation 2.1 – a version that can be estimated using available data, replacing P* with O and adding coefficients to take into the account the fact that R, O, and P have different scales:

$$R_t = a_0 + \beta_1 O_t + \beta_2 P_t + e_t. \qquad (2.4)$$

To be clear: R is the average survey response supporting more or less policy in each year t, P is the amount of policy, O is any number of proxies for P*, for example, economic and national security, and a and e_t represent the intercept and the error term, respectively. Now, the most critical part of Equation 2.4 for our purposes is the coefficient of feedback, β_2: if people respond thermostatically, β_2 will be less than 0. In fact, unless O fully accounts for P*, the coefficient will to some degree encompass both negative and positive feedback, and actually will capture their net effect. There thus is reason to suppose that the coefficient provides minimal estimates of both types of feedback, positive and negative, as discussed in previous work (Soroka and Wlezien 2010).

---

[5] Even where survey organizations ask about absolute preferences, they do not capture people's preferred levels, and it is not clear what responses to questions they do ask tell us about what the public wants, and for three main reasons. First, for those questions that ask support for and opposition to a particular policy, responses can be deceiving about the public's preferences for the policy. Consider Obamacare, which received minority public support in the polls partly because a significant percentage of opponents actually favors a larger government role in health care, not less. (See the series of CNN/ORC International polls between March 2010 and July 2014.) Second, even where responses indicate support for a particular policy, they do not reveal people's preferred levels of policy in the area. For instance, returning to the case of Obamacare, it may be that a person supports the plan but favors more, perhaps much more, of a government role in health care. Third, even if we can tap preferred levels for specific policies in some areas, such as gay marriage, it is difficult to do in many others. Consider, for example, asking people how much spending they want on health care, let alone the many less salient areas in which government spends money and makes (and implements) other policy decisions. For more in-depth discussion of these issues, see Wlezien (2017b).

[6] This actually is quite convenient, as it makes it possible to measure the thermostatic signal the public sends to policymakers – to test the model, we need a measure of relative preferences, after all.

These are the basics of public responsiveness to policy, and they are critical background to what follows, namely, a consideration of the source of that public responsiveness. How does the public receive information about government policy outputs? Let us take initial steps toward conceptualizing how media coverage might serve this function.

2.2 A MEDIA-CENTERED ACCOUNT OF PUBLIC RESPONSIVENESS

Recall that our media-centered account of public responsiveness supposes the following: (a) public responsiveness to policy requires only basic levels of knowledge about policy and policy change, (b) this basic information is readily available in media content, and (c) citizens can recognize and respond to these informational media cues. How might this work? The sections that follow outline our reasoning in detail.

2.2.1 Public Responsiveness Is Not that Hard

Let us begin with the first supposition. In contrast to what some analysts seem to think, public responsiveness to policy does *not* require a high level of information. Consider the literature on thermostatic responsiveness, which shows that citizens adjust their preferences for policy change based in part on policy; when policy goes up, preferences go down, other things being the same, that is, the (underlying) preferred level of policy. This public responsiveness requires only that people have a sense for the direction of policy *change* – whether policy has gone up or down – and perhaps the general magnitude – whether it has gone up (down) by a little or a lot. These are rather basic pieces of information that can be gleaned from simple cues available in the media environment (see, e.g., Lupia and McCubbins 1998). To be clear, public responsiveness need not depend on citizens knowing what exactly is happening in a policy domain; it only requires that some know the basic trajectory of policy.

By way of example, consider that it is 2012, two years after the Affordable Care Act was passed. There was of course plenty of public discussion about health care leading up to Obamacare, and there is a lot following its passage as well. Indeed, it seems very likely that most Americans would have at least a vague sense that the Obama administration had done *something* large on health care. Even if citizens have some misperceptions about certain aspects of the legislation (see Mettler 2018), most probably know that there is increasing government action – and spending – on health care. And this very general sense of increasing/decreasing "policy" is all that is required to adjust their relative preferences for policy, and thus to send a signal to government about the direction in which policy should move in the next fiscal year.

Notice that this view of public responsiveness implies a slightly reformulated version of Equation 2.4. In that model, relative preferences were a function of the difference between proxies for preferred levels of policy (O) and policy itself (P). In this revised version, public responsiveness depends on *changes* in each variable, so that *changes* in relative preferences (R) reflect *changes* in policy (P) and proxies for preferred levels (O), as follows:

$$\Delta R_t = a_0 + \beta_1 \Delta O_t + \beta_2 \Delta P_t + e_t. \qquad (2.5)$$

Here, people *update* their preferences for more policy based on changes in policy, though innovations in the underlying preferred levels also matter. People do not have to freshly develop new preferences about policies each year, as these develop over time and reflect a – perhaps very general – sense of how much government should do and has done. But people do update, adjusting their preferences based on new information.[7] This is in our view a relatively straightforward version of public responsiveness. It does not require that we all have a highly specialized knowledge of policy domains. It requires only that we have a sense for whether we'd like more or less policy, and a sense for whether policy is moving toward that position.[8]

In practice, the updating of preferences may involve adjustments to both current changes in policy *and* the disequilibria between policy and the public's (underlying) preferred level, that is, the extent to which policy commitment is too high or low given that preference. This implies an error correction model of preferences, which is the focus of most of our analyses in Chapter 6:

---

[7] Notice that this is exactly what we would expect if the "level" model captured in Equation 2.4 is correct *and* the public responds only to current policy and does so completely within a year (see Wlezien 1995), where preferences at each point in time equal lagged preferences plus any innovations in P^* and P. If responsiveness is not concurrent but is delayed, then this model, which is mathematically equivalent to the explicitly differenced one in Equation 2.5, would misrepresent that responsiveness and actually *understate* it.

[8] Note that this view of responsiveness is in line with work on online processing, which finds evidence that individuals are capable of regularly updating preferences based on relatively simple cues (see, e.g., Taber and Young 2013). Our ability to make inferences from relatively simple, that is, heuristic, cues is also well established (e.g., Kahneman 2003).

$$\Delta R_t = a_0 + \beta_1 \Delta O_t + \beta_2 O_{t-1} + \beta_3 \Delta P_t + \beta_4 P_{t-1} + \beta_5 R_{t-1} + e_t. \quad (2.6)$$

Note that Equation 2.6 incorporates elements of both Equations 2.4 and 2.5. It allows for current changes in O and P to have short-term (differenced) effects on changes in R, while also allowing long-term (lagged level) effects of O and P alongside the history of R as well. Put more plainly: the model on which we rely expects citizens to update their preferences for policy over time, informed by a combination of short-term changes and long-term levels of policy and other factors.[9]

2.2.2 Media Report on Policy, and People Get It

In order for the public to respond to policy, people need information. That information has to come from somewhere, and our second supposition is that at least some – and perhaps a great deal – of that information is transmitted by legacy (i.e., newspapers, television) and new media.

The prospect that media provide the information that drives public responsiveness may seem at odds with common critiques of news coverage, as noted earlier. That said, we have also argued that media can be inefficient and biased in many different ways but still provide the basic information citizens need to assess the direction (and general magnitude) of policy change, at least in very salient policy areas that attract a lot of public, political, and media attention. Put differently, even as there can be inaccurate information in media content, there can also be a good deal of accurate information, including about policy.[10]

This view of media coverage as providing not all but some, and perhaps the most, critical pieces of policy-relevant information fits nicely with work on political knowledge and political learning. A good amount of research suggests that people can and do learn from media content (e.g., Druckman 2005; Jerit et al. 2006). More recent work in the area also highlights the importance of focusing on more than just citizens' ability to recall and learn static political facts. For instance, scholars have shown how learning from media coverage is particularly pronounced for

---

[9] While the equation may be theoretically encompassing, estimation depends on satisfying certain assumptions about the characteristics of (and relationships between) the different variables, which we take up in the context of our empirical analysis of preferences in Chapter 6.

[10] While attention to policy is important (Williams and Schoonvelde 2018), public responsiveness requires accurate information about what governments actually are doing.

policy-specific knowledge and surveillance knowledge (Barabas and Jerit 2009; Barabas et al. 2014).

What might media coverage of policy look like? Note first that, like public preferences, media coverage need not offer a complete picture of policy at every turn – coverage builds on prior coverage and thus often focuses on policy *change*. There will certainly be exceptions to this rule: particularly when entirely new policies are adopted, we expect media coverage to focus on *levels* of these policies, that is, on the specific provisions of the Affordable Care Act. But this should be the exception rather than the norm. Typically, media coverage will focus on change, possibly even for whole new policies. This is in part because, as noted earlier, there is reason to suppose that the public focuses on and responds to information about policy change. It follows that media coverage, the purpose of which is to attract an audience, will most often focus on the information that the audience finds most important. The details of policy are typically myriad and complex; more general accounts of increases or decreases from the status quo are more easily understood, and more likely to find an audience.

Indeed, our own past work finds evidence of a focus on change rather than levels in media coverage of the economy (Soroka et al. 2015; Wlezien et al. 2017). This may come as no surprise to scholars of journalism, the news, and "newsworthiness" (e.g., Shoemaker and Cohen, 2006; Bennett 2016). The notion that news depends on information being new, that is, a change from the status quo, is built into most notions of newsworthiness; and this helps account for why changes in policy receive more attention than levels.

A focus on change is central to a number of prior accounts of media coverage as well. For instance, it is built into Zaller's (2003) "Burglar Alarm" news standard, outlined as a more realistic alternative to what he refers to as the "Full News" standard. Zaller argues that " . . . news should provide information in the manner of attention-catching 'burglar alarms' about acute problems, rather than 'police patrols' over vast areas that pose no immediate problems" (2003:110). Boydstun (2013) argues further that the alarm mode precipitated by changing conditions can lead to a patrol mode in which news fixates on policy response, at least until an alarm goes off in another area. Change from the status quo is central to work suggesting that "deviance" (Shoemaker et al. 1991) or "outlyingness" (Lamberson and Soroka 2018) are critical drivers of newsworthiness as well. There are, in short, many reasons to expect that media coverage of policy focuses on change.

There also is evidence that citizens recognize and respond to this coverage. Some of this evidence has been identified in Chapter 1, but there are other examples as well. Druckman (2005a) finds that media use is correlated with increased knowledge of election candidates' policy positions, for instance. Jerit et al. (2006) find that public knowledge about public policy issues increases alongside media coverage of those issues (especially among educated respondents). Barabas et al. (2014) find reported media use is positively associated with correct answers to a range of political knowledge questions. Our own prior work (Neuner et al. 2019) identifies similar patterns. We find not only that there are a large number of cues about US defense spending in media coverage but that individuals are able to identify these cues. Importantly, relying on a survey question battery unique to the American National Election Surveys in the 1980s and 1990s, we find that self-reported media use is associated with increased responsiveness to policy over time.

It thus seems likely that the public can identify and respond to information about policy change in media coverage;, and that media regularly provide this information. We can portray a "media policy signal" in a way similar to our account of public responsiveness above:

$$^{\Delta}M_t = h\{\Delta P_t, U_0, U_t\}, \tag{2.7}$$

where the superscripted delta ($^{\Delta}$) for M signifies that we are not focused on changes in coverage (ΔM) but rather recognize that M is itself about change. Media coverage of policy change ($^{\Delta}M$) is a function of change in policy (P) for the particular year t. That said, we expect a fair bit of variation in the strength of the connection between $^{\Delta}M$ and ΔP. Some policy domains will receive very accurate coverage, and others will not. There also may be real variation across media outlets, and/or over time – as we have seen earlier, there are considerable literatures outlining systematic biases in media coverage of policy, or simply failures to cover some policy in any detail at all. For this reason, U_0 captures *bias* in media coverage for different outlets taken together, that is, a tendency to overstate or understate what is being done in a policy area, for instance, to consistently convey that government is doing less then when it really is not, and might be doing more.[11] There can be other more random errors in coverage as well, which U_t in Equation 2.7 captures.

---

[11] This kind of bias may be of special importance across media outlets, where some tend to understate policy change and others overstate it.

For the time being, it is important to highlight that the effectiveness of media coverage in informing the public depends on the degree to which it reflects policy. If the impact of ΔP_t outweighs that of U_0 and U_t, coverage provides a reasonable signal about policy change. If, by contrast, the impact of ΔP_t is overwhelmed by U_0 and U_t, coverage is less likely to provide what citizens need in order to respond to policy, making it harder for the public to effectively guide policymakers and hold them accountable. Which of these possibilities is the case? This is an empirical question and a focus of the chapters that follow.

2.2.3 Media, Public Opinion, and Policy

Equations 2.1 through 2.7 outline the various components of a media-centered account of public responsiveness. Relative preferences for policy (R) change over time in response to changes in preferred levels of policy (P^*) and policy itself (P), though there may be adjustment to (lagged) disequilibria between P^* and P as well. Recall that since we do not directly observe P^*, empirical estimation must rely on proxies (O). More importantly for our purposes, the degree to which R responds efficiently to P depends on a combination of change in policy as well as news-mediated information about policy change ($^\Delta M$). That information is itself a function of changes in policy alongside both stable and time-varying errors in coverage (U_0, U_t) introduced just above.

We can characterize the relationships with the following adaptation of Equation 2.5:

$$\Delta R_t = a_0 + \gamma_1 \Delta O_t + \gamma_2 \Delta P_t + \gamma_3 {}^\Delta M_t + e_t, \qquad (2.8)$$

where the coefficients γ_2 and γ_3 capture the relative impacts of policy change and the media policy signal on changes in relative preferences (while γ_1 captures the impact of changes in the proxies for the preferred levels of policy). If the public responds thermostatically only to policy and not media coverage itself, then the coefficient γ_2 would be less than 0 and the coefficient γ_3 would equal 0. This would indicate that the public responds to policy and not the rest of media coverage (U_0, U_t), which might not be surprising given that some of the error is due to measurement – where our media policy signal does not fully capture the information people receive, and we don't expect them to respond to that error. Of course, it alternatively may be that the public responds to media coverage in its entirety, that is, both that relating to current policy and the rest of the signal as well. If this is the case, we will observe that γ_2 equals 0 and γ_3 is less than 0.

Given that past work has identified thermostatic responsiveness in salient policy domains, our expectation is that the sum of policy's direct effect on preferences (γ_2) and its indirect effect (γ_3 times the effect of policy on $^\Delta M$ in Equation 2.7) will be negative in these domains. Since people presumably need media reporting to learn about policy change, there may be reason to expect the indirect effect to matter more. But, it is important to recognize that media coverage of policy may not be just about policy outputs in the particular year, as it may reflect actions taken that year for future years. It also may be, as noted earlier, that disequilibria between P^* and P matter, so the cumulation of media coverage over time may figure into public adjustment as well – see Equation 2.6 and the discussion surrounding it. These may produce more complex dynamics, which we pick up later, in our empirical analyses.

For expository purposes, we can represent the model in graphical form. We are motivated here in part by Karl Deutsch's work in *The Nerves of Government: Models of Communication and Control* (1963). Deutsch offers a depiction of foreign policy decisions, replicated here as Figure 2.1, intended as an explication of his approach to understanding policymaking in representative democracies. The figure is unquestionably complicated. But it serves to highlight some of our favorite pieces of his argument.

First and foremost, Deutsch's figure makes clear that information is the raw material of political decision-making. The figure includes flows of information not just between actors but inside actors' minds (e.g., "selective recall" and "selective memory"). We are not sure that the inclusion of political psychology is more helpful than distracting for our purposes, and it certainly makes tests of the model more complex. But we see advantages to thinking about information flows between political actors as being subject to "screens" or "filtering," in roughly the same way as we are used to thinking about individual-level information processing. (For a related psychological account of information processing in institutions, see Bryan Jones' excellent *Politics and the Architecture of Choice*.)

Even as the forefronting of communication and information is a valuable element of Deutsch's account, it nevertheless is the case that mass media are not explicitly featured, either in the figure or in his broader argument. Citizens also play only a peripheral role. Each of these actors is in Deutsch's account an implicit part of the "domestic input" that is considered in making (foreign) policy decisions. We thus want to retain

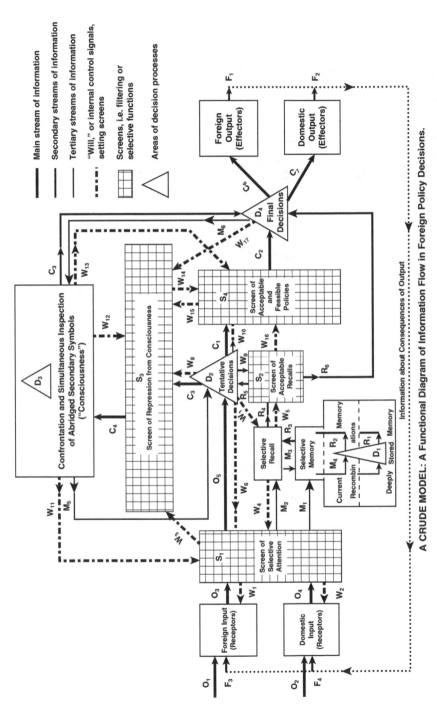

FIGURE 2.1 Deutsch's "A crude model: A functional diagram of information flow in foreign policy decisions"

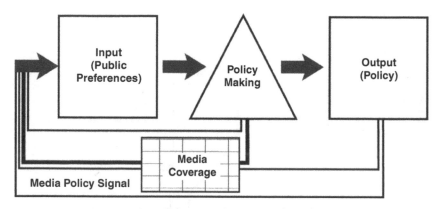

FIGURE 2.2 A media-centered account of a political system

Deutsch's emphasis on information, but make more explicit the roles of the public and media, and the relationships between them that are central to modern representative government, similar to what Easton (1953) did in his depiction of a political system relating inputs and outputs.

Figure 2.2 represents a first effort at doing exactly this. The figure drops the cognitive/psychological aspects of Deutsch's model, although it retains a grid representing a "filter," as well as a triangle representing an "area of decision process." In our simplified model, public preferences are the primary input, and policy is the primary output of the policymaking process. We, and others, have explored elements of this model in prior work. The arrow connecting public preferences to outputs is the central focus of work on policy representation. Research on public inputs, and on public responsiveness in particular, has focused on the different factors shown to influence preferences – both policymaking and policy outputs themselves. But there is little work that explicitly considers the role of media coverage as a critical mechanism and filter, in the connections between policymaking, outputs, and public preferences. Our contention, based on past work (e.g., Soroka and Wlezien 2010), is that the public in most instances responds to policy outputs rather than policy outcomes. There is good reason for this, as outcomes often are difficult to observe and, even when observable, are the result of many factors in addition to policy and so may not provide a good indication of what government has done.[12] And we expect that much of this responsiveness is fueled by

---

[12] They can prove useful where policy information is lacking, however (see Buchanan N.d.). And it is well known that conditions matter for the preferred levels of policy themselves.

information that comes not from policymakers directly but from media content. Hence, we give greater weight to the flow of information from policymaking, through media coverage, in Figure 2.2.

It is worth noting that we regard both Equation 2.8 and Figure 2.2 as stylized accounts of the mediated relationship between public preferences and policy. There are almost certainly many more arrows one could insert in Figure 2.2. Media content can affect policymaking directly, for instance (e.g., Walgrave 2008). Media coverage also can both affect and *reflect* public opinion (e.g., Wlezien and Soroka 2019). We do not want to discount these possibilities, and indeed in later chapters, especially Chapter 7, we will complicate the stylized model set out here. But for the time being, and indeed for much of the book, our primary interest is in capturing the degree to which media coverage reflects policy and informs preferences. We thus view this simplified account as an advantageous starting point.

2.2.4 Media, Public Opinion, and Policy, Over Time

While Figure 2.2 is illustrative of the general relationships between policy, media coverage, and public opinion, we cannot tell from it how the connections play out over time. Figure 2.3 depicts these dynamics.[13] Here, changes in public policy in a particular year positively influence media coverage in that year; relative preferences for policy then respond thermostatically (negatively) to this media signal. Those preferences then positively influence public policy for the ensuing year. The impact of

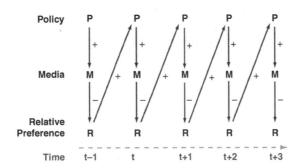

FIGURE 2.3 Information flows over time

---

[13] The figure we use here is an adapted version of Figure 2.3 from Soroka and Wlezien (2010), which depicted the relationships between opinion and policy over time but not the role of the media.

preferences on policy is not a primary concern of this book (but see Soroka and Wlezien 2010); that said, we want to be clear that the lags in the figure are not meant to imply a greater delay in the responsiveness of policy-makers by comparison with the media (and the public). Rather, it is intended to reflect the reality of budgetary policymaking, the focus of our empirical analyses, where spending for any fiscal year is almost entirely decided in the previous year. For example, decisions about spending for fiscal year 2020 were made in 2019 and thus are expected to reflect public opinion in that year, and the resulting policy then impacts media coverage and opinion in the following year, that is, in 2020.

In practice, the relationships between policy, media coverage, and the public may be more complex than Figure 2.3 implies. It may be that media coverage in a particular year reflects not only policy made for that fiscal year but also policy made in that year for future years. Indeed, there is reason to suppose that this better reflects the focus of media coverage of the budgetary process, beginning with the president's budget that usually is released about the same time as the State of the Union Address and continuing with the conflict and cooperation that emerges as the Congressional budget process unfolds. This possibility and others, as well as their consequences for public responsiveness, are considered and assessed in the chapters that follow. In the meantime, Figure 2.3 offers one simplified account of the timing of the interactions between policy, media, and public preferences over time.

The figure provides the basic structure of the model we intend to examine in the remainder of the book. Doing so requires measures of our different variables. Most importantly for our purposes, it requires measures of media coverage of actual policy decisions, something which has not been comprehensively tried in previous research. This is the focus of the chapter that follows.

3

Measuring the "Media Signal"

Testing our media-centered account of public responsiveness requires, first and foremost, measures of media coverage of public policy over an extended period of time and across a broad range of media sources. Recall that we need to measure not just the attention being paid to particular policy areas but the coverage of policy decisions themselves – ideally both their direction and magnitude. This chapter presents the first steps toward developing measures that accomplish this task for the five domains of U.S. federal policymaking that will occupy our attention for the remainder of the book: spending on defense, welfare, health, education, and the environment.

We focus on budgetary policy for various reasons. To begin with, federal government spending is accurately reported by the Office of Management and Budget (OMB), which means we have objective, numeric measures of "reality" with which to compare media coverage. It also allows direct comparability across domains, as policy for each is captured in dollars despite many differences in policy details. In addition, there are regular survey questions asking about support for more or less spending dating back to the mid-1970s, so we have an indication of relative preferences across the five domains over an extended period. Finally, as we shall see, the language of spending is relatively clear, so we are able to extract relevant media coverage. Not all policymaking will be adequately captured by budgetary policy alone, of course, and we consider the inclusion of regulations for environmental policy in particular. For the bulk of our analyses, however, a focus on budgets facilitates measurement across each of the elements of our model: policy, the public, and the media policy signal.

As laid out in Chapter 2, we target our efforts at measuring media coverage of budgetary policy change. We capture the media signal using computer-assisted content analyses of media coverage across seventeen newspapers, in some cases back to fiscal year (FY) 1980, television transcripts for the major networks back to FY 1990, and Facebook content from FY 2010 to 2017. Differences in the time periods for which we capture content on different platforms are determined entirely by data availability; and we will discuss in some detail here exactly what sources are available, when, and why. But the magnitude of our corpora is considerable. To our knowledge, they form the largest policy-focused media database assembled to date.

We will spend the bulk of this chapter outlining what we refer to as a "hierarchical dictionary-based" (Soroka and Wlezien 2019; Dun et al. 2021) approach to content analysis, the primary means by which we build a measure of the media policy signal. In Chapter 4 we turn to more complex supervised-learning approaches to capturing the media policy signal. Before we get to either of these content-analytic methods, however, it is important to describe our database of news coverage across the five policy domains, nearly forty years, and numerous media outlets.

3.1 THE MEDIA CORPORA

There is of course a lot of media content out there, much more than we can possibly collect and analyze. We still can attempt to represent the population of news sources, relying on a broad range of (a) newspapers, (b) broadcast and cable television news programs, and (c) social media content. The following sections describe in some detail each of these corpora.

3.1.1 The Newspaper Corpus

Our full-text newspaper corpus was drawn from Lexis-Nexis using their Web Services Kit (WSK), which was available for the several years over which we gathered data for this project (2015–2018).[1] Unlike standard news indices that allow for limited full-text downloads, the WSK facilitated the downloading of several hundred thousand stories, formatted in xml, in a single search request.

We focused on a set of seventeen major daily newspapers selected based on data availability and circulation, with some consideration

---

[1] It has now been replaced with a Nexis Uni API, although that too may change shortly.

given to regional coverage. The list of papers on which our analyses are based is as follows: *Arizona Republic, Arkansas Democrat-Gazette, Atlanta Journal-Constitution, Boston Globe, Chicago Tribune, Denver Post, Houston Chronicle, Los Angeles Times, Minneapolis Star-Tribune, New York Times, Orange County Register, Philadelphia Inquirer, Seattle Times, St. Louis Post-Dispatch, Tampa Bay Tribune, USA Today,* and *Washington Post.* These are seventeen of the highest-circulation newspapers in the United States, three of which claim national audiences, and seven of which cover large regions in the north-eastern, southern, midwestern, and western parts of the country. (We do not include the *Wall Street Journal* only because it is not available through Lexis-Nexis.) Combining these newspapers, we believe, offers a representative sample of the national news stream, at least where newspapers are concerned.

We begin our data-gathering in FY 1980, but at that time only the *New York Times* and *Washington Post* are available. The *Los Angeles Times,* the *Chicago Tribune,* and the *Houston Chronicle* enter the dataset in 1985 and other papers come online later in the 1980s and into the 1990s. We have sixteen newspapers by 1994, the full set of seventeen by 1999. We then have access to all papers up to the end of 2018.

We do not collect these newspapers in their entirety but rather focus on content related to each of our five policy domains. We do so using a search in the Lexis-Nexis system that combines assigned subject codes and full-text keywords. The subject codes for these domains offer relatively efficient ways of capturing content related to each topic – a fact that we confirmed through preliminary searches comparing subject code results with those using full-text keywords. Even so, we identified some domains in which the subject codes missed content that we thought was central to each domain, and in those cases we either replaced or supplemented subject code searches with full-text keyword searches. The final searches for each domain were as follows:

Defense: "STX001996 or BODY(national defense) or BODY(national security) or BODY(defense spending) or BODY(military spending) or BODY(military procurement) or body (weapons spending)," where STX001996 is the National Security subject code.

Welfare: "N64000CC OR BODY(food stamp) OR BODY(income assistance) OR BODY(social assistance) OR BODY(social security) OR BODY(medicaid) OR BODY(medicare)," where N64000CC is the Social Assistance and Welfare subject code.

Health: "STX000833 OR BODY(health care)," where STX000833 is the Health Care Policy subject code.

Education: "STX000558 OR BODY(education funding) or BODY (school funding) or BODY(education reform) or BODY(education regulation) or BODY(education policy)," where STX000558 is the Education Funding subject code.

Environment: "STX001940," where STX001940 is the Environment & Natural Resources subject code.

These searches were intended to be relatively broad – we used expansive searches, capturing some irrelevant content but also the vast majority of relevant content. We did this because our focus is not on entire articles but rather on relevant sentences that we extract from this downloaded content – and our selection of sentences relies on relatively narrow set of domain-specific keywords. We address this in more detail when we outline the hierarchical dictionary method later. In our minds, it is better to capture any content that might be relevant, and then assess relevance once we have it. Our searches lead to databases that include the following number of newspaper articles in each domain: Defense: 2,171,189; Welfare: 422,454; Health: 680,474; Education: 325,948; Environment: 2,463,687. These articles, roughly 6 million in total, are the raw material used for all the analyses of newspaper data that follow.

3.1.2 The Television Corpus

Our corpus of television news broadcasts also is extracted from Lexis-Nexis, again using the WSK. Television transcripts are stored in Lexis-Nexis in a somewhat different format than newspaper articles. In some cases, content is stored at the story level, like newspapers; in other cases, content is stored at the show level, for example, there is a single transcript for an entire half-hour program. This makes a subject-focused search across networks rather complex: for the major broadcast networks the search identifies individual stories, and for the cable networks the search identifies entire shows. Because we eventually focus on relevant sentences, however, our approach to television transcripts can be inclusive. We can download all transcripts, story- or show-level, and extract relevant sentences afterward.

For the three major broadcasters, ABC, CBS, and NBC, we download all available content from 1990 onward in any morning or evening news broadcast or major "newsmagazine" program. The cable news networks, CNN, MSNBC, and Fox, do not have traditional half-hour news programs – indeed, those networks do not clearly separate news from half-hour commentary programs. Thus, we cannot quite get comparable programming from the cable networks, but we can download all available content, drop infrequent programs, and keep the major recurring ones. These are not directly equivalent to the ABC, CBS, and NBC evening news broadcasts – just as newspapers and evening broadcasts are dissimilar "platforms," so too are broadcast and cable news programs. That said, the sentences that we extract from CNN programs are representative of news coverage on that channel, just as the sentences that we extract from ABC are representative of the news on that channel.

The "major" programs that we keep from each television station are as follows:

ABC: ABC World News/Saturday/Sunday/This Morning, World News Tonight/Saturday/Sunday/This Morning, Good Morning America (306,738 entries of story-level data)

CBS: CBS Evening News, 60 Minutes, CBS This Morning, CBS Morning News (283,237 entries of story-level data)

NBC: NBC Nightly News, Dateline NBC, Today, Saturday/Sunday Today (303,699 entries or story-level data)

CNN: CNN Today, Inside Politics, Crossfire, The Situation Room, World News, Prime News, News, Newstand, Newsnight, Newsmaker, News Hour, Newsday, Morning News, Moneyline, and other shows including the following commentators in the show title: Cooper, King, Tapper, Woodruff (251,205 entries of show-level data)

MSNBC: Countdown, Hardball, MSNBC "Special," The Last Word, Saturday Final, and other shows including the following commentators in the show title: Hayes, Maddow, Williams (18,933 entries of show-level data)

Fox: all shows including the following commentators in the show title: Baier, Cavuto, Gibson, Hannity, Hume, O'Reilly, Van Susteren (88,296 entries of show-level data)

3.1.3 The Facebook Corpus

It has become increasingly difficult to gather data from Facebook. Indeed, at the time of writing there was no straightforward means by which to capture large quantities of public Facebook posts. Thankfully,

Dan Hiaeshutter-Rice was gathering data on public Facebook pages leading up to, and through, the 2016 election. His database ends in 2017, but goes back to 2010, the near-beginning of Facebook, and has been used in Hiaeshutter-Rice and Weeks (N.d.) and Hiaeshutter-Rice (N.d.). Both papers include much more detail about the data and use it much more intensively than is our objective here. Even so, we have kindly been given access to the data and so are able to extend our analyses to Facebook.

The corpus itself includes all posts from roughly 500 top public-affairs-oriented public pages on Facebook. This includes most major news agencies, alongside a good number of "fringe" news outlets. The total number of entries in the Facebook database is 13,086,250. The top twenty contributing sources, listed in descending order based on the number of posts during this time period, are as follows: UFP News, Patriot News List, Barracuda Brigade, Business Insider, Jews News, KHOU11, Huffington Post, *Daily Mail*, Fox Carolina News, *NY Daily News*, *Time*, CNN Monday, End Time Headline, Q13 Fox, ABC 13 Houston, *The Telegraph* (UK), Huffington Post UK, Pix 11 News, NBC Chicago, and AOL. This is an amalgam of major broadcasters and news outlets, alongside some zealots and racists.

Of course, not all sources will post about public policy, so some (including Jews News, which, as you might have guessed, does not have helpful news for Jews) drop out of our working data entirely. And the sites that post the most also are do not necessarily include the most read or recirculated posts. Our data include information on the number of reactions that each post receives, where reactions include likes, the various other emoji responses, comments, and shares. If we base our top-20 list on total reactions over the time period, the top content producers are: I Freaking Love Science, Fox News, Occupy Democrats, Huffington Post, ABC News, Official Right Wing News, Buzzfeed, CNN, The Patriot Review, *People Magazine*, Today, The Mind Unleashed, BBC News, *USA Today*, *Daily Mail*, Upworthy, Barack Obama, The Political Insider, Breitbart, and the Conservative Tribune. This list includes some more mainstream left- and right-leaning news sources than does a list based on the number of posts alone.

Given the way in which news content finds its way into individuals' Facebook streams, reactions-weighted data may offer a better reflection of the Facebook policy signal than raw data. We will consider this in our closing chapter when we turn to the impact of the changing media environment on media accuracy and public responsiveness to policy.

3.2 EXTRACTING POLICY-RELEVANT SENTENCES

Not all of the content we amass is focused on budgetary policy, of course. Particularly in the case of television transcripts and Facebook content, for which we are not extracting content on the basis of topics, our corpora include a large amount of content that is in no way relevant to our work here. Moreover, the raw units of analysis that we have from each medium are not directly comparable.

We solve the problems of unit incomparability by focusing not on stories or shows or posts but on sentences. This is appropriate in large part because the quantity in which we are interested – changes in budgetary policy – will often be transmitted in a single sentence. This is in contrast to more complex or emergent quantities such as issue frames. We might expect a welfare article to be framed as an issue of race in oblique ways over the course of sentences, paragraphs, or entire stories, for instance. Budgetary policy is more specific and self-contained. We are interested in whether media content includes spending, and in particular whether it includes increases or decreases in spending. Has defense spending gone up? Was welfare spending cut? Answers to these questions can be – and often are – communicated at the sentence level.

The analyses that follow are thus not based on articles/transcripts/posts in their entirety but rather all *sentences* in a corpus that focus on spending. To be clear: our working database in the analyses that follow is at the sentence level, where sentences are extracted from the larger databases described earlier using a simple keyword-in-context (KWIC) search identifying all sentences with a keyword related to government spending. For this, we use a Spend dictionary, which includes the following words:

Spend: allocat*, appropriation*, budget*, cost*, earmark*, expend*, fund*, grant*, outlay*, resourc*, spend*

This dictionary search (and each subsequent dictionary search) is implemented in the quanteda package (Benoit et al. 2018) in R. Note that the dictionary has been subjected to testing in the defense domain in Soroka and Wlezien (2019) and was constructed from our own reading of KWIC retrievals, augmented by thesaurus searches.

There are reasons to expect that not all words in the Spend dictionary will work with equal validity and reliability, so we reconsider the use of each word in each of our five domains. In instances where a word does not consistently capture spending, we drop it from consideration in that domain. We discuss this process further later.

In the case of newspapers, then, we have a corpus of articles about defense, for example, from which we extract all sentences that use any of the words in our Spend dictionary. Given that these sentences are drawn from articles that are at least tangentially (and most likely primarily) about defense, there are good reasons to expect that these sentences will be about defense. But this is not necessarily the case. Some articles are only partly about defense, after all, and some might consider defense spending relative to welfare spending. We thus need a way of identifying sentences that mention spending *and* are clearly about the policy domain on which we are focused.

We accomplish this by applying an additional dictionary to each sentence. We first extract all sentences matching our Spend dictionary and then keep only those sentences that also contain a word from each of the following subject-specific Policy dictionaries:

Defense: army, navy, naval, air force, marine*, defense, military, soldier*, war*, cia, homeland, weapon*, terror, security, pentagon, submarine*, warship*, battleship*, destroyer*, airplane*, aircraft, helicopter*, bomb*, missile*, plane*, service men, base*, corps, iraq, afghanistan, nato, naval, cruiser*, intelligence
Welfare: welfare, social assistance, food stamp*, social security, income assistance, security income program, ssip, infants and children program, earned income tax credit, eitc, temporary assistance, tanf
Health: healthcare, health care, obamacare, affordable care act, medicare, medicaid, health insurance program, chip, health administration
Education: education, school*, elementary, secondary, universit*, postgraduate, post-graduate, college*, math, science, stem, arts, music
Environment: environment, water, wildlife, ozone, acid rain, warming, pollution, energy, ocean*, forest*, air, endangered, epa, protection*, sustainability, sustainable

These dictionaries were developed through our own review of KWIC extractions of spending sentences in each domain. We were in the first instance building these dictionaries by looking at the words that most frequently occurred in sentences about spending in each domain. We likely miss some relevant sentences by failing to identify words that should be but are not included in our topic dictionaries. In other words, we err on the side of precision over recall in this instance. (We provide more detailed discussion of these terms later in the chapter.) That said, as we shall see, the words in the dictionaries (a) are in a significant portion of spending sentences in each corpus and (b) reliably distinguish between spending mentions that are judged by human coders to be relevant and irrelevant.

Note that applying the Policy dictionaries serves two purposes. First, in newspaper content, it helps to ensure that sentences extracted from topic-related stories are indeed about the domain in question. Second, in television and Facebook content, where the corpus is not subject specific, it is the only means by which we separate domain-relevant information from all other news content.

The combined application of the Spend and Policy dictionaries is a central feature of what we have referred to as our hierarchical dictionary approach to content analysis. Applying the two dictionaries together is critical to identifying material that is both spending-related and policy-relevant. Using the Spend dictionary on its own will identify material related to defense spending, for example, but not as reliably as it will if we use it in conjunction with the Policy dictionary, which will narrow the substantive focus. Likewise, the Policy dictionary will identify material relevant to defense, but the addition of the Spend dictionary filters out policy content not related to spending. This is of some significance in the building and testing of the dictionaries: our aim is not necessarily to build a Spend dictionary that perfectly captures spending on defense but to build a Spend dictionary that does so in conjunction with the Policy dictionary.

Note that our approach here is identical to the use of hierarchical dictionary counts as implemented in Young and Soroka (2012) and Belanger and Soroka (2012). We also regard this application of dictionaries as very similar to the "learning" inherent in supervised learning methods used for large-N content analysis (e.g., Jurka et al. 2012; see Grimmer and Stewart 2013 for an especially helpful review). Our previous research details how the application of successive dictionaries works (Soroka and Wlezien 2019); other papers further highlight the strong connection between this dictionary-based and human coding (Neuner et al. 2019; Dun et al. 2021), an issue we take up again later.

For the time being, note that our interest is to build and use the Spend and Policy dictionaries alongside another Direction dictionary – a basket of words identifying increases or decreases:

Up: accelerat*, accession, accru*, accumulat*, arise, arose, ascen*, augment*, boom*, boost*, climb*, elevat*, exceed*, expand*, expansion*, extend*, gain*, grow*, heighten*, higher, increas*, jump*, leap*, multiply*, peak*, rais*, resurg*, rise*, rising, rose, skyrocket*, soar*, surg*, escalat*, up, upraise*, upsurge*, upward*)
Down: collaps*, contract*, cut*, decay*, declin*, decompos*, decreas*, deflat*, deplet*, depreciat*, descend*, diminish*, dip*, drop*, dwindl*, fall*, fell, fewer, lose*, losing, loss*, lost, lower*, minimiz*, plung*, reced*, reduc*, sank, sink*, scarcit*, shrank*, shrink*, shrivel*, shrunk, slid*, slip*, slow*, slump*, sunk*, toppl*, trim*, tumbl*, wane*, waning, wither*

Again, note that our objective is to find words that reliably capture increases and decreases *in conjunction with* the other dictionaries. We are not interested in capturing any sentence with the word "expansion"; these sentences surely will be on a wide variety of topics. But we are interested in identifying the sentences that use a Spend keyword *and* a Policy keyword *and* "expansion." (Note that the ordering of the dictionaries does not matter, as they are not really nested but are applied jointly.) Those sentences, our human coding suggests, are reliably about increases in spending.

Just how much content matches these conditions? Figures 3.1–3.3 focus on content that satisfies both the Spend and Policy dictionaries; they show the number of policy-relevant spending sentences extracted from newspapers, television transcripts, and Facebook. Since the number of news outlets changes in the early years of our dataset, Figure 3.1 shows the average number of sentences per outlet. This effectively removes the overtime increase in the 1980s and 1990s that is a product of the increasing number of newspapers in our dataset, rather than increasing attention to budgetary policy. Perhaps surprisingly, this has little consequence for the media signals themselves, as we will see in Chapter 4.

In the top panel of Figure 3.1, increases in the volume of coverage of defense spending are evident at the times we might expect – during the defense build-up in Reagan's first term in office and again following 9/11. In the second panel, welfare spending is most salient in the early 1980s, likely a consequence of spending decreases rather than increases, and a useful reminder that salience and direction are rather different things (also see Jennings and Wlezien 2015). Health spending sees a spike in coverage during the Clinton presidency and again at other moments of major health-care policy change. Education spending receives heightened coverage surrounding the No Child Left Behind Act of 2002 and environment spending is heavily covered when environmental policy was on the political agenda, briefly in the early 1980s and again in the early 1990s, and then once more later in that decade and into the new millennium, after which it leveled off and then declined.

Figures 3.2 and 3.3 depict the television-related data over shorter time periods owing to limited availability of content. Figure 3.2 shows the average number of sentences on a television network in a given fiscal year. By comparison with newspaper coverage, there is lot less television coverage of budgetary policy overall, only about 10 percent of the number of spending sentences on average, and more year-to-year variation. Indeed, there are years in which budgetary policy barely finds

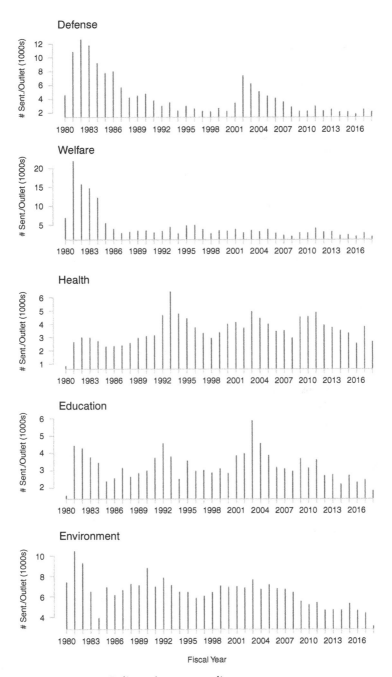

FIGURE 3.1 Policy-relevant spending sentences, newspapers

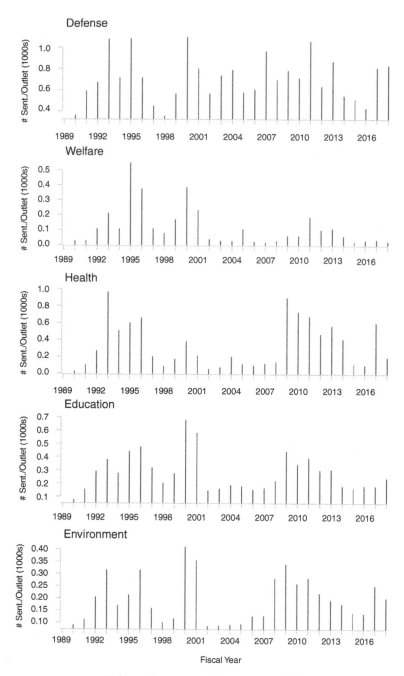

FIGURE 3.2 Policy-relevant spending sentences, TV transcripts

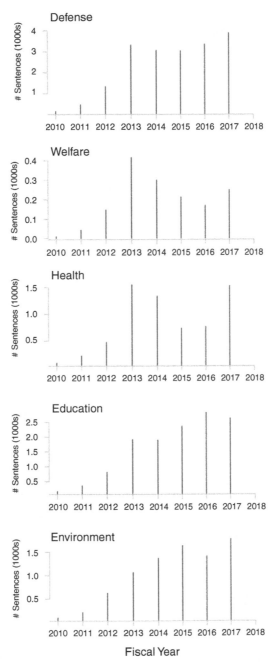

FIGURE 3.3 Policy-relevant spending sentences, Facebook posts

its way into television coverage at all, but also years in which spending in some domains is mentioned over 1,000 times per news outlet.

The trends we see in policy mentions on Facebook, in Figure 3.3, are more about the increasing use of Facebook from 2008 to 2012 than about policy coverage per se. Before 2012, most media outlets were using the platform only sporadically. After 2012, the volume of policy content is greater, though it is difficult to directly compare information about Facebook with the other media outlets. For newspapers or television, figures show the number of relevant sentences the regular audience for a single newspaper or television station would receive, on average, over the time period. For Facebook, it is not clear that there is a "regular audience" for the news stream in its entirety. Consider that Figure 3.3 depicts the volume of spending content for a user who received all posts from the top 500 news outlets.

Note that Figures 3.1 to 3.3 illustrate how much attention was given to budgetary policy in each domain, but they do not tell us anything about coverage of policy change itself, most importantly for our purposes whether spending has increased or decreased. To reiterate, the figures show the number of sentences with Spend and Policy words in them *without* Direction keywords.

Table 3.1 gives us a better sense for the volume of content identified at each step of our hierarchical dictionary analysis. The first three columns of data in the top panel show the number of sentences identified in each domain that include a Spend word, then the number that remain once we apply the Policy dictionary, and finally the number that remain when we add the Direction dictionary. To be clear: there were over 1.7 million sentences in defense articles that use a spending keyword, over half a million of these also include a policy keyword, and 206,426 of those include a signal about the direction of spending change as well.

The final three columns of Table 3.1 express the data in what might be a more intelligible quantity: the average number of sentences in a given outlet in a given year. There are on average 395 sentences in defense articles in a given newspaper over the course of a fiscal year that include keywords in each of the Spend, Policy, and Direction dictionaries. This is a sizeable amount of coverage, on average, just over one spending mention per day. Of course, coverage is not spread evenly across articles and time – there will be some articles with multiple sentences about spending, and these articles likely occur at times when there are policy changes being discussed and/or implemented. There also are domains in which there is markedly less coverage, especially welfare.

TABLE 3.1 *Relevant sentences*

Newspapers

	Total sentences			Weighted sentences (by outlet/ year)		
	Spend	+ Policy	+ Direction	Spend	+ Policy	+ Direction
Defense	1,775,008	521,265	206,426	3,400	999	395
Welfare	1,662,425	31,850	15,580	3,185	61	30
Health	1,922,813	294,683	146,463	3,684	565	281
Education	1,659,397	629,898	265,479	3,179	1,207	509
Environment	3,193,504	362,985	106,689	6,118	695	204

Television

	Total Sentences		Weighted Sentences (by outlet/year)	
	+ Policy	+ Direction	+ Policy	+ Direction
Defense	105,239	32,878	711	222
Welfare	14,999	6,334	101	43
Health	47,703	21,218	322	143
Education	40,783	13,590	276	92
Environment	28,976	9,251	196	63

Facebook

	Total Sentences		Weighted Sentences (by year)	
	+ Policy	+ Direction	+ Policy	+ Direction
Defense	18,563	5,960	2,320	745
Welfare	1,547	709	193	89
Health	6,713	2,688	839	336
Education	12,956	4,133	1,620	517
Environment	8,164	2,401	1,020	300

The middle and lower sets of panels in Table 3.1 include similar descriptive data for the television and Facebook corpora. Recall that in these cases we identify sentences from all available content using a combination of the Spend and Policy dictionaries, so there is no data in the left-hand columns for sentences only mentioning spending, nor are there corresponding averages on right-hand side of the table. Even so, the final two columns show the number of relevant "spending" plus "policy" sentences on average across TV stations and years and then the average number of Facebook sentences per year.

Our primary interest in Table 3.1 is (a) the general trend in sentence identification as we apply successive dictionaries and (b) the overall volume of relevant coverage. Where the general trend is concerned, the application of multiple dictionaries greatly reduces the number of sentences that are considered relevant to the media policy signal. This is as it should be. We cast a relatively wide net in each dictionary, and rely on the combination of dictionaries to extract the most relevant content. Where the overall volume of coverage is concerned, there is in some domains a fair amount of content about budgetary policy change. Consider that there are 395 sentences relating to defense spending change in each newspaper in each year, on average, 222 such sentences in each TV network's news programs on an annual basis, and 745 such sentences in yearly public Facebook posts. This is critical, of course: in order for media to facilitate public responsiveness to policy, there has to be a reasonable amount of policy coverage. For health care, the numbers are 281, 143, and 336. Coverage of other policy areas is in some instances sparser, especially for welfare. We nevertheless take Table 3.1 as providing a strong indication that budgetary policy coverage exists. Media *do* report on changes in spending in some prominent domains, and this coverage is not rare. Public responsiveness to media coverage thus is a possibility.

3.3 A PRELIMINARY MEDIA POLICY SIGNAL

The primary purpose of the sentence extraction and coding outlined earlier is to identify a "media policy signal," a summary measure of the information that media are providing about the direction of spending change in each policy domain. This signal is central to our work in the remainder of the book. We will compare the media policy signal to actual spending change to gauge the accuracy of media coverage. We will do so not just with media as a whole but for individual media outlets as well. We also will use the signals as predictors of changes in the public's relative preferences for policy, to test the possibility that the news plays a role in facilitating public responsiveness.

The construction of our media policy signals is straightforward. Having extracted sentences about spending in each policy domain, we use the Direction dictionary to code each sentence as indicating either upward change (scored as +1), downward change (scored as −1), or no change (scored as 0). We then take the sum of all of these codes for each fiscal year. In years in which upward change sentences outnumber downward change sentences, the measure is positive. In years in which downward change sentences outnumber upward change sentences, the measure is negative. This obviously is a (very) basic approach to coding coverage, but it is highly intuitive and seems to us a useful starting point.

Note that summing the codes also means that we capture the magnitude of coverage of change in each direction. In a year in which there are 1,000 upward sentences and only 100 downward sentences, the media policy signal is +900. In another year in which there are only 100 upward sentences and 10 downward sentences, the media policy signal is +90. The ratio of upward to downward sentences is in these two instances the same. But there is much more coverage of defense spending change in the first instance, and our additive measure will capture this difference. We construct the measure in this way because we suspect that the magnitude of spending change will be correlated with the magnitude of media coverage. When there are large changes in spending, we expect large volumes of coverage of those changes. Our measure of the media policy signal takes this into account. In short, our measure likely captures both the direction and magnitude of spending change, though this can be settled empirically.

The additive construction of the media policy signal has one disadvantage when comparing across media (and outlets). Because there is much more content in newspapers than on television or Facebook, we cannot readily make comparisons across media (and outlets).[2] Comparisons across domains also may be difficult, since defense and health care receive markedly more coverage than the other domains. We thus make one additional change to the media policy signal: we produce a "normalized" signal by dividing each signal by its standard deviation. This does not change in any way the overtime trends in the series, of course, but it does mean that all series are expressed in standardized units, making them more directly comparable.

Figure 3.4 shows preliminary media policy signals across each domain, for all sentences from newspapers (black), television (light gray), and Facebook (dark gray). We refer to these data as preliminary because we will make some refinements below based on a series of reliability and validity tests. That said, Figure 3.4 offers a first look at the measure that plays a starring role in subsequent chapters.

---

[2] The variation in coverage also differs within media platforms, of course.

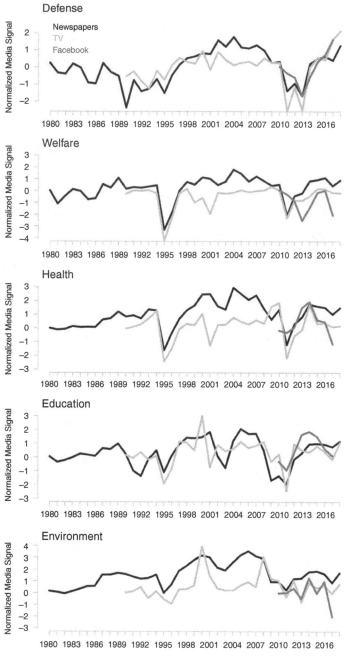

FIGURE 3.4 Preliminary estimates of the media policy signal

A few major changes in coverage already stand out, and we discuss these in greater detail in Chapter 5. For now, the primary feature of Figure 3.4 is the high similarity in the signals based on newspapers and television, and Facebook as well, albeit over a much shorter period of time. There are to be sure some differences across the signals; and as we will see later there are differences across outlets as well. We also have yet to examine the degree to which any of these series line up with actual spending change in each domain – the critical tests of the role that media play in enhancing or confusing accountable representative governance. That our signals produce roughly the same trend across very different news sources already offers an indication of the concurrent validity of our approach, however.

3.4 THE VALIDITY OF THE DICTIONARY-BASED APPROACH

The dictionaries described earlier were developed over several years of extracting, reading, revising, and re-extracting policy sentences. We did not simply invent a list of words and hope for the best. In each case, we rely on our own reading of dictionary-classified sentences – and that of various research assistants – to confirm the inclusion of words and to identify gaps in the dictionaries. We test each dictionary independently and then in conjunction with the other dictionaries, and subject our results to several robustness checks.

First and foremost, we check our dictionary-based results against human coding. This already is documented in previous work focused on news coverage of defense spending (Neuner et al. 2019; Dun et al. 2021). Here, we provide additional tests, not just for defense but across all five policy domains. Our corpus of human-coded content is considerable. We have two bodies of human-coded data. The larger database includes sentences coded in several waves of data-gathering through online crowd-sourced coding, in this instance Amazon Mechanical Turk (MTurk). Each wave of data-gathering focused on a single policy domain. We first defined the domain for online coders. We then asked them to code five sentences. In each case, they are shown a sentence and then asked:

(1) Is Sentence 1 relevant or not relevant to the topic of [domain]? [relevant, not relevant, cannot tell]
(2) Does Sentence 1 show an increase or a decrease in government spending [or regulations]? [increase, decrease, neither]

Note that the second question includes mention of "regulations" only for the environment. It does so because, especially in the case of the environment, increases and decreases in "policy" may not be captured adequately by spending alone; *and* because it is unclear whether survey respondents, when expressing a preference for more or less policy, will be able to distinguish between spending and regulations in this domain. We accordingly collect and code sentences that include regulation words ("regulation*", "regulatory") for the environment. We of course can choose to use these regulation sentences or not use them in the media signals we construct. (As it turns out, this makes little difference to the estimated media signal, which we discuss further in the Appendix to Chapter 4.) For the time being we focus only on spending sentences in all domains.

We solicit five codes of every sentence, so that in every case we have five different coders' assessments of both relevance (question 1) and direction (question 2). We assign categorical codes to each sentence using the following decision rules: a sentence is relevant if three or more (of the five) coders assess it this way; likewise, a sentence reflects upward or downward spending if three or more coders make this assessment.

We do the same with a subset of sentences coded by trained undergraduate coders. These coders are given the same instructions as the online coders, but there is more training involved, including practice coding with feedback and discussion of sentences. (Training data are not used in our analyses here, of course.)

Table 3.2 shows the total number of sentences coded by both means. Note that in the defense domain we have some sentences coded only by students; in welfare and health our student coders receive subsets of sentences coded by MTurkers. We do not use student coders for education or environment but, as we shall see, our aim with student coders is primarily to confirm the reliability of the crowdsourced data.

TABLE 3.2 *Human-coded sentences*

	All	MTurk	Students
Defense	6,119	5,847	1,488
Welfare	7,488	7,488	841
Health	5,403	5,403	880
Education	5,411	5,411	0
Environment	5,116	5,116	0

We focus here on two indicators of the performance of our automated analysis: *precision* and *recall*. These are commonly used to capture the degree to which content is classified correctly (see, e.g., Lacy et al. 2015). Precision indicates how well an approach avoids false-positive classification, and for our purposes is the number of genuinely relevant sentences identified by our dictionaries divided by the total number of sentences coded as relevant by the dictionaries. A high precision score would indicate that most of our classifications of sentences as relevant, say, to defense spending, are correct. It would not necessarily mean that we have correctly identified most of the genuinely relevant sentences, however. This is where recall comes in, which represents the number of relevant sentences identified by dictionaries divided by the total number of genuinely relevant.[3] Identifying what is "genuinely relevant" is not obvious, and in our analysis is determined by human coders, which is standard in assessments of automated content analysis. If a majority of human coders deems a sentence to be relevant, then we expect the dictionary to do so as well, at least most of the time. We expect the same where not-relevant articles are concerned.

Table 3.3 offers some preliminary assessments of precision and recall regarding the relevance of sentences in each policy domain. We focus initially on the first two columns, which show scores for all sentences in each domain. Note that we obtain very high recall for the identification of relevant sentences – almost all (over 90 percent on average) of the sentences that humans classify as relevant are captured using the hierarchical dictionary approach. Precision is weaker, as the dictionary approach tends to

TABLE 3.3 *Precision and recall for relevancy codes*

	All sentences		Sentences with direction keywords	
	Precision	Recall	Precision	Recall
Defense	0.65	0.96	0.70	0.97
Welfare	0.64	0.85	0.65	0.87
Health	0.75	0.95	0.78	0.96
Education	0.76	0.93	0.78	0.94
Environment	0.40	0.83	0.40	0.87

[3] The two indicators relate to Type I and Type II errors in hypothesis testing.

produce false positives, in which irrelevant sentences are classified as relevant (roughly 33 percent of the time on average across all domains). This is most true for the environment, where only 40 percent of the cases identified as relevant by the dictionaries also are coded as relevant by humans. This may not be surprising given the foregoing discussion about regulation in environmental policy, however. The performance of dictionaries is decidedly better in the other domains, where average precision is 70 percent.

Results in the first pair of columns in Table 3.3 speak to the reliability of the method used to produce the data shown in Figures 3.1–3.3, specifically to the accuracy of dictionary classification given human coding. The series shown in those figures are based on all policy content, however, not just the sentences with up and down keywords; and precision and recall are most important for these directional sentences that fuel our measure of the media signal. For this reason, the final columns of Table 3.3 show precision and recall for this subset of sentences – those that are most relevant to the calculation of the measures we use in the remainder of the book. Keep in mind that our expectation is that using hierarchical dictionaries should improve the performance of each dictionary. In this instance, we expect that restricting sentences to the ones that also include a direction keyword will improve precision and recall. Is this the case? It is, though not for each statistic in each domain. That said, there are marginal improvements in almost every case – exactly as we should expect if the use of each additional dictionary improves accuracy. The exception remains the estimate of precision for environmental sentences.

How might we identify classification problems and improve precision in the identification of environment articles? We first look at average human-coded relevance for each of the words in our *Spend* dictionary, and each of the words in our *Policy* dictionary for the environment. There are no outliers in terms of relevance scores for each word in the *Spend* dictionary. Not all *Policy* words appear with a reasonable frequency in our human-coded data, but if we focus on the ones for which there are more than 100 mentions, there are comparatively low relevance scores for "water," "energy," "air," and "epa." If we produce precision and recall estimates for sentences with each of these words, we obtain systematically high estimates for recall (always >0.80), but low estimates for precision: 0.39, 0.34, 0.40, and 0.48, respectively, by contrast with 0.61 for "environment" and 0.62 for "wildlife," for instance.

We thus cannot simply remove these keywords from the *Policy* dictionary without doing real damage to recall. To be clear: our ability to capture all the relevant cases is contingent on the inclusion of these keywords, even as they tend to also produce false positives and thus push precision downward. There are nevertheless ways to improve the performance of the environment dictionaries. We see two potentially fruitful avenues. The first is to acknowledge that the environment domain, more than any of the others examined here, is as much if not more about regulation as it is about spending. A spending-focused analysis may miss much of what is going on in the environment domain. This is certainly true when measuring policy; it may well lead to error in our measurement of media coverage as well. A second way to improve the coding of environment sentences may be to *add* rather than subtract words from the *Policy* dictionary. Our own careful reading of articles did not suggest additional words, but there are other approaches to automated analysis that take into account a broader set of words than is feasible with dictionary-based analyses.

3.5 THE MEDIA POLICY SIGNAL

We have introduced some preliminary measures of a media policy signal based on the hierarchical dictionary approach. This approach works well in identifying relevant text given human coding, although in some cases it produces a large number of false positives, mainly in the environment domain. That said, we can see trends in media policy signals that (a) are strongly correlated across newspapers, television, and Facebook and (b) reflect a number of well-known real-world events. This suggests that our measure is fairly reliable in the aggregate, particularly for defense and in the main social welfare spending areas.

The contents of this chapter represent what is in our view a significant step forward in research focused on the accuracy of media content. We have argued that concerns about media accuracy are not a recent phenomenon, and that our understanding the nature of both media accuracy and public responsiveness would benefit from looking broadly across both policy domains and time. The methods developed in this chapter have accordingly produced what is to our knowledge the first representation of policy change, across five domains, in nearly forty years of media coverage in the United States. The approach may not be perfect but it appears to capture meaningful information about policy. It is a critical first step toward understanding the role that media coverage plays in facilitating or impeding public responsiveness to policy. There are of course adjustments and analyses that may improve or support the validity of these measures. This is the aim of Chapter 4.

4

Alternative Measures of the Media Policy Signal

Chapter 3 laid out the building blocks for our measures of the media policy signal and presented a preliminary version of that signal across newspapers, television, and social media content. We now turn to a series of refinements and robustness tests, critical checks on the accuracy of our media policy signal measures.

We begin with some comparisons between crowdsourced codes and those produced by trained student coders. Assessing the accuracy of crowdsourced data is important for the dictionary-based measures developed in the preceding chapter and for the comparisons with machine-learning-based measures introduced in this chapter. We then turn to crowdsourced content analyses of the degree to which extracted text reflects past, present, or future changes in spending. Our measures likely reflect some combination of these spending changes, and understanding the balance of each will be important for analyses in subsequent chapters. Finally, we present comparisons of dictionary-based measures and those based on machine-learning, using nearly 30,000 human-coded sentences and random forest models to replicate that coding across our entire corpus. As we shall see, our estimations of the media policy signal change very little.

The objective of this chapter, in short, is to test and refine the measures of the "media policy signal" presented in Chapter 3. That signal is then the central protagonist in the chapters that follow.

4.1 THE QUALITY OF CROWDSOURCED
CONTENT-ANALYTIC DATA

Our tests of precision and recall in Table 3.3 rely on crowdsourced content-analytic results. There are reasons to be concerned about the quality of coding from systems such as Amazon Mechanical Turk, however, and a growing body of literature on mechanisms attempts to improve that coding (e.g., Lovett et al. 2018).

Here, we provide a relatively simple test of the quality of our crowdsourced data: we compare it with data coded by "expert" student coders, ones we hired and trained. As noted in Table 3.2, there are three domains for which we have data coded by students: defense, welfare, and health. The absence of student coding for education and environment is purely pragmatic. We began our student coders with defense, which is why the largest body of student-coded content is in that domain. (Recall from our preface that we started with defense because it is a publicly – and politically – salient domain where there is evidence of thermostatic feedback, and because we expected it to be a best case of sorts from the point of view of coding media coverage.) We then added coding on welfare and health, also salient areas where we see strong evidence of specific thermostatic public responsiveness (Wlezien 1995, 2004). Following tests in those three domains, we decided not to proceed with additional student coding. Given that decision, readers might suspect that our results are pretty clear: we find little difference in the student and the crowdsourced coding, and so, given the increased speed and reduced cost of crowdsourced data, we chose to rely on it for subsequent analyses.

Our system for student coding perfectly mirrors the system we used in MTurk. Students are presented with sentence-level data for which they code relevance to spending in particular domain and then the direction of spending change. As with the MTurk-coded data, we extract codes for every sentence from five different coders and use the majority decision to assign categorical classifications for relevance (yes/no) and direction (up/down/none). The central difference in the student-coded data is that students do not just code five sentences – five students coded the entire dataset. The approach to training in this instance included the following: an initial meeting to discuss the objectives of the study and then to review examples of coding; some practice coding after which we reconvened and discussed coding again; and then regular feedback and discussion online about problem cases raised by coders. Our process in training students

TABLE 4.1 *Comparing student and crowdsourced coding*

	Relevance	Direction	N
All	76%	84%	3,209
Defense	83%	88%	1,488
Welfare	78%	85%	841
Health	64%	80%	880

Cell percentages indicate the frequency of agreement between trained students and crowdsourced coding.

thus mirrors a typical approach to human-coded data, with training and practice before and during the coding process (e.g., Krippendorff 2004).

To what extent do these student-coded data mirror what we identify in our crowdsourced data? Table 4.1 offers a very basic comparison. It shows the percentage of cases in which the coding by students is the same as the coding by MTurkers. The top row displays results across all domains; the following three rows show results broken down by domain. There are relatively high levels of agreement for relevance and especially for direction. Where direction is concerned, there is very little variation across domains. There is somewhat more for relevance, with agreement highest for defense and lowest for health. This makes sense, at least to us – the definition of defense policy is relatively straightforward, whereas the definition of welfare and health seems more complex. Even so, we take results in Table 4.1 as an indication that the difference between student and crowdsourced coding is not great, particularly given the high annual level of aggregation at which we use the data, that is, we expect differences between signals based on aggregated student versus crowdsourced data to be smaller still.[1]

It is important for us to acknowledge that the desire to have crowdsourced results match student-based results is premised on the notion that student coding is better than crowdsourced data. Given our own experience with training student coders, and then with keeping them focused on their work over large numbers of sentences, we are not entirely convinced. It may well be that for relatively straightforward (and boring) coding, aggregating results from MTurkers responsible for just five sentences at a time will be more reliable. We do not have any measure of the "ground

---

[1] Note that this is an untested proposition here, since testing it requires more student-coded data than we have gathered for this project.

TABLE 4.2 *Precision and recall for relevancy codes, students, and MTurkers*

	All sentences, student coding		All sentences, MTurker coding	
	Precision	Recall	Precision	Recall
Defense	0.64	0.92	0.61	0.92
Welfare	0.84	0.85	0.68	0.86
Health	0.56	0.97	0.83	0.97

Cell proportions indicate precision and recall for the hierarchical dictionary analysis relative to either trained students or crowdsourced coding.

truth" for each sentence, of course – just various versions of human coding and a hierarchical-dictionary-based signal. We nevertheless can explore the extent to which our tests of the dictionary differ based on student versus crowdsourced coding. One interpretation of the results focuses on the dictionary itself: Do our estimates of precision and recall differ if we use student coding? Another interpretation focuses on the crowdsourced data: Is the degree to which crowdsourced coding matches up with the dictionary any worse (or better) than student-coded data?

The answer to both questions, in short, is no. Table 4.2 shows precision and recall for the hierarchical dictionary based on student and MTurker coding for each of the three domains for which we have both. Measures of precision and recall for MTurkers is different here than in Table 3.3 since we restrict these estimates only to the reduced set for which we have student codes. Measures of precision and recall in Table 4.2 are thus directly comparable for students and MTurkers. There are some differences in performance – student coding for welfare has higher precision than MTurker coding, while MTurker coding for health has higher precision than that for the students. But the level of recall across students and MTurkers is nearly identical. This analysis thus reveals little difference in coding performance. Most importantly, there is no indication here that student coding produces results that are more in line with the dictionary (one version of "ground truth") than does MTurker coding.

In sum, we see few concerns with using crowdsourced human coding for our analyses of media coverage. This is not to say that crowdsourced data will always be similar or better than student-coded data. For more complex quantities, where more expertise is required, there may be good reasons to avoid crowdsourced coding. And there almost certainly is error in both approaches (and in the dictionary as well). For the comparatively simple sentence-level coding we are focused on here, however, there does not seem to be a major advantage to using trained student coders.

4.2 THE TIME HORIZONS OF SPENDING
SENTENCES IN NEWS CONTENT

Our discussion in Chapter 3 proceeded without giving any consideration to whether the spending sentences that produce our media policy signal refer to current, or past, or future changes in spending. This is of relevance for several reasons. If sentences are not overwhelmingly focused on present changes in spending, then our signal may combine information about past, current, and future policy change. If our signal represents a blurred combination of past, current, and future policy change, then we might have different expectations about the relationship between spending change and the signal, and the responsiveness of the public.

Forthcoming chapters will consider in some detail the timing of the relationship between our media policy signal and measures of policy and public preferences. Here, we take a first step toward considering the temporal focus of media coverage using human-coded data. Our approach is relatively straightforward. We begin by taking a random sample of 500 sentences that are coded as relevant from each domain, that is, they are about spending in each particular area. We then field the coding of these sentences in Amazon Mechanical Turk, using the following instructions:

Consider the following sentences about defense spending in the US. Evaluate each sentence for whether it refers to spending in the PAST (spending that has already happened), spending in the PRESENT (current spending), or spending in the FUTURE (spending that will happen, or that is being proposed to happen).

Coders are presented with five sentences, and for each they must choose one of the three options. We extract five codes for every sentence. We then take the average of those codes, where past is coded as −1, present as 0, and future as +1. The resulting measure ranges from −1, indicating that all five coders agreed that the sentence is about past spending, to +1, indicating that all five coders agreed that the sentence is about future spending. Sentences that all coders agree are about current spending change will have an aggregated measure of 0.

Results are shown in Figure 4.1. Note that in most domains – indeed, all domains except for health – the model category is *not* 0. Most of the time, at least some number of coders believes that the spending change

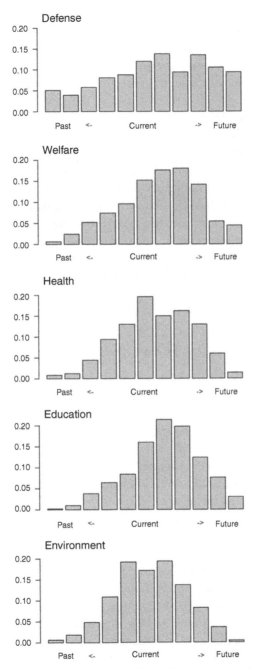

FIGURE 4.1 The temporal focus of spending sentences, by domain

being discussed is either past or future. Defense spending is especially broadly distributed where temporal focus is concerned, as there appears to be a lot of discussion about past and future spending. The bias is toward future spending, however, not just in defense but across all domains except the environment, which is especially well centered around current policy change.

The future-leaning focus of news content makes sense. News generally should be more about what is to come than what is from the past, and our own work on the nature of news coverage of the economy finds similar evidence of a focus on the future (Soroka et al. 2015; Wlezien et al. 2017). Note that reporting on budgetary decision-making will also tend to produce a future-leaning focus in news content, given that decisions typically happen in the fiscal year preceding actual spending change, that is, coverage this year may be as much about spending decisions being made at present for next year as it is about spending being undertaken this year. We set these possibilities aside for the time being but take them up in subsequent chapters, where knowing about the temporal focus of our media signal will be of real significance.

4.3 DICTIONARIES VERSUS MACHINE LEARNING

We have thus far focused on the use of hierarchical dictionaries to capture media coverage of policy change. As we noted in Chapter 3, this approach is rather more complex than the standard, single-dictionary approach to automated content analysis that is (more) common in the literature. Rather than rely on a single dictionary to reliably capture our quantity of interest, we rely on a combination of dictionaries, where we expect the presence of direction and/or topic keywords to augment the validity of our dictionary capturing spending.

There nevertheless are more technically sophisticated approaches to automated content analysis. (See Grimmer and Stewart 2013 for a particularly valuable review of different approaches.) There has recently been a good deal of attention paid to supervised-learning approaches, ones that "learn" from a sample human-coded data and then apply that knowledge to a much larger corpus. Whereas dictionaries necessarily rely on a fixed set of words, supervised learning approaches can take all words in a corpus into account. Moreover, many applications consider not just the frequency of words but the *co-occurrence* of words, even when those words are not proximate within a text. There thus are good reasons to suppose that supervised learning approaches are better able than simple dictionary-based approaches to consider not just the frequency of words but also the context in which those words appear.

Our thinking on this subject is outlined in some detail in Dun et al. (2021). Our intention here is to provide a brief primer on the topic, and then to conduct analyses that compare hierarchical dictionary and machine-learning estimates of the media policy signal. We see this section in part as a methodological discussion of the relative strengths of different approaches to content analysis and in part as a test of the validity of the dictionary-based approach. That said, as will become clear, in these data we find only minimal differences between the two approaches.

We begin by laying out the differences between the two approaches, reproducing a figure used in Dun et al. (2021). Figure 4.2 illustrates the steps taken for the hierarchical dictionary approach alongside what we have called Dictionary-plus-Supervised-Learning approach. The latter is so-named because it too necessarily relies on at least some minimal dictionary-based analysis. Both approaches use word- and topic-based searches for articles in online indices, after all, which is true of many other applications of machine learning. In our case, we let the two approaches rely on a corpus of sentences identified using the "spending" dictionaries. We cannot really proceed otherwise, since the frequency of articles about policy change is low enough that either the population of news articles or a random draw from that population would produce a corpus that is overwhelming not about policy change. Any machine learning, and to a large extent reliable human coding as well, requires

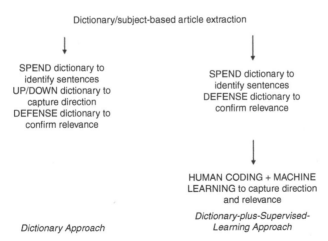

FIGURE 4.2 Dictionary and dictionary-plus-supervised-learning approaches

a more "balanced" sample, that is, one in which there are a reasonable number of cases in each category (i.e., relevant or not). In the absence of balance, the algorithm will tend to predict the predominant response most of the time since doing so will tend to be correct. Achieving balance for most machine-learning approaches often requires the use of a dictionary of some sort.

The means by which we extract human coding has been well described earlier. We rely on the same body of human-coded data used to estimate the precision and recall for the dictionaries summarized in Table 4.2. Here, however, those human codes become the means by which we train the supervised-learning model.

The data used in supervised learning are as follows. We "stem" all words, removing suffixes so that our analysis focuses on the root of each word, for example, "spend," rather than its many variants including "spends," "spending," and so on. We also remove all "stop words," that is, very common words such as "the" or "a."[2] We then produce a document frequency matrix based on this cleaned text, recording every "feature" across every sentence in the corpus, where features in this instance include both unigrams (single words) and bigrams (every combination of two successive words). To be clear, in the sentence "Reagan increased defense spending this past year," unigrams include each word independently while bigrams include every successive pair of words, that is, "Reagan increased," "increased defense," "defense spending," "spending this," and so on.

We divide the resulting document frequency matrix into training and test sets, where 80 percent of the coded sentences are used for training the algorithm, and a random draw of 20 percent of the sentences is held back to test the precision and recall of the trained algorithm. For the sake of parsimony (and thus processing time), we remove all features in the document frequency matrix that occur fewer than two times in the training dataset.

We conduct each of these steps separately for each of the five policy domains. All of these decisions are pretty standard in the literature, and identical to the process used in Dun et al. (2021). The supervised learning itself then employs a random forest model, carried out using the *randomForest* and *rfUtilities* packages in R. We selected the random forest classifier (Breiman 2001) because it is generally considered one of

---

[2] We rely on the standard set of stop words included in the quanteda (Benoit et al. 2018) package in the statistical software environment, R.

the more accurate and efficient multi-class algorithms. Our own prior work also found that the random forest approach made more accurate predictions than a multi-class support vector machine (SVM) approach, another common classification algorithm. The difference between the two systems is likely less important here than the general idea behind the one that we use.

The objective of a random forest model is to find language that is as uniquely associated with each category, for example, a spending increase or spending decrease, as is possible. A random forest model is composed of a large number of decision trees, that is, ways of distinguishing categories based on observed word occurrences and co-occurrences. Each decision tree relies on a different random subset of human-coded sentences. The combination of these many decision "trees" is the random "forest," then, an algorithm that is able to use the language associated with human-coded sentences to classify many more as-yet-uncoded sentences. For more technical detail on random forest models and their application, see, for example, Montgomery and Olivella (2018) and Siroky (2009).

There are two decisions that researchers must make in the application of a random forest algorithm: the number of "trees" to be used and the number of "variables" to be considered within each tree. Typically, researchers are interested in an approach that maximizes accuracy as much as is feasible, given constraints on processing time. (More trees and/or variables will increase processing time.) We did not face major constraints in processing time, partly because of the relative simplicity of our data – by comparison with massive databases of social media content, for instance – and partly because we were able to rely on access to a supercomputer through the Texas Advanced Computer Center at the University of Texas at Austin. Even so, a single random forest estimation typically took between 2 and 6 hours to estimate, sometimes more.

We decided on model specification based on preliminary models that made predictions using different combinations of trees and variables.[3] In each case, we prioritized prediction accuracy over computer time. Note that prediction in this instance is focused on four categories, reflecting the

---

[3] Testing models with various trees and variables is time-consuming, but was automated using the tuneRF() function in the *randomForest* package. The final models rely on tree/variable combinations that are as follows: defense, 250 and 416; welfare 250 and 234; health, 250 and 208; education, 150 and 428; environment, 150 and 210.

combined application of the Spend, Policy, and Direction keyword dictionaries. Those categories are assigned as follows:

a. If <60 percent of MTurkers say a sentence is relevant, the sentence gets a 0;
b. If ≥60 percent of MTurkers say a sentence is relevant but <60 percent of MTurkers agree on a direction, the sentence gets a 1;
c. If ≥60 percent of MTurkers say a sentence is relevant and ≥60 percent of MTurkers say spending is going down, the sentence gets a 2; and
d. If ≥60 percent of MTurkers say a sentence is relevant and ≥60 percent of MTurkers say spending is going up, the sentence gets a 3.

The random forest model weights samples drawn from each training category (0, 1, 2, and 3) in inverse proportion to how often they show up in the training set. We do this because the training set is unbalanced – we still have too many 0s – and inverse weighting should lead the random forest model to produce more accurate predictions in uncategorized data.[4]

Recall that we train the machine on 80 percent of our human-coded sample, holding back 20 percent of that human-coded data for tests of precision and recall. Those tests are presented in Table 4.3, which shows results for sentence-level coding from both the machine and the dictionary. Again, we reestimate precision and recall for the dictionary using the same cases as we use to test precision and recall for the machine, so the results across the two approaches in Table 4.3 are directly comparable. We also now show precision and recall for each of the four categories used in machine learning.

There is significant variation in precision and recall both across policy domains and across categories within policy domains. There are some domains in which precision and recall are relatively high (defense), and others where it is decidedly weak (environment). The coding of 0s (not relevant) and 1s (relevant, no direction) is typically stronger than the coding of 2s and 3s – though note that the latter reflect two coding decisions (relevance + direction), and we should expect more error as a result. As with most automated approaches, there is a lot of error in

---

[4] In fact, we had repeated failures in which our random forest estimation did not converge in the environment domain due to a high proportion of 0s – a problem we fixed only by collecting additional crowdsourced data and then dropping some of the 0s from the training set.

TABLE 4.3 *Precision and recall, dictionary versus machine learning*

	Dictionary		Machine	
	Precision	Recall	Precision	Recall
Defense				
Not relevant	0.87	0.63	0.80	0.84
Relevant, no direction	0.55	0.67	0.62	0.58
Relevant, downward spending	0.40	0.66	0.56	0.59
Relevant, upward spending	0.50	0.42	0.48	0.46
Welfare				
Not relevant	0.54	0.68	0.58	0.64
Relevant, no direction	0.69	0.51	0.66	0.66
Relevant, downward spending	0.32	0.50	0.41	0.39
Relevant, upward spending	0.28	0.30	0.29	0.22
Health				
Not relevant	0.27	0.87	0.70	0.69
Relevant, no direction	0.73	0.37	0.70	0.71
Relevant, downward spending	0.29	0.27	0.35	0.25
Relevant, upward spending	0.42	0.24	0.38	0.40
Education				
Not relevant	0.66	0.59	0.72	0.64
Relevant, no direction	0.67	0.63	0.71	0.74
Relevant, downward spending	0.34	0.50	0.33	0.36
Relevant, upward spending	0.36	0.40	0.45	0.42
Environment				
Not relevant	0.58	0.62	0.58	0.63
Relevant, no direction	0.37	0.53	0.46	0.46
Relevant, downward spending	0.17	0.15	0.19	0.11
Relevant, upward spending	0.35	0.14	0.42	0.42
Total (average by category)				
Not relevant	0.58	0.68	0.68	0.69
Relevant, no direction	0.60	0.54	0.63	0.63
Relevant, downward spending	0.30	0.42	0.37	0.34
Relevant, upward spending	0.38	0.30	0.40	0.38
Total (average across all categories)	0.47	0.48	0.52	0.51

Cell proportions indicate precision and recall for the hierarchical dictionary and machine learning analysis relative to crowdsourced human coding.

TABLE 4.4 *Correlation between dictionary- and machine coding*

	Defense	Welfare	Health	Education	Environment
Sentence-level, Dictionary versus ML	0.31	0.43	0.26	0.45	0.17
Sentence-level, Dictionary + Domain keywords versus ML	0.35	0.14	0.31	0.42	0.08
FY aggregate measures, Dictionary versus ML	0.91	0.84	0.89	0.82	0.89
FY aggregate measures, Dictionary + Domain keywords versus ML	0.81	0.63	0.74	0.77	0.74

Cells contain Pearson's correlation coefficients between automated coding approaches to estimating a media policy signal. For sentence-level correlations, $N = 1,569,273$ for defense; $1,389,525$ for welfare; $1,639,575$ for health; $1,347,690$ for education; and $2,802,790$ for environment. For all aggregate correlations, $N = 38$.

the sentence-level coding. That said, the error is not obviously lower or higher in the machine learning than the hierarchical dictionaries. The final rows of Table 4.3 show average precision and recall scores for each category across all five domains, as well as average across all categories and domains, the latter of which reveal a slight advantage for machine learning, though more so for precision.

Table 4.4 offers another diagnostic test, this time focusing on both the sentence-level and aggregated indicators resulting from the dictionary and machine-based coding, not just in the 20 percent "test" dataset of human-coded data but across the entire corpus. The main objective of machine learning, after all, is to apply codes to the entire corpus. Having estimated a model with a given set of parameters, and examining the precision and recall of that model (as in Table 4.3), we are then able to apply the estimated model to the entire corpus, generating predictions for every sentence we have.

Table 4.4 thus is based on predictions across the entire corpus. We begin by coding each sentence as –1 (downward spending), +1 (upward spending), or 0 (no change in spending). This is exactly the coding used in Chapter 3 to estimate the media policy signal; so our dictionary-based measures here are exactly as we have seen previously, and the machine-based measures reflect a recoding of the new machine-learning results described earlier (in

Table 4.3). We then estimate the correlation between the dictionary and machine-based results; first across all sentences in the corpus and then across our media signals based on aggregating dictionary- or machine-based sentence codings by fiscal year.

Sentence-level correlations are in the first two rows. The first row shows correlations between the simple dictionary-based codes and those generated using machine learning, while the second reports the associations between enhanced dictionary-based codes (that take into account relevance codes based on the Policy dictionaries outlined in Chapter 3, section 3.2) and the machine-learning coding. The relationships all are quite modest, revealing that the two general approaches – dictionaries and machine learning – often produce different codes for the same sentence. These correlations are constrained by the fact that we are using variables that take on just three values (–1, 0, +1); even so, the estimates are not especially high, that is, closer to 0 than to 1, and in the environment domain they are strikingly low. Note that all are statistically significant at $p<.01$.

The bottom two rows of Table 4.4 show correlations between the aggregated series, where the sentence-level codings are simply added together by fiscal year, exactly as we did in Chapter 3. Here we see the importance of aggregation. Even as there are frequent errors in the sentence-level coding, aggregation identifies a signal, where the one produced by machine learning is highly correlated with that generated using dictionaries, on average about 0.80. There is one important lesson from the machine-learning analysis at both the sentence and aggregate levels: insofar as the machine-learning signal reflects accurate human assessments of relevance, it appears as though the dictionary-based coding is worsened rather than improved by the addition of domain keywords (in the second row). The dictionary signal without this additional constraint is very highly correlated with the machine-learning signal, 0.87 on average in the aggregate analysis.

Figure 4.3 shows the aggregated media signals over time. Each figure plots three signals for each spending domain: one based on dictionaries, another based on dictionaries with topic keywords, and the third using supervised learning. The strong relationship between the hierarchical dictionary and machine-learning signals here is very clear. There are small differences over time, but the signals tend to rise and fall together. Note that there is nothing in our data analysis which requires that this is the case. The dictionary-based method relies entirely on dictionaries and

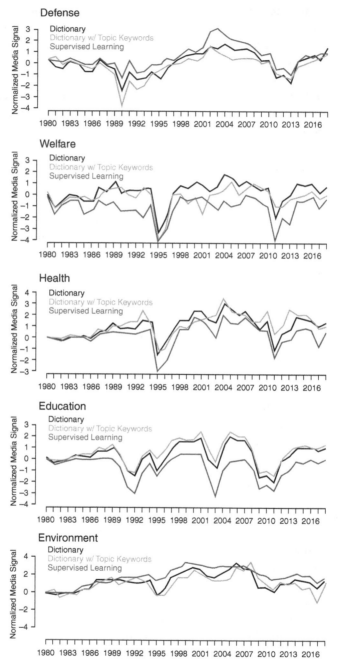

FIGURE 4.3 The media policy signal, dictionary, and supervised learning

the supervised learning method uses human-coded data to train an algorithm. That the two end up with roughly the same aggregate series suggests to us that both methods produce a valid signal, though note that relying on the dictionary to find a balanced sample with which to train the random forest algorithm likely inflates the observed correlation between the two measures.[5]

Some relatively simple and more qualitative analyses give us further reason to be confident in the content-analytic results. We already know the words that are behind the dictionary-based analyses, of course – they are the words in our dictionaries. These words may be different in the supervised learning algorithm, however, since there are no constraints in terms of the words that it uses to replicate human codes. Thinking about the supervised learning results as being driven just by words is a little simplistic (and inaccurate); it is driven by words, but also combinations of words through both bi-grams and co-occurrences of other non-proximate words, as discussed earlier. Even so, looking at the words that are most highly correlated with the coding done by the supervised learning can give us a sense of the degree to which the machine-learning approach ends up focusing on language that is similar or different to what we rely on in the dictionaries.

Table 4.5 provides a glimpse of the words that are most strongly correlated with the machine-learning codes. Identifying these words is relatively simple. We estimate the correlation between every word in the corpus and each of three codes from the machine learning – relevant with no spending change, relevant with upward spending change, and relevant with downward spending change. We then take the words that are correlated at $r = 0.05$ or greater within each of these three categories and present them (in descending order based on the magnitude of the correlation coefficient) in Table 4.5.

We do not expect every word in each category to be perfect markers of that particular category, of course. The random forest model does not assign categories based just on the occurrence of single words, after all. Even so, our expectation is that, to the extent that the machine learning works, each of the lists in Table 4.5 will be full of words that are related to upward or downward spending change. That is, by our estimation, clearly the case.

---

[5] The use of a dictionary to identify a balanced sample with which to train the machine learning algorithm is common, and often critical, in applications of supervised learning. See Dun et al. (2021) for more extensive discussion.

TABLE 4.5 *Words correlated with machine-learning predictions*

Category	Top 20 words
Defense, Relevance	defense, military, war, billion, spending, pentagon, weapons, iraq, force, homeland, cuts, air, billions, reductions, missile, reduction, forces, wars, security, afghanistan, missiles, secretary, soviet, nuclear, troops, department, pentagons, cold, armed, budget, domestic, cut, increase, nato, congress, united, weapon, reagan, aircraft, strategic, buildup, star, militarys, personnel, cheney, bill, contractors, allies, world, civilian, weinberger, fighter
Defense, Down	cuts, reductions, reduction, cut, defense, spending, military, budget, cutting, automatic, acrosstheboard, reduced, cutbacks, reduce, domestic, billion, deficit, reducing, sequestration, proposed, pentagon, savings, deeper, programs, deep
Defense, Up	billion, homeland, billions, increase, security, military, defense, spending, dollars, pentagon, increases, increased, iraq, year, afghanistan, department, request, increasing, war, weapons, bill, missile, next, fiscal, emergency, requested, nearly
Welfare, Relevance	cuts, welfare, cut, spending, programs, food, stamps, cutting, increase, increases, stamp, increased, domestic, budget, reductions, billion, tax, acrosstheboard, automatic, reduction, deep, deficit, proposed, education, aid, reduce, poor, increasing, defense, back, republicans, taxes, program, assistance, block, nutrition, balance, child, reducing, social, recipients, families
Welfare, Down	cuts, cut, cutting, spending, budget, programs, reductions, acrosstheboard, domestic, automatic, deep, deficit, reduction, back, proposed, reduce, billion, defense, republicans, reagan, increases, tax, reducing, hikes, balance, reduced
Welfare, Up	increase, increased, increases, increasing, spending, percent, food, funding, education, increasingly, programs, stamp, credits
Health, Relevance	health, care, costs, medical, insurance, medicare, healthcare, medicaid, patients, coverage, rising, mental, system, services, hospitals, doctors, nursing, employers, providers, benefits, plans, reform, poor, hospital, drug, premiums, reduce, americans, affordable, insurers, elderly, workers, uninsured, preventive, national, employees, people, plan, provide, centers, control, providing, pay, managed, quality, prescription, access, universal, home, physicians, private, cover, patient, reducing, drugs, institutes, skyrocketing, retiree

TABLE 4.5 *(continued)*

Category	Top 20 words
Health, Down	cuts, cut, cutting, reduce, health, care, medicaid, budget, reducing, tax, balance, reduced, deep, spending, programs, medicare, republicans
Health, Up	health, care, rising, increase, million, increased, increases, costs, increasing, centers, mental, rise, institutes, veterans
Education, Relevance	school, education, schools, funding, cuts, college, students, public, teachers, districts, cut, high, colleges, board, district, higher, educational, elementary, system, teacher, student, charter, parents, state, tuition, aid, universities, private, systems, educators, children, cutting, special, unified, local, middle, superintendent, classroom, community, officials, educate
Education, Down	cuts, cut, cutting, budget, deep, reductions, programs, forced, proposed, layoffs, acrosstheboard
Education, Up	increase, education, increased, increases, increasing, million, schools, rate, elementary, school, funding, teachers, tax, earmarked, percent, additional, teacher, seeking
Environment, Relevance	regulations, resources, water, regulators, regulation, resource, environmental, natural, regulate, fund, funding, cut, million, funds, agency, protection, state, cuts, regulated, pollution, federal, wildlife, regulating, projects, energy, emissions, conservation, agencies, air, clean, protect, plants, use, law, laws, act, project, epa, industry, states, plant, power, rules, regulates, california, management, cutting
Environment, Down	cut, cuts, cutting, agencies, agency, budget, agency's, regulations, administration, law
Environment, Up	million, funds, fund, funding, projects, project, millions, additional, program, water, improvements, funded, dollars, addition, year, estimated, research, earmarked, trust, sewer, construction, billion, help, programs, provide, increase, pay, bond, matching, restoration, state, grant, federal, approved, last, park, improvement

Consider, for instance, the words that are most commonly associated with downward spending change (looking across all five policy domains), such as cut/cuts/cutting, reduction/reductions/reducing; or the words most commonly associated with upward spending change, such as increase/increases/increasing. Relevance keywords in Table 4.5 are also very clearly related to each policy domain. One possible use of these word lists is as a way of improving our dictionaries. We have argued elsewhere for the potential advantages of combining dictionary-based and machine-learning approaches (Dun et al. 2021). One possibility, noted earlier, is that dictionaries can be used to produce more balanced samples for training a supervised learning model. Another possibility is that the machine-learning results can identify words that should be included in a dictionary.

There are few hints of words in Table 4.5 that are not but should be included in our dictionaries, however. There are in particular no indications of spending or direction words that are highly correlated with machine-learning results and not already included in the spending or direction dictionaries. This is mildly but not totally surprising; the dictionaries on which we rely were subjected to years of testing and re-testing, after all. But it is reassuring that a machine-coding system does not turn up words that prior work had missed. This helps account for why we find such high correlations between the dictionary- and machine-based media policy signals. In addition, the use of co-occurrences rather than simple word frequencies seems to matter rather little in the aggregate – given the observed similarity of the dictionary and machine-learning signals, simple word counts using hierarchical dictionaries appears in this instance to capture the same over-time variation as the more complex machine-learning approach.

4.4 ADDING NEWSPAPERS OVER TIME

Recall from Chapter 3 that we have data from all television networks over the same time period (1990–2018), but our newspaper database begins in 1980 with just the *New York Times* and *Washington Post*, and does not include all seventeen newspapers until 1999. We have thus far been looking at the signal – produced using both dictionaries and machine learning – without taking into account the growing number of newspapers in the sample. This is because doing so does not make much difference, as we will see. Insofar as different papers tend to communicate the same basic information, there is reason to expect the direction of the newspaper signal to be largely unaffected by the addition of papers. That said, the variation can change with increasing coverage, where we might observe more pronounced indications of policy change over time. This need not be the case, of course, but is important to test because our measure plays a critical role in ensuing chapters.

Figure 4.4 shows trends in two dictionary-based estimations of the media policy signal in each domain: (1) one that relies on just the *New York Times* and *Washington Post*, and thus is consistent across the entire time period and (2) another that excludes these two newspapers and adds others whenever they enter our dataset between 1985 and 1999. The figure focuses on trends from 1985 onward, since 1985 is the first year at which the additional newspapers enter our dataset. Trends for each series are very similar – the lowest correlation between the series is 0.82 (for Education), and there is no hint of increasing variability as newspapers are added to the series. There *are* small differences between the series, of course – newspapers will have slightly different coverage of each policy domain, and that will be reflected in what turn out to be relatively small shifts in the estimated signals. Where measurement is concerned, results in Figure 4.4 suggest that the simple measure we have focused on thus far does not reflect anything unique about the *New York Times* and the *Washington Post*, since the other fifteen newspapers produce a signal that is very similar. That said, there *are* differences between newspapers, as we shall see in the next chapter.

There are other over-time and across-newspaper differences worth considering. One issue is taking the circulation of newspapers into account in the design of the media policy signal. We consider that in the Appendix to this chapter. Another issue is the declining circulation of all newspapers over time, and the difference this might make for public responsiveness to the media policy signal. We consider this in Chapter 7.

4.5 ON MEASURING MEDIA COVERAGE OF SPENDING

What are the lessons of the preceding analyses? What can we take from this chapter into the subsequent chapters, where our focus is entirely on the ways in which the media policy signal is associated with policy change and public preferences? Our reading of the preceding results suggests the following.

First, crowdsourced content analysis does not appear to be more error-prone than the more standard trained student-driven analysis. This finding is important, because we rely predominantly on our (much larger) crowdsourced human coding for both the testing of dictionaries and the estimation of a supervised-learning-based signal.

Second, the estimation of a media policy signal that relies on human-coded data and machine learning is only marginally different from a signal that relies on dictionaries. This increases our faith in the dictionary-based

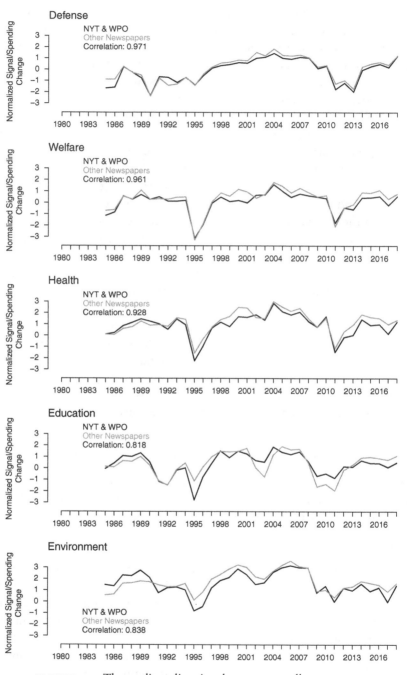

FIGURE 4.4 The media policy signal, two versus all newspapers

approach, as does the realization that the words most correlated with machine-learning results are typically the ones already included in the dictionaries. This simplifies our analysis moving forward, in which we will rely exclusively on the dictionaries for television and Facebook signals, and primarily for newspaper signals as well.

Finally, human coding makes clear that our media signal reflects some combination of past, current, and future spending, with an emphasis on current *and* future spending. This finding is in line with past work on the temporal focus of news content generally, and is what we would expect if coverage follows the policymaking process itself. There also appears to be little difference in our series owing to changes in the availability of newspaper content. Both of these findings will be of real importance to our time-series models, beginning with the relationship between spending and the media signal(s) in Chapter 5.

4.6 APPENDIX TO CHAPTER 4: ALTERNATIVE SPECIFICATIONS OF THE MEDIA "POLICY SIGNAL"

Our main measure of newspaper coverage is simple: it tallies the number of sentences indicating upward or downward changes in spending, by domain and fiscal year. This is true for the measures relying on dictionary-based content analysis; it is true for the measure based on machine learning as well. There are several alternative specifications worth considering, however.

The first is related just to the environment domain. Recall that our content analyses for the environment captured sentences related to regulation as well as spending. We gather regulation sentences because regulation is such a big part of environmental policy; and because citizens may well respond to regulation along with spending. Searches for regulation sentences in the other domains yielded very small numbers of sentences, so we do not worry about regulation in the other domains; but regulation sentences make up 13 percent of all sentences retrieved in the newspaper and television corpuses for the environment.

Note that our analysis of regulation sentences mirrors exactly our analysis of spending sentences, insofar as we capture increases or decreases in policy. It may be that regulation requires a somewhat different analysis, but that is beyond the scope of the content analyses that we have conducted. Where a focus on increases and decreases is concerned, including the regulation sentences in the environment corpus produces aggregate signals that are – in every possible configuration of the media policy signal – correlated with the spending-only measure at $r > 0.99$. This may come as little surprise, given that regulation sentences are a small portion of the environment dataset. There is further work to be done on regulation coverage specifically, we suspect. But in the chapters that follow, we include regulation sentences in the media measures for the environment, knowing that the alternative would produce results that are (nearly) identical.

A second consideration in the design of the media policy signal is the differential audience of different newspapers. All sentences are treated equally in the measures used thus far; they accordingly give more weight to newspapers that produce more coverage, particularly the *New York Times* and the *Washington Post*. Analyses in Chapter 4 have already shown that variation in the measure is not driven just by these papers; indeed, we found virtually no difference in the signal for these two papers and the others, even as data for the latter become available at different points in time.

It thus appears that our simple additive measure of the media policy signal works well to capture trends in coverage across outlets. This is of obvious importance to our research, particularly analyses of the accuracy of media coverage in Chapter 5. But if the objective is to capture the signal that actually reaches people – as is the aim in analyses of public perceptions and preferences in Chapter 6 – then it may be important to also consider the *attention* that different outlets receive.

We focus our analyses here on the newspaper signal, since differences in attentiveness to the three major television networks are more limited. First, let us consider the actual circulation of newspapers. We can do so by weighting each spending sentence by the circulation of the newspaper in which it appears. We use the average weekday circulation during the 2001–2010 period, based on annual Audit Reports for individual newspapers from the Alliance for Audited Media. Newspapers that produce a lot of coverage and also have a large circulation, such as the *New York Times*, carry more weight in the alternative measure of the media signal; those that produce little coverage and have a small circulation, such as the *Denver Post*, carry less weight.

Circulation figures are shown in Table 4.A1. *USA Today* has a massive circulation of over three million, the *New York Times* has a circulation of just under one million; there is a set of newspapers with a circulation of roughly a half a million; and for the remainder, circulation ranges between one and three hundred thousand. Differences between most newspapers

TABLE 4.A1 *Newspaper circulation,*
weekday averages, 2001–2010

USA Today	3,424,951
New York Times	994,453
Los Angeles Times	520,232
Chicago Tribune	477,351
Washington Post	446,887
Houston Chronicle	299,260
Tampa Bay Times	292,680
Minnesota Star-Tribune	278,139
Orange County Register	260,622
Philadelphia Inquirer	246,790
Boston Globe	233,254
Seattle Times	210,258
Denver Post	206,637
Arizona Republic	176,408
St. Louis Post-Dispatch	127,497
Arkansas Democrat-Gazette	126,960
Atlanta Journal-Constitution	120,665

are actually relatively small. Given differences in the volume of coverage, the primary effects of weighting by circulation will be to (a) reduce the impact of the *Washington Post*, which produces a lot of content but is middling in terms of circulation and (b) augment the impact of *USA Today*, which produces limited content but has a circulation more than three times the size of any other newspaper. There will be other changes in the weight each newspaper has on the overall measure as well, of course. Figure 4.A1 offers a comparison between two measures: (a) our original additive measure, in which all sentences are given equal weight and (b) a circulation-weighted measure in which the upward (+1), downward (−1), or neutral (0) sentence codings are multiplied by the circulation of the newspaper. Both series are set on the same scale and plotted in Figure 4.A1.

It turns out that there are almost no discernable differences between our initial measure and one that is weighted by circulation. The first measure, shown as a gray line in Figure 4.A1, is barely distinguishable from the circulation-weighted one, shown in black. Correlations are between 0.96 and 0.99. What accounts for such small changes? As

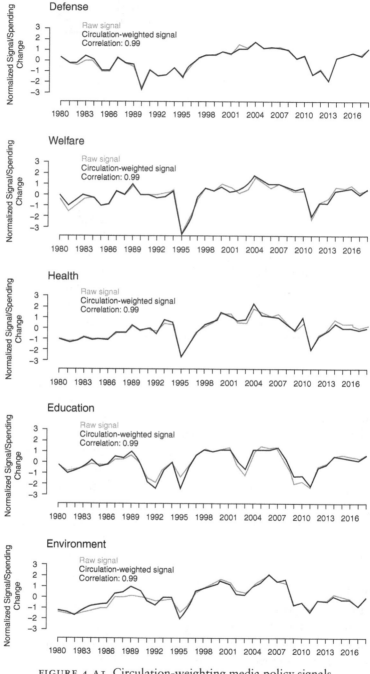

FIGURE 4.A1 Circulation-weighting media policy signals

noted earlier, the relative weight of most newspapers changes relatively little in this circulation-weighted measure. For the most part, the *Washington Post* matters a little bit less and *USA Today* matters a fair bit more – but the impact of *USA Today* on the overall measure is still limited by the relatively small volume of coverage in that paper. There thus is little benefit to weighting by circulation when estimating relationships with budgetary policy and public opinion, which we do in Chapters 5 and 6.[6]

---

[6] Of course, our analyses conceal variation across individuals, which we cannot address in the absence of information about which specific outlets they consume.

5

The Accuracy of Media Coverage

The last two chapters have described in some detail the building blocks of our measures of the media policy signal. The reliability with which we capture that signal is of some significance. It is central to our tests of (a) the degree to which media coverage accurately (or inaccurately) reflects policy change and (b) the extent to which media coverage informs (or complicates) public responsiveness to policy. This chapter focuses on the former. In so doing, we offer what is to our knowledge the first test of the long-term accuracy of media coverage – in this case, across multiple decades, five policy domains, and twenty-three newspaper and television media outlets. (Since Facebook data are available for only eight fiscal years, we do not interrogate them in this chapter, although we do undertake some basic analyses in our concluding Chapter 8.)

Recall from Chapter 2 the burgeoning literatures on inaccuracies in media coverage, particularly in recent years, given concerns about a breakdown in the relationship between the press and governments, and the Trump administration's claims about "fake news." We argued there that media inaccuracies are not new – that concerns about the differences between media content and reality are longstanding. Differences between crime-related media coverage and actual crime rates are well established (e.g., Sacco 1995; Dixon et al. 2003; Soroka 2014), as are failures in media reporting of complex scientific issues (e.g., Bennett 1988), for example. Media coverage of welfare has misrepresented the race of welfare recipients (e.g., Gilens 1999), and reporting on health-care reform may well have hindered informed public attitudes about both the Clinton and Obama administrations' programs (Fowler et al. 2017; Gollust et al. 2019).

What follows is an extension of this past work. How accurate has the US media been in its representation of budgetary policy over the past four decades? How accurate has it been on defense versus welfare? How does accuracy differ across specific outlets? Are national newspapers like the *Washington Post* and the *New York Times* more accurate than local ones? Are broadcast television stations more accurate than their cable counterparts? Among the latter, how accurate is CNN compared to MSNBC and Fox? We attempt to answer these questions in this chapter.

We see the results that follow not just as an exploration into the accuracy of media coverage but also as an important step toward understanding the potential for informed public responsiveness to policy change. As we have discussed, such policy feedback depends on information about policy; that information presumably comes in part if not exclusively from media coverage; so, the accuracy of media coverage is a necessary condition for informed public responsiveness. Just how accurate is media coverage of policy?

We begin with some relatively straightforward graphical and correlational analyses of the relationship between the media policy signal and changes in budgetary policy. We then turn to regression analyses to better tease out the impact of past, current, and future policy change on media coverage. As we shall see, there are domains in which spending is captured remarkably well in media coverage. If citizens follow media coverage even sporadically they will receive relatively accurate information about what governments are doing on defense, for instance. There are, however, other domains in which this is clearly not the case. In fact, media coverage of *each of the domestic domains* is less clearly linked to spending. There are nevertheless reasons to expect that public preferences can be usefully informed by media coverage of health and welfare and perhaps also education and the environment, although our results for the latter two domains are more complex and less encouraging.

5.1 MEASURING MEDIA COVERAGE AND BUDGETARY POLICY

Recall that we have developed four different measures of a media policy signal: (1) a dictionary-based measure of newspaper coverage; (2) a version of the dictionary-based measure that applies an additional dictionary in order to increase the likelihood that sentences are directly relevant to the policy domain; (3) a machine-learning-based measure of the newspaper policy signal that incorporates spending, direction, and relevance considerations from crowdsourced coding; and (4) a dictionary-based measure of television coverage. These measures have been discussed in great detail in Chapters 3 and 4. Analysis in those chapters indicates that the application of the additional relevance dictionary in our dictionary-based measures makes very little difference. We have also seen only small differences between the dictionary-based measures and those based on machine learning. For the sake of parsimony, then, the results below rely primarily on the first newspaper measure and also the one for television news.

We rely on two different measures of spending change: (1) appropriations and (2) outlays. Our use of these two measures is not related to concerns about measuring accuracy but rather about capturing two different types of actions that reflect different "moments" in the budgetary process. There is first the moment when decisions are made, which is reflected in appropriations, the budgetary authority that Congress provides for each policy domain in a given fiscal year. These decisions are mostly made prior to the fiscal year (FY) in which they are spent. As noted in Chapter 2, the budget for FY t typically is proposed, debated, and (usually) decided in FY t-1, although appropriations can be added during FY t as well (see Wlezien 1993). The funding appropriated in FY t-1 need not all be spent in FY t, however. Large infrastructural projects can take years to accomplish, and in this case the appropriations specified in single-year decisions can be spread over multiple years. Outlays are the actual spending outputs that flow from these decisions.

We have in past work explored the differences between appropriations and outlays in analyses of public opinion and policy (Soroka and Wlezien 2010; for more on the relationships between appropriations and outlays and their consequences, see Wlezien and Soroka 2003). The basic difference does not require much statistical analysis, however: appropriations precede outlays, and the difference between the two is typically greatest in domains in which there are large infrastructural projects – a classic example being an aircraft carrier, funds for which are appropriated in a single year but obligated and spent over many ensuing years. Our prior work suggests that the public reacts to policy decisions, at least in salient domains, as responsiveness to appropriations is just as strong as that to outlays. It also is very quick, registered in preferences before most money is actually spent. This makes sense given that decisions are publicly debated whereas expenditures happen more opaquely and are distributed across both space and time. It follows that media coverage may focus on appropriations, as information about policymaking is more visible – and readily available – to journalists. Perhaps most importantly, given the focus of this book, the fact that public responsiveness is driven by spending decisions implies that media coverage reflects appropriations more than outlays. This also has possible implications for the timing of media coverage, which may more closely follow the budget policymaking in year t–1 than fiscal year t itself. We explore these possibilities later in the text.

We measure budgetary policy using data from the Historical Tables produced by the Office of Management and Budget (OMB). Specifically, we use price-adjusted data based on the OMB's Consumer Price Index (CPI). By removing the effects of inflation, we assess changes in budgetary policy in constant or "real" dollars. There are other transformations to the spending series worth considering as well. Some past work uses changes in per-capita spending, controlling for change in the size of the US population, for instance. Diagnostic analyses indicate that making this additional adjustment makes little difference to the results below, and so we opt for the aggregated values in this chapter and those that follow.

We focus specifically on differences in standardized levels of spending from year to year, where levels of spending are expressed as standard deviations from the zero-centered mean, estimated by domain, and based on the observed variation in each domain-specific time series over the roughly forty years examined here. Standardizing the spending series in this way makes no difference to their trends over time, of course; it simply expresses values using a different metric. There are several advantages of doing this, such as a more straightforward comparison of coefficients across domains for which the levels of spending differ quite dramatically. Note that we considered the possibility that, given the substantial growth in spending in most of the domains, media coverage better reflects percentage changes than simple differences in spending. This is not what we observe based on an analysis included in the Appendix to this chapter, and so we proceed with differences in standardized levels of spending later.[1]

5.2 CORRELATING MEDIA COVERAGE AND BUDGETARY POLICY

Figure 5.1 plots the two measures of media coverage we use moving forward – the dictionary-based measures for both newspapers and television – alongside changes in budgetary policy across all five

---

[1] That said, using a percentage change measure does not significantly alter the pattern of the results, which is not surprising, given the correlation between the two variables is 0.91.

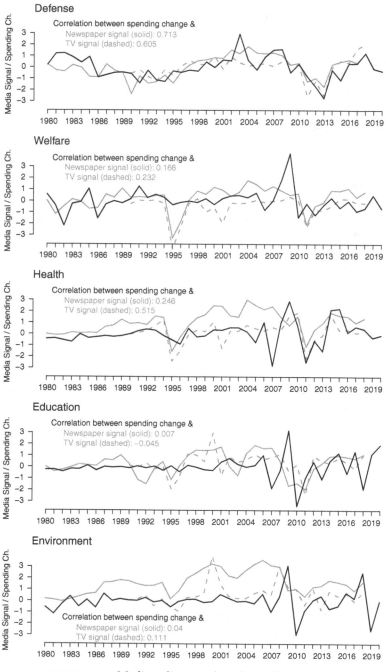

FIGURE 5.1 Media policy signals and spending change

domains. The figure provides a useful first glimpse of relationships between media coverage and spending change. To be perfectly clear, the figure depicts changes in appropriations for a particular fiscal year, say, 1990, and media coverage within that fiscal year, that is, what time series aficionados might refer to as the "current" association between the two series. In order to view overtime variation in all series on the same y-axis, we rely on standardized changes in spending (rather than changes in standardized levels of spending). The figure also includes Pearson's (r) correlations between each of the two media signals and spending change.[2] Since television data are unavailable before 1990, we make all correlations – for both newspaper and television media signals – directly comparable by calculating them using data from 1990 onward only. There are differences across media sources within some domains, and real differences in the accuracy of media coverage across domains. This is evident not just from the correlations but from the plotted trends as well.

The relationships between the media signals and spending change in defense are, we believe, rather striking. The correlations between policy and each media signal are 0.71 and 0.60. This makes sense: much of defense policy is reflected in spending; it is a highly salient domain on which there is a lot of reporting; and it is also highly centralized, driven entirely by national-level spending. Reporting on defense thus appears to be highly accurate. The same is true for health spending, particularly for television coverage ($r = 0.52$), less so for the newspaper signal ($r = 0.25$). Media coverage is more weakly correlated with spending change in the welfare domain, and weaker still for environmental spending. In education, media coverage does not appear to reflect spending change at all.

These are by no means our final analyses, and they are confused by several factors. For instance, although previous chapters have suggested that coverage may reflect some combination of present and future spending, Figure 5.1 considers only concurrent spending policy change, that between media coverage in fiscal year t and appropriations for that same fiscal year. We explore alternatives later in some detail; and analyses there make clear that taking lagged, current, and future spending into account makes a big difference to the estimated correspondence between media coverage and policy change.

There also are two moments in US budgetary history that reduce the correlation between media coverage and spending, concurrent and otherwise. The first of these is the conflict between the Clinton

---

[2] All correlations except those for education are significant at $p < .05$.

administration and the Republican-controlled Congress that produced government shutdowns in 1995–96. The conflict was over differences in spending priorities on the environment, education, and health – three domains for which Republicans favored large spending reductions. The bargain that eventually was reached produced only small decreases in domestic spending, as the trends in Figure 5.1 make clear. But the debate about cuts produced a considerable amount of media coverage. This is clearest in the signals for welfare and health, which spike downward in FY 1995, and to a lesser extent in FY 1996 as well. Media coverage of what were at the time *proposed* decreases seemingly outweighed the eventual, limited changes in spending.

The second moment, readily evident in Figure 5.1, is the government response surrounding the Great Recession. Following decreases in spending on social domains toward the end of the Bush administration, the first budget of the Obama administration, for FY 2009, included marked increases in response to the economic collapse. This is clear across all domestic domains in Figure 5.1. The downward change in FY 2010 then reflects a return to pre-FY 2009 spending levels. These marked but short-lived shocks in budgetary policy are for the most part *not* reflected in the media signal.

We can of course remove or control for these anomalous years in our estimations of the relationship between media coverage and policy; and doing so tends to increase the estimated accuracy of media coverage. For instance, excluding FY 1995–96 and FY 2008–10 makes no real difference to (concurrent) correlations in welfare or education, but it leads to marked increases in correlations between the newspaper signal and spending change in health care ($r = 0.31$ from 0.14) and the environment ($r = 0.27$ compared with 0.06). This may offer additional evidence of the validity of the media signal measures, but it may not be the ideal way to think about – and model – the relationship between media and policy.

Our inclination is to include these anomalous years as moments in which there are marked differences between the media signal and actual policy change. Insofar as public preferences are affected by media coverage rather than policy, we might expect the 1995 and 1996 shutdowns to have produced preferences that are a response to spending decreases that were only partly actualized. We might similarly expect preferences to *not* adjust to the spending changes in FYs 2009 and 2010. In short: we view these gaps between media coverage and spending as not problematic measurement issues but rather a reflection of real disjunctures that can occur between media coverage and policy – ones that may

well reduce the extent to which public preferences are responsive to
actual policy change.

5.3 MODELING MEDIA COVERAGE
AND BUDGETARY POLICY

Results in Figure 5.1 offer only a (very) preliminary analysis of the
connection between spending change and media coverage, as they only
capture the correlations between the media signal and current spending
change. As we have seen in Chapter 4, the media signal reflects spending
change not just in the current year but (to varying degrees) in the prior and
forthcoming years as well. We take this into account here by estimating
some simple statistical models in which we regress media measures on
spending change at different time points. The basic form of the estimations is as follows:

$$Media\ Signal_t = \alpha + \beta_1 \Delta Spending_{t-1} + \beta_2 \Delta Spending_t + \beta_3 \Delta Spending_{t+1}, \quad (5.1)$$

where the *Media Signal* can be any of the four measures discussed earlier,
the measure of *Spending* can be appropriations or outlays, and the timing
of *Spending* can be past $(t-1)$, concurrent (t), or future $(t+1)$ – variables
which we will include both separately and together later.

5.3.1 The Newspaper Signal and Change in Appropriations

Table 5.1 shows results from some simple bivariate estimations of
Equation 5.1, relating the media signal to separate measures of spending
one at a time. Rather than specify a single domain, these are fixed-effects
time-series panel analyses that summarize the relationship between media
and spending variables across all five domains. By contrast with
Figure 5.1, for this analysis and those that follow we standardize the levels
of spending in each domain and *then* calculate changes. As noted earlier,
standardizing makes spending differences more comparable across
domains; it also simplifies analyses of preferences in Chapters 6 and 7,
which incorporate both differences and (lagged) levels of spending into the
estimated models. The dependent variable for these models is the same
newspaper signal (without additional relevance keywords) shown in
Figure 5.1. Columns present separate regressions of the current media
signal on (1) lagged spending change, (2) current spending change, and (3)
future spending change. Since all variables are expressed in standardized

TABLE 5.1 *The newspaper signal and change in appropriations*

	Dependent variable: Media signal $_t$		
Δ Spending $_{t-1}$	0.370*	—	—
	(0.115)		
Δ Spending $_t$	—	0.325*	—
		(0.145)	
Δ Spending $_{t+1}$	—	—	0.474***
			(0.136)
Constant	0.624***	0.624***	0.617***
	(0.071)	(0.071)	(0.070)
Within-panel Rsq	0.029	0.026	0.060
N	195	195	195

Cells contain coefficients from fixed-effects linear models with standard errors in parentheses. *$p < .05$; **$p < .01$; ***$p < .001$.

units, coefficients capture the average impact of a one standard deviation shift in spending on standard deviations of the media signal. Coefficients do not clearly indicate how actual dollars spent relate to the number of upward/downward sentences, then; but using standardized measures allows us to more directly compare coefficients across models.

Results of Table 5.1 are fairly clear: averaging across all domains, the newspaper signal is positively related to past, present, *and* future changes in spending. The coefficient for current spending (at time t) actually is the smallest in these models, and the coefficient for future spending is the largest. The latter should come as no surprise given that (a) there is reason to think that the news focuses on spending policy decisions for fiscal year t +1 when they are being made in the previous year and (b) we have already seen human coding in Chapter 4 suggesting that media coverage is not exclusively focused on current spending change. That said, none of the spending coefficients in Table 5.1 are statistically significantly different from each other. The estimates imply that, on average, a one standard deviation shift in spending in any period produces a corresponding shift of roughly 4/10 of a standard deviation in media coverage.

Note that models in Table 5.1 are descriptive, equivalent to "pooled" correlational analyses across the five domains. The models do not account for autocorrelation in the time series – the tendency for media coverage at time t, for instance, to be strongly correlated with media coverage at time $t-1$, which itself can reflect spending at different points in

TABLE 5.2 *The newspaper signal and changes in appropriations taken together*

	Dependent variable: Media signal $_t$	
Δ Spending $_{t-1}$	0.314*	0.244
	(0.124)	(0.135)
Δ Spending $_t$	0.301*	0.194
	(0.139)	(0.136)
Δ Spending $_{t+1}$	0.334**	0.367**
	(0.113)	(0.125)
Media Signal $_{t-1}$	—	0.558***
		(0.064)
Constant	0.637***	0.260***
	(0.056)	(0.066)
Within-panel Rsq	0.054	0.433
N	190	190

Cells contain coefficients with standard errors in parentheses from (a) fixed-effects linear model with an AR(1) disturbance and (b) a fixed-effects linear panel estimation. $*p < .05$; $**p < .01$; $***p < .001$.

time.[3] Relatedly, and perhaps more importantly, the models do not include the different (past, current, and future) measures of spending in the same model, so we do not know whether each has independent effects. While the results in Table 5.1 provide a basic description of the bivariate relationships between spending and media coverage, then, we need to estimate a single model that both accounts for autocorrelation and includes all three spending measures.

Table 5.2 accordingly shows two models, again pooling data across all five policy domains, but now including spending change for years $t - 1$, t, and $t + 1$ simultaneously. The first, in column 1, is estimated using OLS fixed-effects regression with a single-order autoregressive (AR(1)) disturbance, which corrects for correlated errors. The coefficients thus reveal the impact of each measure of spending controlling for the others, taking into account any residual autocorrelation.[4] These results suggest that media

---

[3] Importantly, autocorrelation does not produce biased estimates but does lead to inefficiency, where the variance is greater, that is, estimates can be larger or smaller than they should be.

[4] Assuming we satisfy the other Gauss–Markov assumptions, the regression gives us the "best" OLS estimates.

coverage in each fiscal year is informed by changes in spending in the past, present, *and* future. Even more so than in Table 5.1, the effects are quite similar, and statistically indistinguishable ($p<.05$). The sum of the coefficients is also 0.95, just less than 1.0, which implies that a one standard deviation shift in spending produces nearly a corresponding one standard deviation shift in media coverage over time. The estimate for future spending still is slightly larger than the others, implying that current policymaking might matter more for current newspaper coverage than spending happening today based on decisions taken in the past. We address this more explicitly later in the chapter.[5] For the time being, however, Table 5.2 reflects what in our view is a rather strong relationship between spending change and media coverage.

Although the analysis in the first column is telling about coverage of government spending, it does not *explicitly* model dynamics. We have reason to suppose that current media coverage is related to previous media coverage, which may itself reflect previous spending decisions but also other things. To address this possibility, we need to incorporate lagged ($t - 1$) media coverage into our analysis, which is what we do in the second column of Table 5.2. Results there support our suspicions, as the large, significant effect (0.56) of previous coverage reveals an ebb and flow in news coverage, where indications of increases (or decreases) tend to be preceded and followed by other such indications.[6] Part of the pattern is due to the ebb and flow of spending itself, as the coefficients for the current (t) and lagged ($t - 1$) spending are markedly smaller than in the first column and no longer statistically significant. This indicates that their effects mostly are reflected in previous media coverage, which then influences current media coverage, at least to some degree. Given previous coverage, *only* future spending matters to current coverage to a statistically significant degree, in effect, to influence innovations in what media report. In other words, journalists do not reinvent media coverage "fresh" in every year. This is the case in newspapers, at least, since we have not yet examined other media.

We do not reproduce models here using all variants of the media signal, since results do not change in any substantive way when other variables

---

[5] As mentioned earlier in this chapter, the results do not change substantially when using the percentage change in spending in place of our first differenced measure. Indeed, as can be seen in the appendix, the latter outperforms the former in analyses of the media signal.

[6] Note the fact that the coefficient less than 1.0 indicates that previous coverage does not fully carry over but tends to diminish over time, where large increases (decreases) usually are followed by smaller increases (decreases).

are used. This is not surprising given the similarity in measures of media signal, as we saw in Chapter 4. Using the dictionary-based measure of newspaper content that relies on additional subject keywords produces roughly the same coefficients as we see in Table 5.1, as does using the machine-learning-based measure. Television signals also do not change the story much, although it is worth noting that they appear to reflect current spending a little more than newspapers. The difference is not due to the fact that we have television transcripts over a reduced time period, as newspaper results are no different if we restrict them to the years in which television content is available. Television just is somewhat less future-oriented in their reporting of budgetary policy, even when compared with newspapers over an identical time period. We illustrate this finding in the section that follows.

5.3.2 Appropriations versus Outlays

Thus far we have considered appropriations, the policy decisions that lead to expenditures. What does the relationship between the media signal and policy look like when we use outlays, which register actual spending, as our indicator of budgetary policy? Table 5.3 offers an illustrative example of the extent to which media content responds to appropriations versus outlays. Column 1 of Table 5.3 shows results from a model that regresses the newspaper signal we have been using on both appropriations and outlays – past, present, and future. Models that focus on either one or some subset of these independent variables produce similar findings, so we focus just on the inclusive version here. Column 2 presents results for the television signal.

Results in Table 5.3 indicate that media coverage responds exclusively to appropriations. No coefficient for the outlays measures is statistically significant for newspapers or for television. Where newspapers are concerned, the effects of past and current appropriations changes fall below standard levels of statistical significance, but future changes are statistically significant. Television news, in the second column of Table 5.3, responds to past, current, and future appropriations. That future appropriations have an independent effect on media coverage is of some significance, given the impact of future appropriations is reduced by the inclusion of outlays. (Compare coefficients in the first column with those in the first column of Table 5.2.) These results highlight the focus of media coverage on appropriations decisions rather than outlays, much as we expected.

The centrality of appropriations is of real significance. Recall also that work on public responsiveness to policy change finds that the public

TABLE 5.3 *Newspaper and television signals and changes in appropriations and outlays*

	Dependent variable:	
	Newspaper signal $_t$	Television signal $_t$
Δ Appropriations $_{t-1}$	0.208	0.546**
	(0.147)	(0.199)
Δ Appropriations $_t$	0.155	0.478*
	(0.167)	(0.201)
Δ Appropriations $_{t+1}$	0.255*	0.541**
	(0.125)	(0.162)
Δ Outlays $_{t-1}$	−0.253	−0.280
	(0.171)	(0.218)
Δ Outlays $_t$	0.052	0.217
	(0.193)	(0.238)
Δ Outlays $_{t+1}$	0.146	0.152
	(0.176)	(0.240)
Constant	0.667***	0.002
	(0.056)	(0.084)
Within-panel Rsq	0.066	0.175
N	190	190

Cells contain coefficients with standard errors in parentheses from fixed-effects linear models with an AR(1) disturbance. $*p < .05$; $**p < .01$; $***p < .001$.

responds more strongly to spending decisions than spending itself (e.g., Wlezien 1995, 1996; Soroka and Wlezien 2010). That prior finding already hints at the likely importance of media coverage in facilitating public responsiveness: How else would publics learn about policy *decisions* even before there are implemented outlays (or consequences for outcomes themselves)? Results in Table 5.3 not only clarify the focus of media coverage of policy, then, they identify a tendency in media content that buttresses past claims about the focus of public responsiveness. The media respond primarily to spending decisions.

5.3.3 Domain-Specific Results

Results have thus far focused on panel data that captures what approximates an "average" result across five domains taken together in a single analysis. We nevertheless expect differences in media coverage from one policy domain to the next. Rather than show more regression tables, Figure 5.2 illustrates the estimated impact of a one-standard-deviation change in spending at $t - 1$, t, and $t + 1$ on the media signal at t. All results are based on Prais–Winsten models that account for first-order autoregressive process in time-series models for which the newspaper or television signal is the dependent variable. (By comparison with the inclusion of lagged dependent variables, this allows us to see more clearly how the different spending measures map into news coverage, as in Table 5.2.) Again, using standardized measures here facilitates comparisons both across domains and media.

The top-left panel of Figure 5.2 shows the estimated impact of past, present, and future changes in defense spending on the newspaper signal for that domain in fiscal year t. Note the inclination toward current and future spending change. This is not the only domain for which reporting is future-leaning, though there are other domains in which coverage is more inclined toward a combination of current and past spending. There are within-domain differences across newspapers and television news as well. The analysis of welfare suggests an orientation toward the future in newspaper coverage but a focus on the past in television coverage. Newspapers and especially television are more reflective of current changes in health spending.

Figure 5.2 nicely captures differences in the responsiveness of media coverage to policy change in each domain. It can be seen that coverage of spending on education and environment is much more muted than for the other three domains. There are hints of a future orientation in environmental policy coverage, but only a weak influence of spending policy on coverage overall. Education coverage is only slightly (and not significantly) better. For both domains, television coverage appears to reflect spending change more reliably than newspaper coverage does. This may come as a surprise to some, given that there tends to be more detailed coverage of most events in newspapers than on television. The current-affairs, non-editorializing orientation of the three broadcast networks may be an advantage here. Regardless, there is reason to suppose that the results in Figure 5.2 mask differences across individual sources. We explore this possibility next.

5.3.4 Source-Specific Results

Not all newspapers or television networks cover spending policy to the same degree; nor do they necessarily have the same focus on past, present,

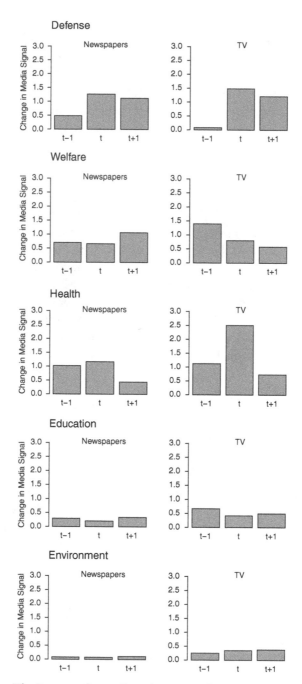

FIGURE 5.2 The impact of spending change on the newspaper and television signals

and future spending. We have thus far explored the relationship between media coverage and policy using results that aggregate policy cues across *all* newspapers or *all* television networks. We can produce media policy signals for each individual source as well, of course. Doing so does not impose serious data limitations – as we have seen in Chapters 3 and 4, there are plenty of policy cues in each source, especially once we aggregate by fiscal year. So, what do media policy signals look like for individual sources? Or rather, what is the accuracy of coverage in the different sources?

We have data from seventeen newspapers and six television networks, so we do not attempt to show results for all sources here. Rather, we illustrate focusing on just five newspapers in Figure 5.3: three national papers – the *New York Times* (NYT), *USA Today* (USA), and the *Washington Post* (WPO) – and two fairly large regional ones – the *Atlanta Journal-Constitution* (AJC) and the *Chicago Tribune* (CTR). Again, we plot the estimated impacts of standardized changes in past, present, and future spending on current coverage. We continue to use the standardized measures of spending, but we now use the raw media signals that reflect simple article counts in order to highlight differences in the volume of coverage across outlets. Coefficients thus represent the impact of a one-unit change in standardized spending on the balance of upward and downward sentences about spending in each newspaper. For example: a one standard deviation change in defense spending in fiscal year *t* shifts the balance of upward versus downward spending sentences in the *Washington Post* by roughly 600 sentences in a given fiscal year. This is among the largest effects shown in Figure 5.3. (It quite literally is off the chart given that we restrict the *y*-axis in order to better illustrate smaller effects in other newspapers.)

The impact of policy change tends to be larger for the *Washington Post* and *New York Times*, and this is because these newspapers have far more policy content than the others – a fact that is lost when we use fully standardized measures but is readily evident in Figure 5.3. Do note that not all coefficients in Figure 5.3 are statistically significant, and so we need to be careful about very specific conclusions. That said, results in Figure 5.3 suggest that coverage in the *Atlanta Journal-Constitution* is marginally more responsive to spending change in defense and health. The *New York Times* and *Washington Post* appear to be less responsive to policy change on education and the environment. Although there are hints of a bias toward current and future policy change overall, there are newspaper/domain combinations in which current and past spending

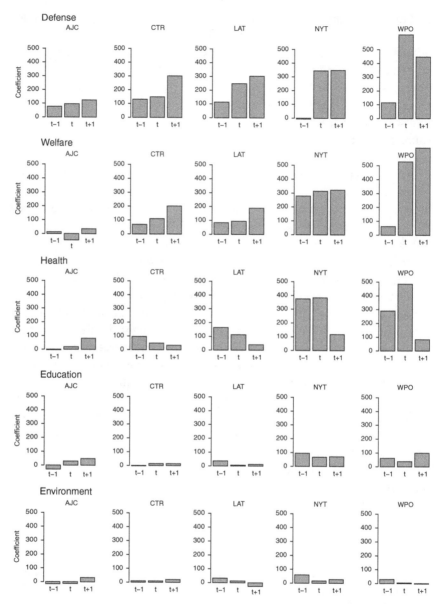

FIGURE 5.3 Media responsiveness to change in spending, by source and policy domain

appears to matter most. There is, in short, a lot of variation in media coverage across both domains and sources. Given that most people will learn about policy change from just one or a few sources, these differences in coverage may influence whether and how people respond to policy change, which we revisit in Chapter 7.

Figure 5.3 offers a first look at differences across sources, but the total number of source-domain differences – across five domains and twenty-three sources – is too large to offer a particularly useful visualization here. That said, it is possible to capture source-level differences by estimating models that capture each source's responsiveness to policy, averaged across all five domains. This is the purpose of Figure 5.4,

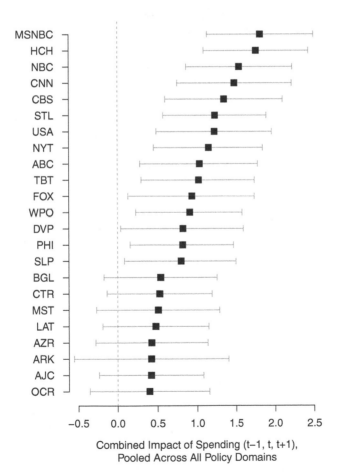

FIGURE 5.4 Media responsiveness to change in spending, by source

which shows results from separate models for each source, both newspapers and television outlets, based on a panel estimation that includes an AR(1) process. The models include appropriations change in years $t - 1$, t, and $t + 1$, as earlier, but rather than present each of those coefficients separately we show the combination of those three coefficients and its associated 95 percent confidence interval.[7] The point estimates shown in Figure 5.4 thus capture the combined impact of spending decisions in the past, present, and future, summed across all five policy domains. We regard this as a reasonably good approximation of the accuracy of each source's coverage of policy over the past several decades.

Sources are listed based on the descending size of the combined coefficient. By this measure, MSNBC has produced content that best captures past, present, and future policy change across all five policy domains. The *Orange County Register* has by contrast produced the least reflective coverage. Table 5.4 provides a basic summary of results by media type. There are hints that television coverage better conveys spending policy than newspapers do, and that national papers do a better job than regional ones, but there is a lot of variation within each of the groupings, particularly cable television and regional papers. Few of the differences we see in Figure 5.4 or Table 5.4 are statistically significant – except for those at the very top and bottom of the figure, most estimates are within the 95 percent confidence intervals of most other estimates.

TABLE 5.4 *A summary of newspaper and television responsiveness*

	Mean combined coefficient	Standard deviation
Television	1.36	0.33
Broadcast	1.31	0.26
Cable	1.41	0.44
Newspapers	0.79	0.39
National	1.09	0.17
Regional	0.73	0.39

[7] We use all years available for each source, so it is worth recalling that some newspapers are available for longer than others; and the television series are available from 1990 onward. Restricting the analysis to the period over which all sources are available has only a small impact on the results in the figure.

Differences between individual sources, too, are in most cases relatively small – and these coefficients mask all sorts of variation in the impact of past, present, and future spending change in each domain. Our summary assessment of Figure 5.4 alongside the results that precede it are that media coverage does regularly reflect policy and that there is a general tendency toward coverage of decisions (appropriations) about future spending. But, while this tends to hold across outlets, there is a good deal of variability in the magnitude with which coverage in any one source accurately reflects policy change. This may be of consequence for consumers.

5.4 ON SPENDING AND MEDIA COVERAGE

Do news media provide accurate signals about policy change? The preceding results indicate that there is not a simple answer to this question – there is, rather, a lot of variability in the accuracy of media coverage, across both policy domains and outlets. There nevertheless are some general patterns worth highlighting.

Most importantly, media coverage does on average reflect policy change. The media thus provide at least some, if not a lot, of the information required in order for citizens to update their policy preferences and hold governments accountable. There is on average an inclination toward coverage of policy *decisions*, that is, appropriations, rather than outlays. There also is a tendency to focus on current and future policy change rather than past policy, which implies that the news focuses mostly on what recently has been or is being decided.

That said, these general findings conceal a good amount of variation. Defense, the domain in which policy itself is most centralized and seemingly most spending-focused, reveals very high levels of media accuracy. Education and the environment in which policymaking is highly decentralized and often focused on non-spending items (like regulation), produce rather low levels of media accuracy. It may be that we are looking for media accuracy in the wrong place – perhaps local news provides a more accurate view of local education policy, for instance. Where our media signal is concerned, however, it appears to be rather difficult to stay informed about national education policy change, at least as regards spending. Even where there are substantial connections between spending and media coverage, the match between the two is imperfect. And the focus of coverage also can differ, for example, news about health spending focuses more on past policy change than it does on other domains.

The seeming absence of policy-related media coverage does not preclude the possibility of a responsive public, of course. To begin with, we must be modest about our media measures, which contain a good amount of measurement error. While we have clean measures of spending, despite our best efforts, the media signals we have produced contain both signal and noise. What news the public receives about policy may provide a clearer indication of what the government is doing than our measures – and their relationships with spending – would lead one to think. Additionally, we suspect that citizens learn about federal policy change at least partly if not mostly from media, but local media may matter, as might friends and family. There may be other "cues" that help citizens adjust their perceptions of (and preferences for) policy as well: knowing that Republicans or Democrats are in power might be enough to at least party adjust preferences to (unknown) policy change. It thus is important to remember, as we move to analyses of public opinion, that the public can exhibit some level of responsiveness even in the absence of accurate media, measured or not. But we expect that this responsiveness should be weak and less reliable by comparison with domains in which there is a strong and reliable media policy signal.

Media also can lead citizens astray, and we have already seen hints of this possibility. The absence of media coverage is a problem in some domains, but the presence of inaccurate media coverage is a problem in others. "Inaccurate" might not always be the right way to think about gaps between media and policy either. Some media coverage probably is just plain wrong, but some of the "other stuff" that shifts the media policy signal away from actual policy change may be substantive, and actually related to policy. We consider this in greater detail in Chapter 7.

The extent to which the public responds to both components – the spending and non-spending aspects – of media coverage is the focus of the chapter that follows.

5.5 APPENDIX TO CHAPTER 5: POLICY CHANGE AND MEDIA COVERAGE – DO MEASURES MATTER?

The body of this chapter (and the ensuing chapters) relies on the difference in spending from year to year in our analyses of media coverage. That is, we subtract spending in the previous fiscal year from spending in the current fiscal year, keeping in mind that we first adjust spending for inflation and then standardize those numbers by domain before taking differences, as discussed in the text.

TABLE 5.A1   *The impact of spending change on media coverage*

	Dependent variable: Newspaper signal $_t$		
%Δ Appropriations $_{t-1}$	—	0.008$^+$	−0.008
		(0.004)	(0.010)
%Δ Appropriations $_t$	—	0.008$^+$	0.001
		(0.005)	(0.011)
%Δ Appropriations $_{t+1}$	—	0.011**	0.004
		(0.004)	(0.010)
Δ Appropriations $_{t-1}$	0.314*	—	0.513$^+$
	(0.124)		(0.288)
Δ Appropriations $_t$	0.301*	—	0.254
	(0.139)		(0.331)
Δ Appropriations $_{t+1}$	0.334**	—	0.221
	(0.113)		(0.271)
Constant	0.637***	0.603***	0.642***
	(0.056)	(0.058)	(0.059)
Within-panel Rsq	0.054	0.041	0.060
N	190	190	190

Cells contain coefficients with standard errors in parentheses from fixed-effects linear models with an AR(1) disturbance. $^+p < .10$; $^*p < .05$; $^{**}p < .01$; $^{***}p < .001$.

We know that spending levels in most of the areas we analyze have increased substantially over time, even after we adjust for inflation (and population as well). Given the trends in spending, there is reason to think that the effect of a fixed increase (or decrease) in spending, say, of $1 billion, on media coverage may have declined over time, as it represents a smaller and smaller share of the budget. That is, it may be that media coverage reflects changes *relative to* the level of spending. We can directly assess this using a spending measure based on percentage changes.

We do so by calculating the percentage change in spending: ((appropriations $_t$ − appropriations $_{t-1}$)/appropriations $_{t-1}$) × 100, and reestimating the equation for newspaper coverage in the first column of Table 5.2 using percentage changes in place of the differenced variables. For the sake of comparison, the first column of Table 5.A1 repeats the results from the first column of Table 5.2, and the second column then shows results using the percentage change measures. There, the coefficients for the latter all are smaller owing to differences in measurement; what matters most is that the reliability of the percentage change variables is lower than that for the differenced ones, and the overall fit of the model is lower as well, for example, the R-squared drops from 0.054 to 0.041.

We can also estimate an equation including both the percentage change and differenced variables. Because of the multicollinearity introduced by including the measures together, the standard errors all are three times as large. Even so, the results – shown in the last column of Table 5.A1 – suggest that the differenced variables are more predictive than are the percentage change measure, as all of the coefficients for the former are positive and more reliable. The lesson seems to be that media coverage does not take into account the amount of spending in its reporting and focuses primarily on the actual increases or decreases instead. This may not be what we want of our media coverage, but it appears to be what we get.

6

Policy, the Media, and the Public

Does media coverage matter for the functioning of representative democracy? Do people notice news coverage? Do they take it into account? In particular, do citizens use the information that media content conveys to update their policy preferences? These questions are the central motivation for this book. They are critical to assessing the role of media as a functioning Fourth Estate. They are equally critical to assessing the functioning of representative democracy because a public that responds to accurate media coverage of policy is central to effective accountability and control. In this chapter we try to provide some answers.

To backtrack slightly, recall that we began to study the coverage of policy because we wanted to understand how people received information about what government is doing. We know that people do have some information and that they use it, that is, this information produces thermostatic shifts in public preferences for policy (in some domains at least). It is not complete, "perfect" information to be sure. It also may be at a very general level, maybe just the direction of policy change and approximate magnitude, for example, "President Trump cut taxes, by a lot" or "President Clinton cut defense spending and by a good amount," not specific details. We know that people have some information not from responses to surveys asking them directly about their knowledge of government actions, but from analyses of public preferences and spending. And we also know that the dynamic is not restricted to a select few hyperattentive citizens – it is evident across various subgroups of the population, including education and income levels, and even party identification.

The information people receive must be mediated in some way, as we cannot directly observe what policymakers are doing in person or on our mobile phones. To what extent is it mediated by news coverage? And if news coverage is what matters, does the *entirety* of that coverage influence what people perceive and prefer? Important here is that media coverage of policy does not solely register what policymakers have done: the preceding chapters show that media coverage partly reflects what policymakers have done and are doing. But, other things factor into media coverage, including events and political debate. This component of media coverage – the part that is unexplained in the models from Chapter 5 – may be of real significance. Media coverage captures a wide range of things beyond just policy decisions, after all, and this may inform public preferences. Or not.

We consider these possibilities later, as we focus on whether and how news mediates public responsiveness to policy. We begin by introducing our principal measures of public preferences from the General Social Survey. We then consider a smaller, unique body of data on public perceptions of policy change, from the American National Election Studies. These data allow us some preliminary insight into whether the public notices government spending and media coverage of government spending. The remainder of the chapter then presents results of analyses of public preferences, first to establish the effects of spending on preferences, and then to assess the role of the media signal. Results document thermostatic public responsiveness, as found in previous research, and also that news coverage is a critical mediating force. As we will see, it is not only spending-focused media content that drives public opinion – the other policy-relevant information conveyed in media coverage can matter too. This is of real importance, and leads us to further questions about the relationships between the politics, the media, and the public.

6.1 MEASURES OF RELATIVE PUBLIC PREFERENCES

Recall from Chapter 2 that we are interested in how relative preferences for spending respond to actual policy change, and so we need measures of preferences for "more" or "less."[1] Ours come from the General Social Survey (GSS), which was fielded from 1973 to 1994 in every year except 1979 and 1981 and then in even-numbered years thereafter. We are able to use data through 2018, based on the last publicly available survey as of this writing. In each survey, the GSS asks about preferences for spending in various spending areas using the following item:

---

[1] Also recall that these are the measures we have, as survey organizations have regularly asked people about whether they want more or less, not how much spending they want.

We are faced with many problems in this country, none of which can be solved easily or inexpensively. I'm going to name some of these problems, and for each one I'd like you to tell me whether we are spending too much money on it, too little money, or about the right amount.

Do you think the government is spending too much, too little or about the right amount on [e.g., health care]?'

Respondents are asked about a range of spending domains, many of which appear in each survey. Some of these match the foci of our media measures: defense, welfare, health, education, and the environment, recalling that we chose these domains in part because of the availability of public opinion data.[2]

Note that the survey question does not point to a particular level of government, and so the reference point is not perfectly clear, that is, we cannot be sure whether responses register preferences about the national government, or some lower-level government, or both. This obviously is less of an issue in areas where policy is centralized, like national defense, than others where there is a good amount of mixing across levels, like health care, welfare, and especially education. There is evidence that people respond to national spending even in these more mixed domains (Wlezien 1995; Soroka and Wlezien 2010). That said, there also is evidence that estimated public responsiveness declines as the level of decentralization of spending – the greater the mix of state and local sources – increases. This is as we have theorized and found previously (Soroka and Wlezien 2010; Wlezien and Soroka 2011), and may be of consequence for models of media coverage as well. Indeed, the decentralization of policy, and correspondingly complex policy "signal," may help account for patterns we observed in the preceding chapter – in particular the more limited connection between media coverage and federal spending on education, by far the most decentralized policy domain examined here.

Although the survey question directly taps relative preferences, responses provide only very general information. We have discussed this at some length in our earlier work (Soroka and Wlezien 2010). What is most important to reiterate here is that many respondents select the

---

[2] We rely on the primary representative sample in each year, ignoring minority oversamples. We do not apply survey weights, which are an issue since the GSS began employing a two-stage subsampling design for nonresponse beginning in 2004, as we have to use the subsample that receives the specific items of interest, for example, the "welfare" spending question instead of the "assistance to the poor" variant. For more information about the GSS methodology, see www3.norc.org/gss. Note that applying survey weights makes little difference to the time series.

middling option, indicating that the government is spending "about the right amount." (Depending on the spending category and year, between 15 and 60 percent of respondents select this position.) Thus, the median respondent frequently appears to be happy with the policy status quo, and this may not change even as conditions and policy change. This apparent support for current spending levels nevertheless encompasses a good amount of variation, from those who are very close to preferring less to those who are equally close to favoring more. As such, the "true" median preference can change over time even as the median response to the question remains the same.

It is possible to identify this public preference – at least the changes over time – by aggregating individual responses and focusing on the mean. We also can take the difference between the percentage of respondents wanting more and the percentage of respondents wanting less – technically, the percentage saying we are spending "too little" minus the percentage saying we are spending "too much." The latter measure is perfectly correlated with the mean over time and provides a more intuitive empirical referent, in terms of actual percentages of the public, and we adopt this approach and refer to the percentage difference measures as indicators of "net support" for spending.

These measures tell us little about absolute preferences at any point in time, however. The fact that net support is positive, that is, more people say we are spending too little than too much, does not mean the average person really wants more spending than is currently in place. Indeed, the average person might want the same or less. Part of the problem is question wording, which matters a lot for the responses we get (Soroka and Wlezien 2010). The classic case is "welfare" and "the poor," where majorities oppose more spending on the former but support more spending on the latter, seemingly contradictory preferences (Rasinski 1989). Of course, it may be that the labels mean very different things to people, but this highlights the uncertainty about what exactly they have in mind when expressing preferences for spending in particular policy areas. Do the programs they are thinking of match with what budget experts think? Policymakers? News reporters?

Another part of the problem with interpretation is that responses register unconstrained preferences, that is, without any trade-offs between spending on different programs, between spending and taxes, or between spending and deficits. In effect, and borrowing from economics, people can express costless preferences for spending on education, health, the environment and other program – the equivalent of free lunches. Hansen

(1998) has shown that taking trade-offs into account can produce very different spending preference distributions, and tends to increase support for the status quo. It thus may be that that the public really is getting the spending it wants, at least given the budget constraints.[3]

Thankfully, even in the face of complexities with question wording and interpretation, these measures of net support for spending are revealing about preference change *over time*. To be clear: even as the wording of questions may "slice" up underlying preferences in different ways, the change in responses over time can reflect real change in public preferences. This is what matters most for our analysis.

Figure 6.1 depicts the measures of net support in our five spending domains beginning in 1976. Dots distinguish the years in which there are surveys, keeping in mind that data are missing in numerous years, and lines connect those dots.[4] Defense preferences show the greatest variation, being most supportive of greater spending in the early 1980s and mostly lower thereafter, albeit with increases following 9/11 and then again through the Clinton and Obama presidencies. (This may be concealed somewhat in the figure because the y-axis for the defense panel has a range of 100 points (from −40 to +60), which is nearly double that for the other panels, where the range is just 60 points.) Welfare preferences show a fair amount of variation and the remaining domains exhibit slightly less, particularly education. That said, there is over-time change in other domains that presumably is connected to real-world events and to policy change: consider the drop in relative preferences for health care spending after the passage of the ACA in 2010, for instance.

The flow of preferences for spending has been the subject of much previous work, reviewed in Chapter 2. That research shows that preferences change in part because people's demand for spending change owing to variation in national and economic security, among other things (Wlezien 1995). For non-defense programs, there is an underlying trend in demand for spending that owes to long-term economic growth (Wlezien and Soroka 2021), but the variation in economic conditions also matters (see as well Stevenson 2001; Erikson et al. 2002). Some of the variation is common across domains, where preferences flow together, but some is

---

[3] That said, the evidence of interdependence in spending preferences indicates that people do make at least some trade-offs (Wlezien 1995; Soroka and Wlezien 2010). See Wlezien (2017b) for more discussion of measurement of policy preferences and its consequences for analysis of policy representation.

[4] Specifically, data are missing in fifteen years between 1976 and 2018: 1979, 1981, 1992, 1995, 1997, 1999, 2001, 2003, 2005, 2007, 2009, 2011, 2013, 2015, and 2017.

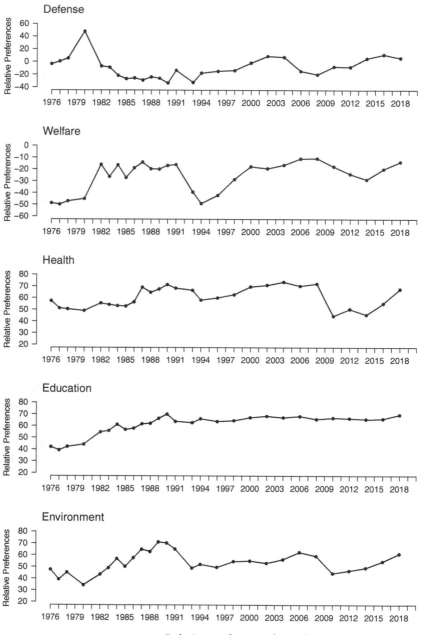

FIGURE 6.1 Relative preferences for policy

unique (Wlezien 2004; Soroka and Wlezien 2010). Analysis suggests that just over 50 percent of the variance in preferences is common but that this varies substantially across domains, being lowest for defense and greatest for the environment.[5] Perhaps most importantly, the previous research has shown that people respond to spending within different domains, particularly defense, welfare, and health. This book is substantially motivated by – and dedicated to accounting for – this fact.

6.2 DOES THE PUBLIC NOTICE SPENDING (AND MEDIA COVERAGE)?

We have seen that spending cues exist and that they reflect policy to some degree. Implicitly, we also have seen from our work with undergraduates and MTurkers that people can understand media cues. We nevertheless lack direct evidence that citizens actually receive and accept the information captured by our media coverage measure; that is, we have not directly tested whether individuals' perceptions of spending change are informed by media content. Building on prior work with Fabian Neuner (Neuner et al. 2019), this section attempts to addresses this issue, at least to a basic degree.

We do so using responses to a rare pair of questions about perceptions of government spending included in seven election waves (both presidential and midterm) of the American National Election Study (ANES), between 1980 and 1992.[6] Respondents were asked the following questions:

Some people believe that we should spend much less money for defense. Others feel that defense spending should be greatly increased. Where would you place what the Federal Government is doing at the present time?

Some people think the government should provide fewer services, even in areas such as health and education in order to reduce spending. Other people feel it is important for the government to provide many more services even if it means an

---

[5] A principal components analysis of the five spending domains over the 28 years we have data suggests that, although preferences in the different domains load on one factor, there is a fair amount of unique variance. The "uniqueness" scores, which range between 0 (low) and 1 (high), are as follows: defense, 0.72; welfare, 0.47; health, 0.48; education, 0.45; environment, 0.17. Note that this pattern differs some to what we observed prior to 2009 (Soroka and Wlezien 2010), as preferences for spending have becomes less correlated with each other (and more unique), especially for health. Also see Figure 6.1.

[6] To be clear, these surveys are repeated cross-sections, in which different people are surveyed in each year; we thus cannot observe whether particular individuals' perceptions actually changed.

increase in spending. Where would you place what the Federal Government is doing at the present time?

Both questions employed what appears to be a sensible 7-point scale, though we note that the response options are phrased in what seem grammatically incorrect ways, indicating "increase" and "decrease" spending a lot instead of "increasing" and "decreasing." This may be because the question was asked together with a similar question about spending preferences, where the wording of the options makes more sense, and they simply duplicated them for perceptions.[7] Regardless, our assumption is that respondents understood the meaning of the question and responded accordingly, and the results support the assumption, as we will see.

The questions were asked only about defense and "services," the latter of which (obviously) is less specific. Reponses thus allow only a limited analysis but the data nevertheless offer the opportunity to directly examine people's *perceptions* of spending change. Most importantly, we can assess whether and how they relate to spending and media coverage itself, and for this analysis we consider aggregate perceptions. Figure 6.2 shows the mean response to both questions using the 1–7 scale, where low values indicate decreases and high values increases, that is, the higher the score, the greater the average perceived increase. The left-hand panel shows defense perceptions in black; the right-hand panel shows services perceptions, also in black. The figure also includes year-to-year *changes* in spending, here in billions of constant US dollars. For the services category we combine health and education spending, in line with the question wording, which mentions those domains.[8] Figure 6.3 shows identical measures of perceptions, this time alongside *levels* of spending, again in billions of constant dollars.

Why do we consider both changes and levels of spending? Thermostatic responsiveness hinges on public recognition of spending change and the ANES questions ask directly about this, so we clearly need to include changes. That said, our prior work with the defense perceptions question suggests that these perceptions of change mostly reflect spending *levels* (Neuner et al. 2019). This kind of mismatch between what a survey question asks and the answers people give is not

---

[7] It also may be that the codebook is incorrect.

[8] We also explored adding welfare spending, but this (slightly) reduces rather than increases the observed correlation with perceptions.

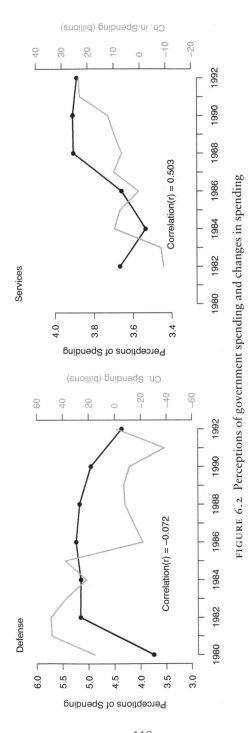

FIGURE 6.2 Perceptions of government spending and changes in spending

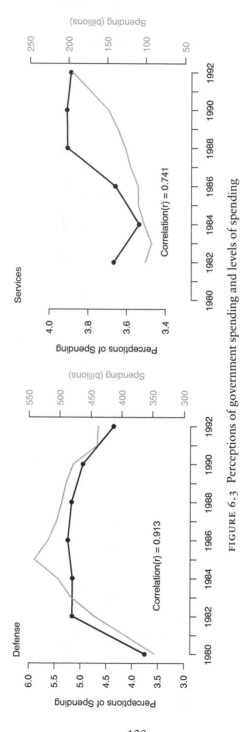

FIGURE 6.3 Perceptions of government spending and levels of spending

uncommon in survey research. Pollsters get to ask the questions but respondents get to answer them.[9]

In the case of these spending perceptions, when asked about whether spending has "increased" or "decreased," it appears that people respond based on whether we are spending "a lot" or "a little." This is clear based on a comparison of results in Figures 6.2 and 6.3. Defense perceptions hardly track spending change in the former figure ($r = -0.07$) but almost perfectly follow spending levels in the latter ($r = 0.91$). A similar dynamic is evident for services, although in this case the difference is less dramatic; the correlation with changes in spending is 0.50 and that with levels is 0.74. There apparently is an association between what the government is spending and public perceptions, just not exactly as we might expect based on the survey question. Nevertheless, Figure 6.3 suggests that people notice what policymakers are doing.

What about news coverage itself? We know from the preceding chapter that coverage tends to follow spending, but do public perceptions follow that coverage? Figure 6.4 again shows the same measure of perceptions, this time alongside a newspaper media signal over the period. Given that perceptions reflect spending levels, not changes, we need to use a media measure that reflects those levels. We did not create such a measure based on the news content and are not sure that we could, as we discussed earlier in the book. We can, however, produce one using the media signal we did create, by summing the values over time. Since we have seen that the yearly signal captures yearly policy change, at least to some degree, the running tally of it should capture the sum of policy change over time, just as the spending level in a particular year is the sum of spending changes in previous years. For example, if the media signal is a +250 in one year, indicating an increase in spending, and then +100 in the next, indicating a smaller increase, and finally –150 in the third year, pointing to a decrease, the cumulative media signal would be 250, 350, and 200 in the three fiscal years. The resulting measure does not directly tap spending levels at each point in time, but it should capture shifts in those levels; and the time-serial correspondence between the cumulative media signal and

---

[9] For instance, in the face of concerns that traditional measures of issue importance, such as those tapping most important "problems," might not reveal what scholars think they do (Wlezien 2005), many researchers have turned to measures of most important "issues." The problem is that responses to the different questions do not differ much, if at all (Jennings and Wlezien 2011). That is, when asked about "issues" people appear to think and respond about "problems."

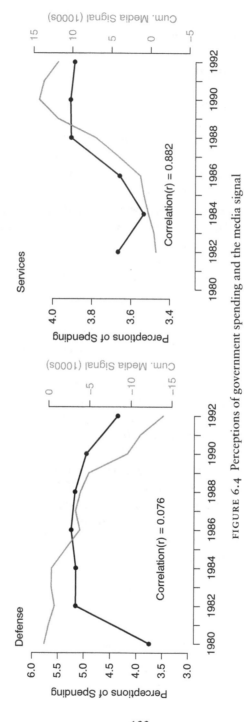

FIGURE 6.4 Perceptions of government spending and the media signal

public perceptions should be high if the public actually notices the ebb and flow of coverage. This is what matters for our analysis.

It is of some significance, then, that we observe in Figure 6.4 a rather strong correspondence between the cumulative media signal and perceptions, at least in the social services domain ($r = 0.88$). The relationship between media and perceptions is much less clear in defense, though note that the low correlation (0.07) is primarily the product of the deviation between the media signal and perceptions in 1980. There may be good reason for this deviation. We already have seen that the focus of media coverage is not only on spending for the current year but also on decisions taken during the year for the fiscal year to come, and this is particularly true for defense. Media coverage also can pick up the effects of events, precipitating increased public demand and political attention. Both of these factors may help explain the seeming disjuncture between media coverage and spending perceptions for defense in 1980, when media coverage pointed toward increases, some of which were in the offing in the coming fiscal year and those that followed. After 1980, the correlation between cumulative media coverage and perceptions is a healthy 0.88, which is larger than that between appropriations and perceptions during the same period ($r = 0.68$).[10]

Results in Figures 6.2 through 6.4 are based on a small number of cases, and so should of course not be taken too seriously. They nevertheless *do* suggest that the public notices spending and media coverage of it – but a more rigorous analysis is needed. Thankfully, it also is possible.

6.3 DOES THE PUBLIC RESPOND?

Perceptions of policy are necessary for thermostatic responsiveness but not sufficient. We want to know whether people actually use the information to inform their preferences. The public can see that spending went up, perhaps, but what do they want after the fact? Are they now less supportive of further increases? And more supportive of decreases? Does this depend on the circumstances, particularly the perceived "need" for

---

[10] Using alternative measures of the defense media signal does not change results markedly. Using the dictionary-based measure that includes relevance keywords produces a post-1980 correlation of 0.94; using the machine-learning (ML) version produces a correlation of 0.90. The story is similar for social spending, at least across the two dictionary measures. Using the combined machine-learning-based measures for health and education produces different results, but this is not surprising given the relatively weak performance of the ML measure for education.

spending? Moreover, is media coverage the mechanism? Do the other factors – besides spending – that influence media coverage also influence preferences? Answers to all of these questions require a more detailed analysis of preferences. We begin by focusing on public responsiveness to budgetary policy, and then turn to the role of media coverage.

6.3.1 Spending and Public Preferences

As discussed in Chapter 2, our analytic approach draws on the thermostatic model of public responsiveness. In the model, the public's relative preference – it's preference for "more" (or "less") – at any point in time is a function of its underlying preferred level of policy and policy itself. Because we do not directly measure the public's preferred level of policy, we have to rely on proxies. We have just seen that pollsters regularly ask about relative preferences, for example, whether we are spending "too little" or "too much." This turns out to be a good thing since what is most important for testing the thermostatic model is a measure of relative preferences – the dependent variable. As outlined in Chapter 2, public preferences at any point in time are given by the following equation:

$$R_t = a_0 + \beta_1 O_t + \beta_2 P_t + e_t. \tag{6.1}$$

Recall that if the public responds thermostatically, increases in spending will lead to decreases in net support for more spending, in which case the coefficient β_2 would be less than 0. Also recall that it is important to account for variation in the public's demand for spending, O in Equation 6.1. For instance, one regular finding in previous studies is that demand tends to trend upward over time across domains, where relative preferences increase unless spending also increases by a sufficient amount (Wlezien 1995; Soroka and Wlezien 2010).[11] Recent research on welfare preferences demonstrates that the (underlying) trend in preferences owes mostly to economic growth, which leads to greater support, though its effect in the United States has been dampened by growing income inequality, seemingly perversely (Wlezien and Soroka 2021; also see Kelly and Enns 2010). Given

---

[11] The tendency for preferences to increase effectively rules out the possibility that the negative effect of spending on relative preferences reflects "undermining" feedback in domains *where spending has increased over time*, which is the case in those we examine, whether measured in current or real dollars, and even when calculated per capita. To be absolutely clear, if spending increases were undermining demand, we would observe a negative trend, not a positive one. Also see Wlezien (2017); Wlezien and Soroka (2021).

this research, we include inflation-adjusted GDP as well as the Gini coefficient in the equations, the latter of which is a common indicator of income inequality.[12] Thus, levels of relative preferences – net support for spending in the different domains from Figure 6.1 – are modeled as a function of spending levels, real GDP, and the Gini coefficient, the latter of which increases as inequality increases, as we have observed in the United States over the preceding decades.[13]

As for our examination of the media signal in Chapter 5, we begin with a "pooled" analysis, combining the five spending domains into one equation, the results for which are summarized in Table 6.1. This is done for expository purposes, not for technical ones, as the diagnostics described earlier (in footnote 13) imply different specifications for education and the environment; note that pooling has little consequence for the results, as we document later and will be very clear when we turn to differences across domains.[14] For the analysis, we impute preference data in the fifteen years

---

[12] Both are the standard series distributed by the Federal Reserve Bank of St. Louis (https://fred.stlouisfed.org).

[13] Consistent with previous research, net support for spending appears to be stationary, exhibiting regression to the mean over time, and this also can be seen in Figure 6.1. All three of the independent variables are expected to be integrated time series, where effects tend to accumulate, drifting up and down in the form of a "random walk." According to our theoretical model in Chapter 2 (see that chapter's footnote 2), these variables – spending, GDP, and the Gini coefficient – also are expected to be cointegrated, that is, where spending follows the economy and the Gini over time such that the linear combination is stationary. Diagnostic tests confirm that GDP and the Gini coefficient are integrated and there is evidence that spending is as well for defense, welfare, and health. (By contrast, spending on education and the environment seem to be trend stationary.) Regressing spending in these three domains on GDP and the Gini coefficient produces residuals that also appear to be stationary, supporting the expectation of cointegration and implying that equation 1 is "balanced" for defense, welfare, and health, that is, both the left-hand and right-hand sides are stationary. (For more on equation balance in time series analysis, see Enns and Wlezien 2017 and Enns et al. N.d.) To be clear, for the foregoing diagnostics, we begin with Dickey-Fuller tests and supplement with KPSS tests, which is a useful check in all cases but particularly where the former are inconclusive, that is, where the estimates comport with our theoretical expectations but do not meet the levels of statistical significance based on MacKinnon's critical values the null hypotheses of the two tests are opposites of the other, where Dickey-Fuller tests against the null of a unit root (or non-stationarity) and the KPSS tests against the null of stationarity. Based on our inferences, we are able to directly interpret the results of the estimated regression for defense, welfare, and health preferences, while analysis for education and the environment requires a slightly different specification, which we address later in the chapter.

[14] If we estimate the pooled model using only defense, welfare, and health the estimated coefficient for GDP is the same, that for the Gini is virtually unchanged (0.72 instead of 0.74), and the effect of spending increases substantially in absolute terms, from –5.39 to –9.33.

TABLE 6.1 *Pooled "thermostatic" regressions of relative preferences*

	Dependent variable: public preferences	
GDP $_t$	0.002***	—
	(0.000)	
Δ GDP $_t$	—	0.001
		(0.002)
GDP $_{t-1}$	—	0.001***
		(0.000)
Gini $_t$	0.744	—
	(0.563)	
Δ Gini $_t$	—	−1.236
		(1.004)
Gini $_{t-1}$	—	−0.175
		(0.328)
Spending $_t$	−5.389***	—
	(1.296)	
Δ Spending $_t$	—	−2.349*
		(0.952)
Spending $_{t-1}$	—	−3.466***
		(0.880)
Preferences $_{t-1}$	—	−0.203***
		(0.039)
Constant	−16.783	1.137
	(6.761)	(9.764)
Within-panel Rsq	0.176	0.174
N	215	210

Cells contain coefficients with standard errors in parentheses from fixed-effects linear models. $*p < .05;$ $**\ p < .01;$ $***p < .001.$

of the forty-three-year span it is missing, using linear interpolation.[15] Because we expect inequality to not matter in defense, we set that variable

---

[15] This makes little difference for the results of the basic static model we begin with in the first column of Table 6.1, as imputation produces similar, statistically indistinguishable coefficients even as it increases the number of observations by more than 50 percent, from 140 to 215. For the dynamic analysis in the second column and in all of the tables that follow, imputation is necessary to produce meaningful estimates, as we otherwise would be left with only twelve cases in each domain and sixty in total, ten per domain and fifty in total for the period during which we have media measures.

to a constant for that domain in these pooled estimations; given that we estimate fixed effects, which controls for systematic differences across spending areas, the resulting coefficient captures the impact of inequality over time for the set of domestic domains.

The first column of Table 6.1 shows a basic equation in which preferences for spending are modeled as a function of concurrent levels of spending (again standardized by domain as in Chapter 5), GDP, and the Gini coefficient. This equation does not take into account any autocorrelation or dynamics, though the analyses that follow do. Here we can see that GDP has the expected positive effect and the coefficient for the inequality measure is positive but insignificant. Demand for spending thus appears to increase as the economy grows over time and ebbs during recessions, per previous research.[16] Spending has a negative effect on preferences, where preferences tend to decrease (increase) as spending increases (decreases), exactly as the thermostatic model predicts. Taken together, the coefficients in the first column of Table 6.1 indicate that the evolution of preferences for more spending depends *jointly* on public demand and policymaker supply, where the economy drives the underlying preferred policy "temperature." We therefore expect spending increases to produce observable downward (upward) shifts in preferences *only* when they are greater (lesser) than we would predict given economic growth. This supports the previous research.

The specification in the first column of Table 6.1 presumes that all effects are contemporaneous, what time-series analysts refer to as a "static model" (see De Boef and Keele 2008).[17] This follows our initial theoretical model, but it may be that the effects are more dynamic, and we can adopt a more general modeling approach that makes it unnecessary to settle things by assumption. To that end, column 2 of Table 6.1 reports results of an error correction model (ECM) of spending preferences. Here, the dependent variable is the current *change* in preferences; independent variables include the lagged (year $t - 1$) level of preferences, the current (year t) changes in spending, GDP, and the Gini coefficient, and the lagged (year $t - 1$) levels of spending, GDP, and the Gini.[18] Separately estimating the effects of current changes and lagged levels of our independent

---

[16] The GDP variable does trend but both that trend and the variation around it impacts preferences in statistically indistinguishable ways (also see Wlezien and Soroka 2021)

[17] As noted earlier, it also ignores dynamics, producing autocorrelation in the errors.

[18] This is mathematically equivalent to estimating an autoregressive distributed lag (ADL) model, which employs level variables on both sides of the equation. See De Boef and Keele (2008).

variables together with the lagged level of preferences allows us to assess their "short-run" and "long-run" effects.

These results comport with those in the first column of Table 6.1, albeit with some important differences. First, we see in the second column that the lagged preference variable has a negative coefficient (–0.203) that is significantly different from 0. This implies mean reversion to the public's support for spending given the effects of the other variables. Second, the coefficients for the two GDP variables are positive while the coefficients for the two Gini variables are negative, though only lagged levels of GDP are statistically significant. This implies that the effect of the economy is not just in the short-run, that is, through current changes, but also in the longer run. In other words, macroeconomic conditions help to determine the equilibrium level of spending needed to stabilize preferences: when the economy is booming, people want more spending and so more spending is needed to bring preferences down or *keep them from going up in the first place*. Third, and relatedly, both spending variables are negatively signed and significant, though the coefficients do differ slightly, where current changes have a smaller effect than lagged levels.[19] The latter is important because the coefficients on the lagged independent variables in the equation define the adjustment of preferences to disequilibria between spending and GDP. If spending is too low (high) given macroeconomics, preferences for more spending are expected to go up (down) in the next year.[20] Note that the effect is robust to the inclusion of variables tapping the party of the president, which underscores public responsiveness to information about spending itself – see the Appendix to this chapter.

Results in Table 6.1 capture the equivalent of an "average" effect of the different variables across the five spending domains. To assess variation, Table 6.2 presents results of estimating the model separately for each domain. These look much like what we saw in the second column of Table 6.1, although degrees of statistical significance vary from one domain to the next. Preferences for spending on health, education, and the environment are less strongly connected to macroeconomics and spending than are preferences for spending on defense

[19] When estimated only for the defense, welfare, and health domains, the coefficients for spending are larger in absolute terms than those in Table 6.1, particularly for current changes.

[20] This is per the thermostatic model (see Wlezien 2004; Soroka and Wlezien 2010), and also see footnote 13.

TABLE 6.2 *Regressions of preferences by spending domain*

| | Dependent variable: Δ Preferences ,, by domain: | | | | |
	Defense	Welfare	Health	Education	Environment
Δ GDP $_t$	−0.010	−0.004	0.009*	0.000	0.006
	(0.008)	(0.005)	(0.004)	(0.002)	(0.004)
GDP $_{t-1}$	0.001*	0.005**	0.002	−0.000	0.−001
	(0.001)	(0.002)	(0.001)	(0.001)	(0.001)
Δ Gini $_t$	—	−2.836	−0.015	0.230	−2.029
		(1.805)	(1.635)	(0.861)	(1.468)
Gini $_{t-1}$	—	−3.693*	−0.967	0.730	−0.188
		(1.384)	(1.194)	(0.732)	(0.985)
Δ Spending $_t$	−12.150+	−13.783***	−6.774	0.014	−0.627
	(6.089)	(4.119)	(4.681)	(0.734)	(1.098)
Spending $_{t-1}$	−5.746*	−8.965**	−5.961	0.098	−3.503*
	(2.361)	(2.780)	(4.004)	(0.894)	(1.302)
Preferences $_{t-1}$	−0.172+	−0.375***	−0.171+	−0.173*	−0.220*
	(0.099)	(0.099)	(0.098)	0.083)	(0.082)
Constant	−14.113+	97.244	26.465	−16.961	9.708
	(7.025)	(46.001)	(40.481)	(24.314)	(35.250)
Rsq	0.277	0.447	0.252	0.167	0.372
N	42	42	42	42	42

Cells contain coefficients with standard errors in parentheses from linear models.
+ $p < .10$; * $p < .05$; ** $p < .01$; *** $p < .001$.

and welfare.[21] In the latter two domains, GDP and spending have clear effects on preferences, and inequality matters in welfare as well. That said, changes in GDP do matter for preferences on health, and here lagged GDP and both spending coefficients are close to statistically significant. Levels of spending also have a significant effect on environment preferences, a result that is borne out using the model specification implied by the time-serial characteristics of the independent variables.[22] The main exception in this table is education, for which

[21] Adding a trend variable to the equations does not meaningfully change the spending coefficients in any of the equations, as the pattern of statistical significance remains the same and the sizes of the coefficients are not different statistically from those in Table 6.2.

[22] That is, the effect remains even when the lagged levels of GDP and the Gini coefficient are dropped from the equation for the environment, which is the appropriate modeling strategy, given that the variables are integrated and not cointegrated. See footnote 13.

spending preferences are unrelated to the economy or spending itself.[23] This results differ from what we found in our previous research based on a shorter time period (Soroka and Wlezien 2010), which suggests that patterns may have changed in more recent years. That is a subject for other research.

What really matters about the results in Tables 6.1 and 6.2 is that public preferences for spending in certain salient domains are thermostatic, reflecting variation in both the demand for and supply of policy over time. This is the critical background for the next step in our analysis, which focuses on the degree to which media coverage is the basis for the apparent public responsiveness to policy.

6.4 DOES MEDIA COVERAGE MATTER?

The information people have about policy has to come from somewhere. As discussed, some of the information might come from personal experience, particularly in domains where people directly consume policy, as in the case of social programs like health and welfare. In other areas, such as defense and the environment, consumption is more "collective," and this is true even for the areas where people participate directly. Most of us do not receive welfare benefits, and even those who do may have and use information about broader policy trends. It is, after all, more difficult to imagine people responding thermostatically based on their own consumption of policy, for example, my benefits went up and so now I am more in favor of spending less on welfare, than on what policymakers are doing more generally.[24] Where do people get this information? We expect that news coverage is part of the story.

To test this possibility, we need to add news coverage to our public preference equations. Given the model, this is not entirely straightforward, as we need to include measures of both the current change and lagged level of coverage, only the former of which we have at hand. As for the analysis of perceptions earlier in the chapter, however, we can rely on the cumulative media signals used in the analysis of perceptions, where we simply sum up the annual media signal across years (see Figure 6.4). While

---

[23] This also is borne out in analysis following the alternative model specification used in the environment domain and described in footnote 22.

[24] Of course, these may be correlated, at least to the extent personal consumption across individuals moves in sync over time.

not a direct measure, recall that the cumulative media signal directly corresponds with the level of spending over time, which is of special theoretical – and empirical – importance in the thermostatic model. In our model of public preferences, we include both the current (year t) media signal and the lagged (year $t-1$) cumulative media signal recalling that these two variables add up to the cumulative media signal in year t.[25] This specification seems to contrast with our expectation that the media and the public focus on policy changes, but is something we foreshadowed in Chapter 2. We consider this further in the discussion of results that follows.

Although we are especially interested in the defense, welfare, and health domains, we begin with the pooled analysis of all five spending areas, per Table 6.1. Since inequality mattered only for welfare preferences in Table 6.2, we include the Gini coefficient only for that domain in the new analysis. Given that media coverage data are available since 1980, we re-estimate the equation from the second column of Table 6.1 for this shorter period of time, and present those results in the first column of Table 6.3. Results adding the media measures are shown in the second and third columns of the table.

Results in the first column are in line with those for the longer time period presented in Table 6.1. The signs and sizes of the coefficients of all variables are similar, and the statistical significance is as well. What happens when we add the media measures? As can be seen in the second column of Table 6.3, including the media variables reduces the size and significance of the spending coefficients. The coefficient for spending change drops by about 33 percent, from –1.85 to –1.23, and is correspondingly less reliable. The coefficient for lagged levels of spending is reduced by 40 percent, from –3.00 to –1.79. Both changes are the result of the lagged cumulative media coverage, the coefficient for which is negative and also highly reliable (-0.22, $p<.001$). This result pretty strongly implies

---

[25] That is, the cumulative media signal in year t equals the cumulative media signal in year $t-1$ plus the media signal in year t. Diagnostic tests indicate that the variable appears to be integrated and there also is evidence of cointegration with spending, GDP, and the Gini coefficient in the defense, welfare, and health domains. Some might wonder whether this is the correct representation, perhaps moreso because we found evidence of cointegration between spending, GDP, and the Gini coefficient earlier in the chapter. Given this, we used Johansen's method to confirm the modeling choice, results of which identified one cointegrating equation in each domain, where there is an equilibrium relationship between cumulative media coverage and the other variables. The estimated equation of preferences including the variables in Table 6 thus appears to be balanced – also see footnote 13.

TABLE 6.3 *Pooled regressions including media measures*

	Dependent variable: Δ Preferences $_t$		
Δ GDP $_t$	0.001	−0.000	−0.000
	(0.002)	(0.002)	(0.002)
GDP $_{t-1}$	0.001***	0.001***	0.001***
	(0.000)	(0.000)	(0.000)
Δ Gini^a $_t$	−3.060+	−3.459*	−3.544*
	(1.800)	1.697)	(1.696)
Gini^a $_{t-1}$	−0.426	−1.088**	−1.165**
	(0.382)	(0.391)	(0.395)
Δ Spending $_t$	−1.848*	−1.231	−1.464+
	(0.887)	(0.860)	(0.880)
Spending $_{t-1}$	−3.000***	−1.789*	−1.168
	(0.833)	(0.823)	(0.964)
Preferences $_{t-1}$	−0.306***	−0.360***	−0.364***
	(0.037)	(0.038)	(0.038)
Media signal $_t$	—	0.776+	0.871*
		(0.426)	(0.432)
Cumulative media signal $_{t-1}$	—	−0.224***	—
		(0.049)	
Predicted Cum. media signal $_{t-1}$	—	—	−0.283***
			(0.068)
Residual Cum. media signal $_{t-1}$	—	—	−0.164*
			(0.069)
Constant	1.431	7.031+	7.789*
	(4.061)	(4.001)	(4.043)
Within–panel Rsq	0.327	0.410	0.415
N	190	190	190

Cells contain coefficients with standard errors in parentheses from fixed-effects linear models. + $p < .10$; * $p < .05$; ** $p < .01$; *** $p < .001$.
^{a} Included only in the welfare spending domain.

that news coverage matters for thermostatic public responsiveness, predicated on the strong relationship between spending and the cumulative media signal.[26] But, to be clear, lagged cumulative media coverage of policy change matters for public responsiveness *above and beyond* the

[26] Spending accounts for just less than 50 percent of the over-time variance in the cumulative media signal across the five spending domains.

effect of spending itself.[27] By contrast, the current media signal actually has a positive effect on preferences. The estimate is not highly reliable, in large part because the effect does not hold generally across all of the spending domains, which we document later in the chapter.

For now, what is most important about the results is that the news appears to effectively communicate information about spending to the public. That mediation is not perfect, as some effects of spending remain even when the news variables are included. This is not surprising given the (substantial) measurement error in our media variables and the focus of coverage, recalling that the news does not solely reflect current trends in spending: it reflects past and future spending as well, and it contains other information that is not associated with spending trends at all. The public also has separate sources of information about what government is doing. The point of all of this is that we do not expect the news to completely mediate spending decisions and the public, and in the second column of Table 6.3 it clearly doesn't. Even to the extent the news does drive thermostatic public responsiveness to policy, it occurs not because of coverage of current policy change. Instead, the public adjusts its relative preferences based on differences between the cumulative spending signal in the previous year and the level it should be given the economy and other factors. If that cumulative signal is greater than it should be given those factors, the public adjusts its preferences for more spending downward in the future; if the signal is lesser than it should be, preferences shift upward. Of course, if the policy signal is in equilibrium, we expect no such adjustment. The results thus imply that the media signal matters to the public differently to what we originally hypothesized, in the form of either a running tally of coverage of previous policy changes or to coverage of policy levels themselves.

The third column of Table 6.3 captures the mediation of policy information more directly. Here we separate the cumulative media signal into two components, one predicted by spending over time and the rest of the coverage, that is, the residual component. This allows us to compare the effects of spending-related coverage and the rest of the news signal. To create these variables, we estimate a regression of cumulative media coverage on spending separately for each of the domains, which accounts for differences in the connection between spending and the media signal. We generate predicted media coverage using the coefficients on the spending variables; the residual

---

[27] These results also are robust to the inclusion of presidential party variables, as can be seen in the appendix.

component is just the level of cumulative coverage minus that predicted by spending.[28] To assess their separate, potentially different effects, we substitute the lagged values of these two variables – Predicted Coverage and Residual Coverage – for the lagged cumulative media coverage.[29]

The estimates for the other (non-media) variables in the third column of Table 6.3 are very similar to those in the second column, and the differences owe entirely to variation in the effects of spending on media coverage across the domains. Results in this column suggest an even stronger effect of the news, one that more effectively mediates the effect of spending on preferences, as the direct effects of lagged spending levels are smaller and miss standard ($p=.05$) levels of statistical significance. Results also suggest that it is the media content related to spending that matters most for preferences – while both coefficients are negative, that for Residual Coverage is less robust and roughly 3/5 the size of the coefficient for Predicted Coverage (-0.16 vs -0.28). This implies that the public may update its preferences based more – although not exclusively – on coverage that is related to spending.[30]

These results likely overstate the degree of mediation since, as we have seen in the second column of Table 6.3, spending has a direct effect on preferences independent of the news. Not all of the impact of spending happens through our measure of media coverage, and causal mediation analysis suggests that just over 50 percent of the effect is mediated.[31] That the residual component matters does highlight the influence of media coverage on public opinion, as the public seemingly is not just responding to spending; it is responding to media coverage itself, whether predicted by spending or not. The results thus raise questions about what actually determines this "residual" coverage, ones that we delve into more deeply in Chapter 7.

There is reason to think that results in Table 6.3 conceal variation across domains, however. Chapter 5 shows that there are differences in

---

[28] This may appear to contrast with our analyses in Chapter 5 showing that the media signal in each year can reflect change in the preceding and subsequent years, but here we are attempting to unpack the relationship between spending levels and the cumulative media signal in the current year, following the second equation in Table 6.3.

[29] The predicted component is based on separate regressions of cumulative media coverage on spending in each domain, the R-squared from which ranges from .58 to .95.

[30] The difference in coefficients is not statistically significant ($p = .22$).

[31] This is based on application of the Hicks and Tingley (2012) Stata package, where spending is the treatment variable and cumulative media coverage the mediator and using fifty simulations: the average causal mediation effect (ACME) is -1.83 out of a total effect of -3.69.

TABLE 6.4 *Regressions of preferences with media measures by spending domain*

	Dependent variable: Δ Preferences $_t$, by domain:				
	Defense	Welfare	Health	Education	Environment
Δ Spending $_t$	−12.309*	−9.649*	−3.706	.259	.565
	(5.491)	(3.923)	(4.753)	(.631)	(1.256)
Media signal $_t$	2.904+	−.0656	.043	.405	1.273
	(1.535)	(1.010)	(1.210)	(.397)	(1.148)
Predicted Cum media signal $_{t-1}$	−1.428*	−2.332**	−.649+	.155	.156
	(.635)	(.714)	(.364)	(.228)	(.354)
Residual Cum media signal $_{t-1}$	.411	−1.501**	−.815+	.097	.315
	(.760)	(.517)	(.428)	(.256)	(.353)
Within-panel Rsq	0.680	0.687	0.329	0.473	0.4571
N	38	38	38	38	38

Cells contain coefficients with standard errors in parentheses from fixed-effects linear models. Full models use the same controls as in Table 6.3; only spending and media variables are shown here. + p <.10; * $p < .05$; ** $p < .01$; *** $p < .001$.

the accuracy of media coverage, after all, and results in Table 6.2 indicate that responsiveness also varies. To what extent are these results connected? For analyses in Table 6.4 we follow the approach in the third column of Table 6.3, which allows us to more effectively identify the separate effects of spending-related coverage and "other" coverage. In these analyses it is necessary to remove lagged spending because it is perfected correlated with the Predicted Signal, which is generated based on by-domain analysis.[32]

The results in Table 6.4 reveal a good amount of heterogeneity across domains. From the estimates for the Predicted Signal, there is evidence of news-related effects in defense and welfare, and only slightly less reliable effects in health as well. There are no such effects in the environment domain or education, the latter of which is as we have seen throughout the analyses in this chapter. The pattern of public responsiveness in Table 6.4 is largely as we should expect given the results in Table 6.2. The main exception is the environment, where earlier results showed negative

---

[32] That is, spending is perfectly correlated with the predicted signal in each domain.

feedback of spending; here, we find no responsiveness, a consequence both of the shortened time period and collinearity between the variables.[33]

The finding that predicted cumulative media coverage matters for public responsiveness in defense, welfare, and health is important, but it is only moderate evidence of real mediation.[34] Although the information must come from somewhere, and we know that the media signal does follow spending in those three domains, we cannot be absolutely sure that coverage is what matters. Even to the extent the public is responding to news coverage, do notice that our models do not perfectly account for it, particularly in defense and to a lesser degree welfare, where we continue to see effects of spending change even when taking into account the media signal. This may have to do with the limits of our measures but also our model specification, and there is some evidence of the latter.[35]

But what about the impact of the cumulative media coverage that is not associated with spending decisions? Does the public respond to this "residual" news? Results in Table 6.4 suggest that preferences for defense respond exclusively to the media coverage that is directly associated with spending, not the residual coverage, as the coefficient for the latter is positive, though not statistically significant. This implies that media coverage that is uncorrelated with spending on defense does not contain meaningful information to the public about the direction of policy in the domain. Measurement error again is a possibility, as is the specification of media effects, but it also may be that the content of coverage communicates other information that just does not produce the equivalent of a thermostatic response.[36]

For welfare and health, by contrast, there is evidence of responsiveness to both components. In the welfare domain, the coefficient for residual media coverage not only is negative but roughly 3/5 the size of the coefficient for media coverage directly linked to spending, and the estimates are

---

[33] Note, however, that when media variables are dropped from the regression and lagged spending is added back in, the latter has a modest effect that is on the cusp of statistical significance ($p = .08$). This holds when dropping lagged GDP from the equation, per footnotes 13 and 22, and also when excluding the lagged media variables.

[34] Also note that the pattern of results in each of the domains is robust to the inclusion of a linear trend variable.

[35] For instance, the effects of current spending change drop substantially when including the lagged media signal (Media Signal$_{t-1}$) in the model, suggesting that the public responds more to it than it does to the remainder of the lagged cumulative media signal.

[36] The pattern of results is not entirely surprising, given other research (De Boef and Kellstedt 2004) showing that the public does not respond to all media coverage relating to the economy.

not significantly different (p=.30). In health, the coefficient for residual spending also is negative and actually a little larger (in absolute terms) than the coefficient for predicted coverage, though these are quite similar and again not significantly different (p=.62). Based on these results, the public appears to respond fairly equally to spending-related and other, non-spending-related coverage in these domains. This is strong evidence of media effects. They imply that there may be policy-relevant information in the "other" coverage that the public takes into account. There are less sanguine possibilities, of course. The results highlight a need to further explore the sources of this coverage and its effects, a topic we take up in Chapter 7.

For now, we can say that the public does not respond to the *entirety* of media coverage in all spending domains. There is variation in the impact of each component of media coverage – the predicted and residual cumulative signals, as well as the current media signal (in year t). Note from Table 6.4 that the latter is weakly significant, and *positive*, only in defense. This effect, like those for the residual cumulative signal in welfare and health, is intriguing in a different way, as it implies that the public responds in quite opposite fashion to current media signal and the cumulation of past signals. What could explain this difference? There are two main suspects, we think.

The first is the policy focus of media coverage revealed in Chapter 5. There we found that current coverage is as much about policy*making* this year (for next year) as it is about this year's spending (decided last year). As such, it might be that media coverage is positively related to changes in preferences precisely because the latter are actually driving media coverage (and policymaking) during the year.[37] The estimated equation may consequently have the causal direction backward, at least in terms of this particular effect. We can test this possibility, and do so in Chapter 7, where we further unpack the dynamics relating policy, media coverage, and the public.

The second suspect is the possible focus of media coverage on changes in the *need* for defense spending over time, which also may influence public preferences (Wlezien 1996; Soroka and Wlezien 2010). It may be, for instance, that a national security event leads politicians to clamor for more spending, which in turn influences media coverage and public

---

[37] Recall that the General Social Survey (GSS) is typically in the field in the first half of the year, and preferences captured at that time have been shown to influence appropriations' decisions taken later in the year.

opinion. Again, the consequence would be a positive association between current media and current opinion, and *future* spending. This possibility emphasizes the importance of events, but note that the causes of media coverage need not be entirely exogenous to the political process. Consider that politicians may argue for more spending without a precipitating event, and this can impact public preference as well. Even if there is a significant event, politicians' behavior can matter for public the public response, as Brody (1991) found in his analysis of rally around the flag effects.[38] This set of possibilities is quite different to the first, as it sees the causal flow as going from the media to the public, even if only as a conduit, not the other way around. We consider these alternatives in Chapter 7 as well.

6.5 ON MEDIA COVERAGE AND THE PUBLIC

This chapter demonstrates that media coverage about public policy matters for public responsiveness. It offers what is to our knowledge the first evidence that people notice and respond to media coverage of policy across multiple domains. The news mostly serves to provide people with information about spending change, to effectively mediate between policymaking and the public. There are hints of a positive concurrent relationship with perceptions of spending change, at least in defense. But there is more robust, cross-domain evidence of a negative relationship between the cumulative media signal and preferences, where people adjust their preferences downward (upward) in response to the cumulation of signals that policy has increased (decreased) over time. This is not the case in all spending domains, but it is in the most salient ones – the same ones in which previous work and our own reanalysis finds evidence of strong thermostatic responsiveness.

Media coverage appears to matter for preferences independent of spending as well. In both the welfare and health domains, media content that is *uncorrelated with spending* has an effect much like that for spending-related coverage. What exactly does this residual media content contain? In defense, the current media signal also has a positive relationship with preferences that contrasts with the negative feedback of cumulated coverage, as if the news both informs the public about government actions and

---

[38] Brody demonstrated that presidents' approval ratings benefited from military actions only when other politicians did not oppose that action. The behavior of politicians itself may reflect anticipated public reactions, of course – it is not clearly exogenous.

drives public demand (or preferences drive the news). Both of these effects warrant further scrutiny. They and other issues in the relationships between policy, media coverage, and the public are the focus of Chapter 7.

6.6 APPENDIX TO CHAPTER 6: PARTY OF THE PRESIDENT AND PUBLIC RESPONSIVENESS

There is reason to suppose that the seeming public responsiveness to spending masks responsiveness to the party control of government, which itself influences spending, particularly the party of the president (Wlezien 1995, 1996; Soroka and Wlezien 2010; Wlezien and Soroka 2021). Although much of this previous research finds an independent effect of spending, it is worth demonstrating how exactly party variables impact the estimates for spending and media coverage. To do this, we include variables for the party of the president in models of preferences. We do so by creating a dichotomous variable that takes the value "1" in fiscal years during which Democrats are in office, and "0" for Republicans. We might expect the public to react in opposite ways to Democratic (and Republican) presidents in the defense and non-defense domains, but diagnostic analyses reveal that the public's defense preferences do not respond to party control, that is, the effects are entirely in the social spending domains. Given this, we recode the party control variable to 0.5 for all years in the defense domain, and then add two associated variables into our models: (1) the first difference of party control, which takes the value "1" in years Democrats takes office, "–1" when Republicans take office, and "0" when there is no change in party; and (2) the lagged level of party control. Table 6.A1 presents results that include these variables in a pooled model of preferences that does not include the media variables, and then a model that includes them.

The first column in Table 6.A1 presents results of re-estimating the first model of preferences in Table 6.3. Here we can see that the party of the president does matter for public preferences in ways that we expect; that is, under Democratic presidents, preferences for more non-defense spending tend to decrease, approximately four points per year, other things being equal. Including the party control variables actually increases coefficients for spending – the estimate for differenced spending rises from –1.85 in Table 6.3 to –1.94 in Table 6.A1, and that for the lagged level of spending goes from –3.00 to –3.16. While party matters to the public, then, and immediately after presidents take office, it does not dampen public responsiveness to policy itself.

TABLE 6.A1 *Regressions of spending preferences including the party of the president*

	Dependent variable: Δ Preferences $_t$	
Δ GDP $_t$	0.002	0.001
	(0.002)	(0.002)
GDP $_{t-1}$	0.001***	0.001***
	(0.000)	(0.000)
Δ Gini $_t$	−2.130	−2.564
	(1.714)	(1.627)
Gini $_{t-1}$	−0.192***	−0.8571**
	(0.365)	(0.375)
Δ Spending $_t$	−1.943	−1.242
	(0.851)	(0.830)
Spending $_{t-1}$	−3.160***	−2.021
	(0.792)	(0.788)
Preferences $_{t-1}$	−0.355***	−0.390***
	(0.038)	(0.038)
Media signal $_t$	—	0.404
		(0.414)
Cumulative media signal $_{t-1}$	—	−0.214***
		(0.047)
Δ Party of the President $_t$	−3.899**	−3.700***
	(1.159)	(1.106)
Party of the President $_{t-1}$	−4.127***	−3.709***
	(0.947)	(0.916)
Constant	0.130	5.034
	(3.851)	(3.834)
Within-panel Rsq	0.405	0.472
N	190	190

Cells contain coefficients with standard errors in parentheses from fixed-effects linear models. * $p < .05$; ** $p < .01$; *** $p < .001$.

The results in the first column of Table 6.A1 are important to be sure, but they largely support previous research, and in this book, we are primarily focused on public responsiveness to media coverage, not spending per se. To assess whether the party control variables impact these media effects, the second column of the table re-estimates the second model of preferences in Table 6.3 with media variables included. These results again reveal sizable effects of party control, ones that have only modest consequences for our estimates of media influence. The critical coefficient on the cumulative media variable drops trivially from –0.224 to –0.214, which is less than 5 percent. The coverage of policy evidently is fairly independent of party control and the public pretty clearly responds to that coverage when adjusting its preferences.[39] There is a more sizable and meaningful (nearly 50 percent) shift in the coefficient for the current media signal, which remains positive but no longer is significant in the presence of the party variables. This change is more statistical than it is substantive, however, as that media effect is evident only for the defense domain, where the party variable does not vary in our analysis here. For more on the effect of the current media signal on defense spending preferences, see the analysis and discussion in the later sections of Chapter 6 and the exploratory analysis in Chapter 7.

---

[39] Patterns are very much the same when focusing on the three most salient domains – defense, welfare, and health – where the specifications in Table 6.A1 are most appropriate; although the coefficients for party and especially cumulative media coverage are larger, the inclusion of the former has minor impact on the estimate for the latter, which drops from –0.39 to –0.38.

7

Diagnosing and Exploring Dynamics

Preceding chapters have provided evidence that media coverage frequently reflects public policy, and that public preferences respond to the media "policy signal." Those results speak to some important questions about the nature and functioning of representative democracy, we believe. A good number of questions remain, however, and this chapter attempts to address some of what seem to us to be the most pressing issues.

First, we consider the impact that trends in media consumption have on public responsiveness. Most of the preceding analyses rely on a newspaper-based measure of media content, but there has been a steady decline of newspaper circulation in the United States, dropping from a peak of about 63 million in 1984 to under 30 million by 2018. Has the impact of newspapers declined correspondingly? If so, it may be that the newspaper signal has less influence on the public's perceptions of government policy actions and also its preferences.

Second, we consider heterogeneity in public responsiveness to the media policy signal. Analyses in Chapter 6 focus entirely on preferences (and perceptions) for aggregates of all Americans taken together, which may conceal interesting and important differences across subgroups of the population. There may be reason to presume that responsiveness to media coverage is more pronounced for those who are especially attentive to the news, for instance (see Neuner et al. 2019). There also may be differences across groups based on education levels and/or party identification. As discussed in previous chapters, prior research identifies "parallel publics" in preferences for spending (and other policies). Even so, we consider here the possibility that responsiveness to media and policy varies across levels of media use, education, and party identification.

Third, we reconsider the causal relationships between policy, news coverage, and the public. Most of the preceding analyses are based on the presumption that the flow of information is from policy to the news and then to the public. Results in Chapter 6 have already hinted at other possibilities, however. We are particularly interested in the possibility of a reciprocal connection between policy and the news. Does policy really cause news coverage? Or is it that media coverage itself causes policy? And how do public preferences figure in? These questions are not easily sorted using observational data, and experiments involving policy are difficult to imagine, let alone implement. We can however gain some insight into the timing of the relations (i.e., their sequencing) with the data we have, and we explore this later in the chapter.

Fourth and finally, we investigate several of the domain-specific media effects identified in Chapter 6. Media coverage of policy matters, but to varying degrees and in different ways, and we provide additional analyses here to help illuminate some of these domain-level differences in information flows.

All of these analyses focus on the three domains in which we have found consistent connections between policy, media coverage, and public opinion: defense, welfare, and health. They broaden and deepen our understanding of media influence in the United States, as the results support and strengthen the claims proffered in previous chapters.

The sections that follow will pull us in different directions, to be sure. But we see the take-home message of this chapter as being relatively straightforward: even in a changing media environment, the "policy signal" in media content informs, and also may in part reflect, public preferences for policy across a broad spectrum of the American public.

7.1 MEDIA CONSUMPTION AND THE IMPACT OF THE MEDIA SIGNAL

The Appendix to Chapter 4 considers in some detail differences in the circulation of the newspapers that we rely on for our media policy signal. Taking differences in individual newspapers' circulation into account turns out to make little difference to the estimated media policy signal. There is however one other way in which we want to consider newspaper circulation.

FIGURE 7.1 US newspaper circulation, 1980–2018

The overall circulation of newspapers has been declining for some time. Figure 7.1 illustrates the trend in circulation over the past forty years, some of which has to do with the rise of online news, both news outlet- and social media-based. (Data are drawn from Pew 2019c; for recent data on access to online news, see Pew 2019a; on the rise of social media use, see Pew 2014, 2019b.) That said, recent surveys indicate that nearly half of the American public relies on television for their news, a third currently uses news websites, and only 16 percent claim to read newspapers – slightly less than those who depend on social media (see, e.g., Shearer 2018; Pew 2018b). One reasonable supposition is that the impact of newspapers on public preferences has decreased over time.

There also are reasons to think otherwise. Insofar as different media platforms are sending similar policy signals, the circulation of newspapers may not matter, at least for our estimation of media effects. Put differently: insofar as a newspaper-based signal captures the nature of policy information across *other* media, then the impact of the measure need not be affected by the circulation of newspapers. They may be steadily replaced by televised or online content, but much the same information – captured here in newspapers – may still be reaching citizens. Indeed, this seems likely. We already have seen in Chapters 3 and 5 that the policy signal differs only a little between newspapers and television news, for instance. We also know that much of the content that is circulated online, either through website or social media, is from traditional news sources such as major newspapers and television broadcasts (see,

TABLE 7.1 *The impact of newspaper circulation on public responsiveness to the media signal – defense, health, and welfare spending domains*

	Dependent variable: Δ Preferences $_t$
Δ GDP $_t$	–0.004
	(0.003)
GDP $_{t-1}$	0.001**
	(0.000)
Δ Gini $_t$	–3.848*
	(1.861)
Gini $_{t-1}$	–1.547**
	(0.483)
Δ Spending $_t$	–8.204**
	(2.492)
Spending $_{t-1}$	–0.850
	(1.382)
Preferences $_{t-1}$	–0.321***
	(0.052)
Media Signal $_t$	1.567**
	(0.681)
Circulation $_{t-1}$	–0.075
	(0.182)
Cumulative Media Signal $_{t-1}$	–0.305*
	(0.130)
Circulation * Cum Media Signal $_{t-1}$	–0.008
	(0.007)
Constant	14.900
	(11.140)
Within-panel Rsq	0.537
N	114

Cells contain coefficients with standard errors in parentheses from fixed-effects linear models. $*p < .05$; $**p < .01$; $***p < .001$.

e.g., Maier 2010; Pew 2011; Bonazzo 2018). Declining newspaper circulation may thus be of little consequence for the estimated impact of our media policy signal.

This is testable. Table 7.1 shows a pooled model of public responsiveness to policy and media, almost exactly as we have seen in Chapter 6, but focused here only on those domains where we observed mediation – defense, health, and welfare. The model closely follows the second model in Table 6.3; the only changes here are the inclusion of lagged newspaper circulation (in millions) and an interaction between that variable and the lagged cumulative media signal.

Note in this model that the coefficients for spending are negative (as expected) but only the impact of changes is statistically significant, much as we saw when media measures were included in Chapter 6.[1] We subtract the minimum in-sample value from the circulation measure, so the coefficient for the cumulative media signal captures thermostatic responsiveness when circulation is at its lowest. That this coefficient is statistically significant makes clear that the newspaper-based media signal continues to structure public responsiveness at the end of our time series. The interaction term also is negative, pointing to the possibility that public responsiveness to media content was greater when circulation was higher.

Although the coefficient for the interaction is not significantly different from 0, we need to consider the combined additive and interactive effects of the cumulative media signal. Newspaper circulation in 1980 was roughly 62 million; by 2018 it had dropped to about 28 million (see Figure 7.1) Based on the coefficients in Table 7.1, the estimated effect of the cumulative media signal in 1980 is –0.589 (s.e. = 0.162), nearly twice the estimated effect in 2018, –0.305 (s.e. = 0.130). This implies that declining circulation may have dampened public responsiveness to media coverage of spending over time.

There are two reasons to not have too much faith in these estimates. The first is fairly straightforward: none of the yearly estimates are significantly different from any of the others, e.g., the *p*-value for the largest difference in estimates (0.293), which is between the peak of circulation in 1985 and the low point in 2018, is only 0.22. This casts doubt on the effect of circulation on public responsiveness. Second, even to the extent that responsiveness has declined over time, it may capture change in something besides newspaper circulation that also has trended over time.

One possibility is government spending itself, which has tended to increase over the 39 years examined here. So does the cumulative media signal, not surprisingly, as it sums the media signal, which follows spending change (see Chapter 5). A consequence of the increasing level of (and variance in) the cumulative variable is that the coefficient may have shifted

---

[1] Much of thermostatic responsiveness thus is evident from the negative coefficients attached to the (lagged) cumulative media signal, keeping in mind that this provides only a coarse estimate of the effect given the correlation with concurrent spending levels.

over time as a result – they may have declined – and that change may be captured, at least in part, by a circulation variable that trends downwards over time.[2] To be clear: the decline in media effects reflected in the estimates from Table 7.1 could reflect trends in the cumulative media signal itself.[3]

One hint of this alternative hypothesis comes from estimating models like the one in Table 7.1 in the separate domains. The cumulative media signal trends strongly upwards in the domestic domains but hardly in defense and even in the domestic domains the trends are most pronounced for health and to a lesser extent welfare. And when the equation is estimated separately for each domain, the size and significance of the interactive coefficient increases with the degree of upward trend in coverage. Moreover, there is no such effect at all for defense, a domain in which the media signal has barely (and not significantly) trended over time. In the absence of a pronounced trend in spending, therefore, the impact of media coverage appears to be approximately the same.

These results suggest that the public responds to the ebb and flow of coverage in a fairly consistent way over time, i.e., that public responsiveness to the newspaper signal does not depend on newspaper circulation. We do recognize that newspapers probably have had a declining influence over time, and it may be that this decline is genuinely of a limited magnitude in the period examined here. But our suspicion is that these results are a product of similarities between the newspaper signal and information conveyed on other platforms, particularly television. The media environment is changing to be sure, particularly over the past decade; and there are good reasons to expect that the information we receive about policy through social media, for instance, is different from what we capture in a newspaper-based policy signal. We consider this possibility in Chapter 8.

7.2 HETEROGENEITY IN PUBLIC RESPONSIVENESS TO THE NEWS

The thermostatic responsiveness we have posited and demonstrated is not a high information exercise. As we spelled our earlier in the book, all that

---

[2] This suspicion is supported by analysis that includes the log of the lagged cumulative media signal, which outperforms the raw measure in the welfare and health spending domains.

[3] Note that the pooled correlation between the cumulative media signal in the three domains and circulation is –0.52; the average by-domain correlation is –0.73.

it requires is that the public receives (and accepts) basic cues about policy over time. (Also see Soroka and Wlezien 2010.) Earlier chapters of this book document the availability of information, which may help explain the parallelism in preferences that is evident in the literature on public opinion (especially see Page and Shapiro 1992). It also may help explain the similarity in public responsiveness to policy across subgroups in the United States that has been found in previous work (e.g., Soroka and Wlezien 2008; Kelly and Enns 2010; Ura and Ellis 2012).

We consider here differences in responsiveness across levels of (a) newspaper consumption, (b) education, and (c) partisanship. Figure 7.2 shows trends in net preferences for spending on defense, welfare, and health for these subgroups from 1976 to 2018. For the sake of parsimony, the analyses that follow rely on models estimated across the three domains

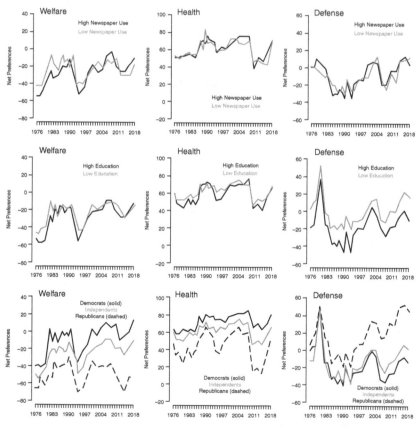

FIGURE 7.2 Net preferences for subgroups, 1976–2018

pooled together, though we note important differences in the text and footnotes. Details about the construction of subgroups, and comparisons across those groups, follow.

We are most interested here in the possibility that public responsiveness varies with levels of news consumption. We do not have media consumption variables for all respondents in the GSS, but there is a newspaper use variable that is captured relatively regularly over time: "How often do you read the newspaper – every day, a few times a week, once a week, less than once a week, or never?" (That we cannot tap television or digital news consumption may be of some consequence; even so, it is all that is available over an extended period in the GSS data.) The variable is asked of all respondents in most surveys until 1988, at which point it is asked of roughly two-third of the sample every time the survey is fielded. The distribution of the variable changes over time as newspaper readership declines, so we divide our respondents at the median in each year, producing roughly equal groups of low- and high-frequency newspaper readers. The preferences of high- and low-newspaper users are illustrated in the top three panels of Figure 7.2. There is scarcely any difference in the preferences of these two groups and they clearly move in parallel over time in all three domains, with an average correlation of 0.82. Table 7.2 offers a more formal test of the possibility that the groups respond differently to spending change and the media signal.

Table 7.2 show results of estimating models of public preferences across the three domains, this time for low- (column 1) and high- (column 2) frequency readers. Note that most coefficients are not strikingly different across the two groups, though results regarding the Gini coefficient suggest that the effect of income inequality on welfare preferences is mostly driven by low-frequency readers. There also is evidence of a concurrent positive effect of the media signal on these readers, suggesting that demand may be more fluid for people with less information, which would come as little surprise to public opinion scholars. The irony is this could be true despite seemingly lower news exposure.

Indeed, the coefficients for the cumulative media signal suggest that the impact of coverage may be slightly greater for low-level readers and that spending levels matter more for high-level ones. Given the standard errors, however, none of these differences are statistically significant. Thus, a more cautious (and accurate) interpretation of Table 7.2 is that the two groups are roughly equally responsive to policy and the media policy signal, at least putting aside the positive effect of the current signal, which

TABLE 7.2 *Public responsiveness and media use*

	Dependent Variable:	
	Δ Preferences, Low News Use $_t$	Δ Preferences, High News Use $_t$
Δ GDP $_t$	−0.006$^+$	−0.001
	(0.003)	(0.003)
GDP $_{t-1}$	0.001**	0.001***
	(0.000)	(0.000)
Δ Gini $_t$	−3.938$^+$	−3.263
	(2.280)	(2.157)
Gini $_{t-1}$	−1.346*	−0.556
	(0.627)	(0.558)
Δ Spending $_t$	−5.328$^+$	−8.119**
	(3.026)	(2.865)
Spending $_{t-1}$	−1.054	−2.202
	(1.567)	(1.491)
Media Signal $_t$	1.828*	0.761
	(0.784)	(0.765)
Cumulative Media Signal $_{t-1}$	−0.306*	−0.224$^+$
	(0.128)	(0.118)
Preferences $_{t-1}$	−0.360***	−0.245***
	(0.070)	(0.061)
Constant	13.378	−3.733
	(9.544)	(8.586)
Within -panel Rsq	0.270	0.287
N	114	114

Cells contain coefficients with standard errors in parentheses from fixed-effects linear models. $^+ p < .10$; $^* p < .05$; $^{**} p < .01$; $^{***} p < .001$.

we have seen is concentrated in the defense spending domain. We will have more on this later in the chapter.

For now, it is important to underscore that there are only slight differences in the reactions of our groups of newspaper readers to media coverage of spending. The result appears to contrast with our own previous research showing greater responsiveness among those with high levels of media exposure (Neuner et al. 2019). Our suspicion is that this is a function of (a) differences in survey measures and (b) differences in time periods. The prior study incorporated reported consumption of both newspapers and television news, and (many) more people rely on the latter than the former, as discussed. There thus is reason to suppose that the groups of high-frequency newspaper readers and high news consumers are quite different, and that this matters for the results of analyses. The Neuner et al. study also is focused on data from 1982 to 1992, when there was a far simpler media environment, in which television and newspaper exposure would accurately capture access to news. Measuring media exposure has always been difficult, but it has become especially fraught over the last decade with the rise of digital media (see, e.g., de Vreese and Neijens, 2016). It may be that identifying differences based on media exposure requires much more robust measures of exposure than exist in the GSS – and this is putting aside the limitations of self-reports. Of course, we cannot test this here and so cannot be absolutely sure.

Table 7.3 repeats the analysis in Table 7.2 but divides respondents based on education. The GSS measures education using a different set of codes over time, and the distribution of education changes as well. We divide the sample at the median, by survey, into high- and low-education groups.[4] Preferences for the two groups are shown in the second row of panels in Figure 7.2. That figure shows that preferences for the two groups are quite similar for welfare and health but that low-education respondents are on average more supportive of defense spending than high-education respondents. Despite these differences, the series shift in parallel over time in each domain, even more so than we saw for self-reported newspaper consumption, as the average correlation is 0.92 (by comparison with 0.82). Not surprisingly, results in Table 7.3 reveal a high level of similarity across groups. Both are responsive to the cumulative media policy signal, and about equally; if anything, the low-education group is more responsive, though the difference is not statistically significant. There also are hints that the highly educated are independently responsive to (levels of) spending, but this is not statistically significant either. Although it may be tempting to conclude that those with higher levels of education are more responsive to the coverage of spending and less

---

[4] The cumulative GSS combines education questions into a single item that captures respondent' number of years of school. The median actually varies only a little over the time period, from twelve to fourteen years, corresponding to completing high school or having completed one or two years of college or university.

TABLE 7.3 *Public responsiveness and education*

	Dependent Variable:	
	Δ Preferences, Low Education $_t$	Δ Preferences, High Education $_t$
Δ GDP $_t$	–0.003	–0.002
	(0.026)	(0.003)
GDP $_{t-1}$	0.001***	0.002***
	(0.000)	(0.000)
Δ Gini $_t$	–3.458+	–4.072+
	(1.829)	(2.174)
Gini $_{t-1}$	–1.787***	–1.220*
	(0.473)	(0.563)
Δ Spending $_t$	–6.976**	–9.236**
	(2.435)	(2.911)
Spending $_{t-1}$	–0.127	–2.418
	(1.267)	(1.523)
Media Signal $_t$	1.316*	1.391+
	(0.624)	(0.768)
Cumulative Media Signal $_{t-1}$	–0.435***	–0.341**
	(0.098)	(0.116)
Preferences $_{t-1}$	–0.351***	–0.341***
	(0.0347)	(0.052)
Constant	16.436*	1.954
	(7.290)	(8.749)
Within-panel Rsq	0.517	0.486
N	114	114

Cells contain coefficients with standard errors in parentheses from fixed-effects linear models. $^+ p < .10$; $^* p < .05$; $^{**} p < .01$; $^{***} p < .001$.

responsive to the rest of the media signal, we stop short of drawing this conclusion given that the differences are not highly reliable.

There may be special reason to expect responsiveness to vary across partisan groups (see, e.g., Druckman et al., 2013; Mullinix 2015), who not only may have different information about policy change (Benkler et al. 2018) but may also react differently to the same information (e.g., Branham 2018). We distinguish partisans based on the 7-point party identification variable, asked of all GSS respondents every year. We combine weak and strong partisans and leave "leaners" as Independents, the latter of which ensures that we have a reasonable number of respondents in that category in each year. The corresponding preference series are shown in the bottom panels of Figure 7.2. There quite clearly are differences across partisan groups, where Democrats are most supportive of domestic spending and Republicans most supportive of defense spending, and these differences grow some over time. But again, preferences largely move in tandem with an average correlation of 0.80.[5]

Table 7.4 presents analyses of the three series. Here, there is stronger evidence of difference across groups: Republicans are more responsive to the cumulative media signal than Independents and especially Democrats. Indeed, preferences for the latter do not reliably reflect media coverage ($p = 0.15$). Thus, by contrast with the mostly modest effects for reported newspaper consumption and education, party really seems to matter for the information citizens have and use. It does not fundamentally condition thermostatic feedback, however, as the direct effect of spending when media variables are excluded is essentially the same.[6] Put differently, all partisan groups respond to information about spending; it's just that Independents and Republicans, particularly the latter, are responsive to the other media coverage that is not correlated with spending.

We see parallels between the results in Table 7.4 and the burgeoning literatures on misinformation and "filter bubbles." Concerns about inaccuracies in media coverage and misinformation, alongside selective exposure and motivated reasoning, fueled by partisan polarization, exploded leading up and to and following the 2016 election of Donald Trump. We suggested in the opening chapter of this book that accuracy in media coverage is not just a recent concern, however. There have always been domains in which media coverage is inaccurate; and, as Chapter 5 has highlighted, media outlets that are more or less accurate as well. Results in Table 7.4 highlight the possibility that differences in partisans' reactions to media coverage *not* directly linked to actual policy change may also be

---

[5] The correlation is lower on average (0.67) when comparing preferences of Democrats and Republicans. Still, in a simple ANOVA of annual defense preferences, modeled as a function of fiscal year and party, both as categorical variables, roughly 51 percent of the variance is accounted for by fiscal year, 40 percent by party, and just 9 percent by the interaction between fiscal year and party; for the domestic domains, the figures are 31 percent, 63 percent, and 6 percent, respectively. These results make clear the extent to which annual net preferences measures vary across years and/or parties, *not* in differing partisan trends over time.

[6] That is, the estimated effects for the change in spending are −10.80 for Democrats and −9.53 for Republicans and those for the lagged levels are −4.65 and −4.60, respectively.

TABLE 7.4 *Public responsiveness and partisanship*

	Dependent Variable:		
	Δ Preferences, Democrats $_t$	Δ Preferences, Independents $_t$	Δ Preferences, Republicans $_t$
Δ GDP $_t$	–0.005	–0.001	–0.001
	(0.003)	(0.002)	(0.003)
GDP $_{t-1}$	0.001***	0.002***	0.002***
	(0.000)	(0.000)	(0.000)
Δ Gini $_t$	–3.956*	–2.668	–5.074*
	(2.177)	(1.739)	(2.358)
Gini $_{t-1}$	–0.562	–1.192**	–2.884***
	(0.582)	(0.450)	(0.643)
Δ Spending $_t$	–9.344**	–7.043**	–6.763*
	(2.890)	(2.325)	(3.161)
Spending $_{t-1}$	–2.457	–1.111	0.264
	(1.555)	(1.208)	(1.627)
Media Signal $_t$	1.658*	0.836	1.158*
	(0.743)	(0.599)	(0.818)
Cumulative Media Signal $_{t-1}$	–0.171	–0.378***	–0.637***
	(0.119)	(0.093)	(0.134)
Preferences $_{t-1}$	–0.384***	–0.315***	–0.264***
	(0.052)	(0.045)	(0.046)
Constant	0.657	4.614	25.234**
	(8.876)	(6.952)	(9.611)
Within-panel Rsq	0.499	0.517	0.412
N	114	114	114

Cells contain coefficients with standard errors in parentheses from fixed-effects linear models. $p < .10$; *$p < .05$; **$p < .01$; ***$p < .001$.

a longstanding issue. It is of some significance, then, that the partisan differences reflected in Table 7.4 do not disappear when we focus on years before the use of social media exploded.[7] Put differently: the public response to media in general and across partisans that we demonstrate is

[7] For instance, when dropping the years after 2010, the pattern of results remains substantially the same.

not simply the consequence of recent developments in media content and public opinion.

There may well be differences in groups' responsiveness to coverage in specific policy domains, but we do not explore it in any detail here. Rather, our focus has been on whether responsiveness generally – to both spending and media content – is isolated to a specific subset of citizens. We find some significant differences across partisans, but little evidence of other heterogeneity. Even accepting these differences, what is striking to us is the parallelism across groups, especially those relating to new exposure and education. Public responsiveness not only is possible; as we have hypothesized, it seemingly is not that difficult.

7.3 ON THE CAUSAL CONNECTIONS BETWEEN POLICY AND THE NEWS

Our analyses demonstrate that the public receives and responds to policy information in news coverage. When the news signals an increase in spending, preferences for more spending go down, other things being equal. This holds for various subgroups of the public. It does not mean that direct news consumption is required for people to respond, of course, since they can get the information in other ways. The news nevertheless is critical. Without it, we cannot see how even the most interested and attentive people would be able to discern what is happening with government policy. We suspect that there is little doubt about this connection; indeed, many of you, like us, may have assumed that it must be true. In other words, our "priors" about the causal relationship between the news and thermostatic public responsiveness were very strong, and the results of our analyses provide even stronger "posteriors."[8]

We suspect that there is greater uncertainty about the relationship between policy and the news. While it may be that policy actually causes news coverage, it also may be that the news causes policy. That the news may impact public policymaking may be unexpected given our focus in Chapters 5 and 6, but there is some valuable research on the subject, some of which we recognized in earlier chapters (e.g., Carpenter 2002; Walgrave 2008; Boydstun 2013; Walgrave and val Aelst 2018). Most of this work focuses on the policy agenda, not policy outputs *per se*; but the media may be a source of information for politicians about the need for

---

[8] Were the observed relationship positive instead of negative, this would be different, as we would be tasked with disentangling the direction(s) of causality.

policy and the amount (and type) of policy as well. It even may be that news coverage effectively captures public demand; there presumably is a reason that media organizations have regularly surveyed the American public, that is, to see what the public is thinking and reflect it in their reporting. News content thus may be a means by which politicians learn about (and then respond to) public preferences.

Let us reconsider our original depiction of a political system relating inputs and outputs in Figure 2.2. There we posited that policymaking and the outputs it produces influence media coverage, which in turn informs future public preferences thermostatically. Now, it alternatively may be that media coverage influences policymaking, positively impacting what policymakers do. The news still may effectively inform the public about government, aiding effective policy feedback on preferences, which we saw in Chapter 6. But it may be doing this while also driving what policymakers do. Indeed, it may be, as we have just suggested, that the news in part captures public demand for policy, and so serves as a mechanism of policy responsiveness to public opinion as well as policy feedback. Figure 7.3 represents this alternative model based on Figure 2.2, which differs only by the addition of an arrow running from media coverage to policymaking.

Definitively sorting out the causal relations between policy and media is not an easy task, of course, although there are some approaches that might help. One is Granger causality from time series analysis. This involves assessing the relationships between variables over time, where the current value of a variable of interest, for instance, media coverage, is modelled as a function of previous values of that variable and some other

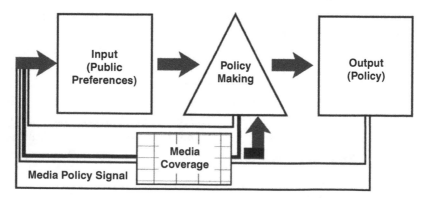

FIGURE 7.3 An alternative media-centered account of a political system

variable, say, budgetary policy. The approach allows us to determine whether the latter has an effect independent of the history of the former, e.g., whether policy change "causes" media coverage. Typically, an equation is estimated in both directions, sometimes referred to as a "cross-lag" model, which is especially appropriate for our purposes given the uncertainty about whether policy causes the news or the other way around. While appealing, it is important to note that the approach is a conservative one, with a tendency toward Type II error, where researchers may fail to find a true effect of a variable, as it may already be reflected in the lagged value of the dependent variable. Given this, positive evidence is to be taken seriously, though it is not the equivalent of a smoking gun.

Implementing Granger causality in our case is not entirely straightforward. Consider that we are interested in how media coverage in a particular fiscal year relates to spending policy made that year for the following fiscal year. It thus would make little sense estimating an equation for spending change in fiscal year t with media coverage in fiscal year $t - 1$ on the right-hand side, as this is part of the relationship that we want to unpack. That is, we want to know whether policymaking made in year $t - 1$ for fiscal year t causes media coverage in year $t - 1$, or whether it is the other way around. We consequently need to estimate a spending equation that includes media coverage in year $t - 2$, and a media equation that includes spending change made in year $t - 1$ for fiscal year t. Table 7.5 shows the results, with the media equation in column 1 and the spending equation in column 2.[9]

Results in the first column provide evidence of policy "causation" of media coverage, as the coefficient for spending change is positive and statistically significant $(p<.04)$. This means that policy made last year (for this year) influences the news in this year independently of the news last year. As noted above, this is fairly strong evidence of spending effects, as it may be that last year's decisions are reflected in last year's news, which is what we have hypothesized and for which we found some evidence. There thus is reason to suppose that the effects of policy on media coverage are greater than the analysis in Table 7.5 would lead us to believe.

The results in the second column of Table 7.5 suggest that media coverage also may Granger cause spending. The coefficient for the media signal is appropriately positive and also fairly reliable $(p =.01)$,

---

[9] Note that all of the variables in these equations are stationary time series, which is necessary to estimate the regressions and interpret the results.

TABLE 7.5 *Granger tests for media and spending*

	Dependent Variable:	
	Media Signal$_t$	Δ Spending $_t$
Media Signal $_{t-1}$	0.514***	—
	(0.084)	
Media Signal $_{t-2}$	—	0.058*
		(0.023)
Δ Spending $_t$	0.747*	
	(0.356)	
Δ Spending $_{t-1}$		0.161$^+$
		(0.096)
Constant	0.185*	0.024
	(0.083)	(0.022)
Within-panel Rsq	0.366	0.122
N	114	117

Cells contain coefficients with standard errors in parentheses from fixed-effects linear models. $p < .10$; *$p < .05$; **$p < .01$; ***$p < .001$.

which means that media coverage in the year before spending decisions are made (for the following fiscal year) predicts those decisions independently of previous spending decisions. This can be taken to imply that policymakers actually respond to media coverage and the information it contains when making policy, but it is important to note that the effect disappears when we include year $t-1$ media coverage in the model.[10] This matters because coverage at that point in time reflects fiscal policy decisions made in that year for year t, and coverage in successive years is highly correlated ($r = 0.65$); in other words, policy change for year t is not independently responsive to coverage in year $t-2$. Given this, there is little basis for concluding that media coverage in year $t-2$ actually causes policy change in year t.

That said, we might expect a relationship between media and policy change if the news reflects public preferences, and the latter influence what policymakers do. This may not be conventional wisdom in

---

[10] The coefficient for coverage in year $t-1$ is 0.07 (s.e. = 0.02), about the same as that for coverage in year $t-2$ (0.06) in Table 7.5, the latter of which drops to 0.02 (s.e. = 0.03) when both are estimated together.

communications (or political science), where media content is typically seen as a determinant of public opinion. To consider the possibility, we first need to assess the relationship between public preferences for spending and media coverage. Keep in mind that we are thinking here about the *levels* of the public's relative preferences, which indicate demand for more spending, as we expect a positive association between support for policy change and signals about policy change.[11] These spending preferences and the media signal are correlated at 0.49 ($p<.00$) in our data, so the news tends to signal increases when the public prefers them. (We have seen that those signals in turn produce thermostatic response, where public preferences go down in the next year.) But is it that the media influence preferences? Or is it that public preferences influence media coverage? Although the literature tends to assume the former, there is increasing evidence that the latter is true (e.g., Soroka et al. 2015; Wlezien et al. 2017; Wlezien and Soroka 2019). Of course, both may be at work. To provide some answers, we again conduct Granger causality tests relating the two variables, the results of which are described in Table 7.6.[12]

TABLE 7.6 *Granger causality tests for preferences and news coverage*

	Dependent Variable:	
	Preferences $_t$	Media Signal $_t$
Preferences $_{t-1}$	0.711***	0.021**
	(0.054)	(0.007)
Media Signal $_{t-1}$	0.477	0.471***
	(0.663)	(0.084)
Constant	−3.525**	0.203
	(1.113)	(0.141)
Within-panel Rsq	0.676	0.391
N	114	114

Cells contain coefficients with standard errors in parentheses from fixed-effects linear models. $p < .10$; *$p < .05$; **$p < .01$; ***$p < .001$.

[11] This is borne out by separate diagnostic analysis of changes in preferences, which are negatively related to the lagged media signal, seemingly owing to thermostatic response.

[12] All of the variables in the equation are stationary.

These results indicate that preferences seem to be driving the news. In the analysis of preferences in the first column of Table 7.6, the coefficient for media coverage (0.477) is appropriately positive but not highly reliable ($p=.47$). By contrast, in the second column, the coefficient for preferences in analysis of the media signal is both positive *and* significant ($p<.01$), and this holds even when lagged and current spending changes are included in the equation.[13] What these results demonstrate is that when the public wants more policy, the news reflects that public demand. The coverage then may influence future changes in spending, which in turn feed back negatively on preferences, producing thermostatic response, though it is important that the evidence of media influence on policy is not robust, as we have seen. There is evidence in our previous research (Soroka and Wlezien 2010) that preferences influence policy change, however, and we can confirm that this holds even when controlling for the news.[14] What matters most to us is that there is strong evidence that the news reflects public policy decisions and this informs the public. It underscores the importance of free, fair, and accurate media to effective accountability and control in the US, indeed, in any polity.

7.4 INTERPRETING CONNECTIONS BETWEEN THE NEWS AND PUBLIC PREFERENCES

We have thus far focused on general patterns of media influence, particularly on the mediation between spending policy and the public. Doing so has provided, we think, a sense for the role that media coverage plays in facilitating thermostatic public responsiveness. But as we have seen, coverage matters in other ways, particularly in those domains where we observe mediation – health, welfare, and defense. In Chapter 6, we found that the "other" component of the cumulative media signal, i.e., the part that is not correlated with spending decisions, influenced public preferences much like spending-correlated coverage in the health and welfare domains. We posited that this part of the signal might contain information that is relevant to spending, and so responsiveness may be beneficial. Of course, it also may contain error, in which case public responsiveness would be less salutary. We also found in Chapter 6 that the current

---

[13] This is based on separate analysis, where the coefficient for lagged preferences drops only slightly, from 0.021 to 0.019, and the p-value remains below .01.

[14] When we estimate a model of spending change in fiscal year t that includes media coverage in year $t-1$, the coefficient for preferences in year $t-1$ is positive and significant ($p = .01$).

media signal has a unique, positive effect on preferences in the defense spending domain. We suggested that this could be due to media reaction to events that impinge upon national security.

While we have identified effects and raised possible explanations, we have not yet presented empirical analyses assessing the latter. We do so now in a basic way, providing some illustrative case studies that demonstrate some of the ways in which media coverage can inform (or misinform) the public about what government is doing.

7.4.1 Health Care

We begin with health care, by focusing on trends in media content and health spending from 2005 to 2017. We focus on this time span because it highlights two periods during which the media signal does *not* neatly follow spending. The first is the aftermath of the Deficit Reduction Act (DRA) of 2005 and the second the period after which the Affordable Care Act (ACA) was signed in 2010. We have already showed graphs of the normalized media signal, capturing policy change, alongside actual changes in appropriations in Chapter 5. Since our models of public preferences also have relied on the *cumulative* media signal, we now show that measure in Figure 7.4 together with the level of health appropriations in constant dollars. Note that the two series are on different scales (and axes), so we cannot make much of when one series is above or below the other. We *can* compare the trends in the series, however.

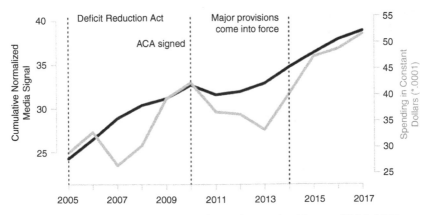

FIGURE 7.4 The media signal and spending on health care, 2005–2017

Following the enactment of the DRA, a decrease in spending was evident across most (if not all) domestic policy domains. In health care, the decrease occurred in 2007, as can be seen in Figure 7.4. Even though appropriations dropped in that year, and fairly sharply, the media signal does not reflect decreased spending in that year or those that followed. The news signal actually registered increases throughout the period and up to the passage of the ACA. Why might this be the case? One possibility is that media coverage simply failed to capture a significant decrease in spending. Another is that the prominence of health care proposals in the drawn-out Democratic nomination process and presidential election (see, e.g., Maioni 2009) produced coverage that focused on *proposed, future* increases in health spending. These discussions may well have factored into citizens' considerations of health care policy, though we cannot be sure based on this analysis.

A similar gap in media coverage is evident between 2010, the year the ACA was signed, and 2014, the year that the major ACA provisions came into force. During this period health appropriations actually decreased; meanwhile, the media signal flattens out before increasing as the ACA comes into effect. Given what we learned in Chapter 4 about the future focus of media coverage, this may be understandable. In the lead-up to the largest change in US health care at least since the 1960s, media content appears to have emphasized prospective increases in spending, even as current spending shifted downwards. The drop in spending was temporary, of course, and the overall trend in the media signal over the period shown in Figure 7.4 does move alongside policy. This is one reason why public responsiveness to health policy is evident in Chapter 6. But media coverage can reflect other policy-relevant information as well, and that information can factor into public preferences, and this appears to have been the case for Obamacare (also see Morgan and Kang 2015).

7.4.2 Welfare

While disjunctures between the media signal and policy can inform the public about what government is doing (or going to do), they also can distort what is happening, and trends in welfare coverage and spending may be an example of exactly this. In Figure 7.5, we again present the cumulative media signal, now for welfare, alongside appropriations in that domain, focusing on the period following the Deficit Reduction Act. There it is clear that the media signal (in black) trends upwards even as

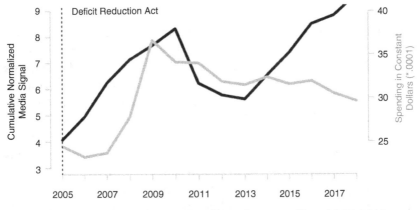

FIGURE 7.5 The media signal and spending on welfare, 2005–2018

welfare spending policy decreases after the legislation was enacted. This is very much like what we saw for health care. By 2009 the welfare budget had recovered, but at this point it begins a slow and steady decline for the next decade. Media coverage follows briefly, declining alongside spending until 2013 at which point media coverage turns sharply upwards.

There is to our knowledge no pivotal moment in welfare politics that can account for this shift in media content. One possibility is that welfare budgetary policy followed economic conditions, which deteriorated in 2008 and 2009 before beginning a long recovery, and the news did not reflect this. It may be that increases in welfare at the state level but not in evidence in federal welfare spending are reflected in the media measure. Another possibility is that even as media coverage has over the past four decades been reasonably representative of welfare policy change, coverage has mis-represented policy in the recent past, coincidentally with the Obama's second term. Regardless of the source, based on our analysis in Chapter 6, the disjuncture is important: we have seen that media coverage of welfare matters to public preferences, after all. (We have also seen in the Appendix to Chapter 6 that this effect is independent of the party of the president.) When news coverage signals increases in spending that are not actually occurring, the public reacts as if they are, and adjusts preferences thermostatically. Given this, we expect that the public was less supportive of increases in welfare spending than they might otherwise have been.

7.4.3 Defense

Our interest in the defense domain is somewhat different. Here we want to account for the positive relationship between the current media signal and public preferences. This is evident only in defense, and it suggests a relationship between the media signal and preferences that runs counter to the thermostatic response that preferences exhibit towards the cumulative media signal. In Chapter 6, we suggested two possibilities. First, the coefficient might capture the effect of preferences on media coverage, not the effect of the latter on the former. There was some evidence of this dynamic in our analyses of causal relationships in the previous section of this chapter, though such a connection is not found specifically in the defense spending domain.[15] Second, the effect may reflect media reactions to events producing changes in national security threat over time, causing demand for spending to increase or decrease accordingly. Such shocks to need and spending demand are not surprising in this domain by comparison with the others in our analysis, as events can and do occur and can be consequential for both need and actual spending.

To better understand the effect of the current media signal on defense preference, we first separate it into two components, one predicted by spending change, which we documented in Chapter 5, and the other, residual component. We are interested here in the effect of the latter component of the current media signal, and what it might reflect. Figure 7.6 accordingly plots that residual component of the media policy signal over time, beginning in 2000 and continuing through 2015. This part of the signal clearly varies a good amount over time. Values tend to be slightly higher during the President George W. Bush years (2001–2008) than in the Obama years that followed, but this does not reflect a broader partisan pattern.[16] It may be that events help us explain the variation we observe. Consider that 9/11 happened toward the end of fiscal year 2001, and we see a sharp upward spike in the defense media signal in the following year, leading up to the invasion of Iraq in 2003. Not surprisingly, we see a sharp increase in defense appropriations in fiscal year 2003, during which the measured media signal increased (see Chapter 5) but the

---

[15] The coefficient is appropriately positive but small (0.01) and does not approach conventional levels of statistical significance ($p = 0.34$). Of course, this does not definitely rule out a current effect, though we do wonder why it would be seen only in the defense spending domain.

[16] The correlation between the variable and the party of the president (Democrat = 1, Republican = 0) is slightly negative (–0.13) but not close to statistically significant ($p = .43$).

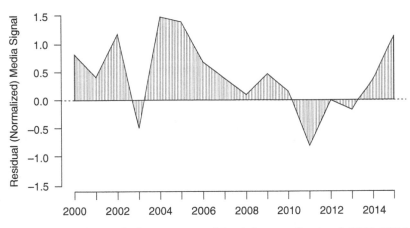

FIGURE 7.6 The residual component of the defense media signal, 2000–2015

residual component declined, possibly registering a reduction in the need for additional spending increases. Thereafter we see positive signals, which may pick up increased need – given spending levels – associated with the ongoing war. Of course, these are just possibilities, and we cannot be absolutely sure based on the analysis; they may, however, highlight ways in which events influence media coverage and public preferences too.

The component of media coverage shown in Figure 7.6 is by construction not correlated with current spending change, but it does match other policy-relevant quantities, including shifts in public preferences, and the nature of national security threats (and commitments) over this time period.[17] Recall that previous research shows that those preferences matter for future spending decisions themselves (Wlezien 1996; Eichenberg and Stoll 2003; Soroka and Wlezien 2010). We thus see the defense results, together with those in health and welfare, as a useful reminder that media coverage includes information that is not necessarily related to current budgetary policy flows (and decisions) but may be relevant to the public and policy nonetheless. Put differently, the other, non-spending

---

[17] When the predicted and residual components of the current media signal are included in the analysis of defense spending preferences in column 1 of Table 6.4, the coefficient for the latter is positive and statistically significant ($p = .07$). As we have seen in previous chapters, the media signal in one fiscal year may correlate positively with spending in the following year precisely because the news covers decisions when they are made. Also, as discussed in the Section 7.3 of this chapter, it may be that the news reflects those decisions because it causes them, though we did not see convincing evidence of that effect.

component appears to includes information about the actual need for and supply of policy. As we have seen for welfare, it also may contain information that is less enlightening.

7.5 THE MANY WAYS THAT THE MEDIA MATTER

The analyses in this chapter have largely supported the Chapter 6 findings, but they also reveal a more powerful, if complex, role of the media in American politics. The information that media coverage provides matters for public opinion. It helps drive – and account for – the thermostatic public responsiveness to policy that we observe. It also has other less obvious effects. In some cases, specifically, health, coverage may – and appears to – provide information about policy commitments that are not directly evident from actual policy, at least measured concurrently. In other cases, namely welfare, coverage may distort what government is doing at the same time – and as much as – it illuminates. In yet other cases, as for defense, it seems to provide information about the need for spending moving forward. The news thus serves to influence the public in different ways.

The news appears to penetrate fairly deeply into American society. Coverage matters fairly similarly across levels of people's media consumption, at least the self-reported use of newspapers, and formal education as well. There are interesting, potentially important differences owing to partisanship that warrant additional investigation, but even here thermostatic public responsiveness is almost identical across partisan subgroups. There is work to do documenting the mediation and how it varies across individuals, which remains a subject for future research. There is also work to do in accounting for the changing media environment, which we consider in Chapter 8.

8

Policy and the Media

Past, Present, and Future

Preceding chapters confirm the critical importance of media coverage to representative democracy. Consider the three-point media-centered account of public responsiveness introduced in Chapter 2: (a) public responsiveness to policy requires only basic levels of knowledge about policy, (b) this basic information is readily available in media content, and (c) citizens can and do recognize and respond to these informational media cues. We have relied on existing work to demonstrate (a), and then have found evidence in our data for both (b) and (c). Results show that media coverage can help ensure the informed electorate that is required for effective accountability and control of elected officials. Media can help make representative democracy "work."

This may seem far too Pollyannaish for some readers. And a lot of research supports such suspicions. We know that the public is often poorly informed, sometimes even misinformed, about politics and policy. We know that the media sometimes are to blame because coverage is lacking or inaccurate. We also know that media coverage can (and does) play a central role in highlighting scientific dissensus on issues where there is in fact very broad consensus, and impedes public attention to critical domestic and global issues through a lack of coverage – to name just a few well-established problems with news content. There are lots of problems with media coverage!

Even as media often fail, they also sometimes succeed. This is our central contention. It should not be confused with an entirely positive view of media, though note that it is consistent with previous research demonstrating a connection between real-world conditions and media coverage (see Chapter 1). According to our analyses, media do not always provide accurate information about policy, and even where they do there are inaccuracies as well. And what our analysis demands of media is limited: we focus only on whether basic factual information about spending policy is communicated to the public. Is spending going up or down? By a little? By a lot? In Chapters 3, 4, and especially 5 we found that media can and often do provide this information. Some outlets provide a lot more, of course; but this basic information appears to be widely available across a range of newspapers and broadcast and cable news programming. We regard these simple, clear signals evident in media coverage as critical cogs in the representative democratic machine.

Analyses in Chapters 6 and 7 also strongly suggest that the news effectively mediates between policy decisions and the public – it is how people get information about what government is doing. Public responsiveness to the media signal holds across subgroups of the American public. There are some differences across subgroups and domains, to be sure, but in salient policy domains all subgroups do respond; and it even appears that self-reported newspaper consumption does not matter much. The latter is not surprising given evidence about what self-reports really tap (see Prior 2009), and the fact that people acquire information about policy from various sources, including television outlets, social media, and in other ways. As we have noted, a newspaper-based measure may well capture the policy signal in these multiple sources as well. What we consider most compelling about our results in Chapters 6 and 7 is that they reveal that media effects are widespread. This helps explain the "parallel publics" that Page and Shapiro (1992) documented long ago and continues – if to a lesser degree – in the present day even in the wake of growing partisan polarization and media fragmentation. The tendency serves to strengthen democratic accountability, which is not dependent solely on a highly attentive and informed issue public.

There are some important caveats. If the previous chapters made clear that media can help make democracy work they also signaled that failures in media coverage can impede public responsiveness, and by implication policymaking and government accountability. We have seen that relationships between policy, the media, and the public vary across domains, after all. The quality of coverage is better in certain politically salient spending domains – defense, welfare, and health – and public responsiveness in these domains is correspondingly more pronounced. The connections are by contrast much weaker for education and the environment. This is not unexpected, as these areas have been shown to be less politically salient in the United States, and the public has also been less responsive to spending in these domains (Wlezien 1995; 2004; Soroka and Wlezien 2010). A weak media signal in these areas almost certainly does not help.

The lack of both a media policy signal and significant public responsiveness in these domains may well be a function of factors not explored here. For education, federalism may weaken effective responsiveness, as spending in the area is made at many levels of government in the United States, and such mixing of governments already has been shown to weaken the responsiveness of public preferences at particular levels. The basic idea is that the involvement of multiple governments confuses responsibility for citizens (Wlezien and Soroka 2011), a confusion that could exist even where media coverage perfectly reflects what the different levels of government are doing; but the news may also add to the confusion.

For the environment, by contrast, the policies that the national government makes are not primarily about or necessarily evident in spending. Although expenditures matter, regulations do as well, and seemingly to a greater degree (see, e.g., Andrews 2018; Galeotti et al. 2020).[1] Thus, even if the news accurately reflects what the government is doing with spending, it might tell us only a little about what the government is doing on the environment. It is for this reason that our measure of the environment media signal includes regulation in the environmental domain; but we are not confident that we capture regulation with the same accuracy with which we capture spending.[2] For our analysis of public responsiveness, this is of special importance. To the extent that the public responds to coverage of regulatory action in their expressed spending preferences, we should see weak effects of budgetary policy and perhaps of the measured media signal as well.

In the domains where news coverage does give rise to thermostatic public responsiveness, Chapter 7 has shown that the news also communicates *other* information that is relevant to spending preferences. To be clear: the component of media coverage that is *not* linked to spending change sometimes matters for public responsiveness. While all the content

---

[1] Consider what commonly are considered the leading pieces of environmental legislation in the United States: the Clean Air Act, the Endangered Species Act, the Montreal Protocol, the Clean Water Act, and the Reformation Plan No. 3 of 1970, the last of which gave rise to the Environmental Protection Agency. Each of these is first and foremost about regulation, with spending implicated in implementation and monitoring.

[2] Our suspicion is that we do capture sentences about regulation fairly reliably, but that the upward and downward keywords may not be an ideal way to capture regulatory change. We have not yet examined this possibility in any detail, however.

we analyze is necessarily related to spending, these sentences need not be *just* about spending change; and the relevance of that content to budgetary policy varies as well. The "other" part of the media signals may communicate relevant information – perhaps budgetary decisions in advance of the spending itself, as in the case of Obamacare, or perhaps relevant information that is largely outside the budgetary process, such as national security threat. But the "other" part of the media policy signal may communicate irrelevant or confusing information as well, which is what we may have seen with welfare. Media content does not entirely account for public preferences, however, as there is variation that remains unexplained by our models. Accounting for this variation strikes us as an important subject for future research.

The relationships between the public, media coverage, and policy are even more complex, particularly as they play out over time. What we have summarized thus far focuses mostly on the "output" side of the process, where media content reflects policy change, which informs public preferences, producing thermostatic change in opinion. But there is an "input" side as well, where the public and media may impact on policymaking itself. Based on our analysis in Chapter 7, it appears that lagged public preferences positively influence current coverage, which may in turn influences policy change. This would place the media in an even more central position in the policymaking process, where they both communicate public preferences (and other information) to policymakers and effectively inform the public by signaling policy actions. Our data provide limited evidence of media *influence* on policymaking, however, so we stop short of fully crediting this formulation – though it is consistent with some recent research, and remains another important subject for future work (see, e.g., Walgrave and van Aelst 2016). Even to the extent coverage mostly serves to reflect policymaking in US spending domains, we have provided very general parameters across fiscal years, and what is happening within those years is not clear. Although we have thought about this and touched on it in earlier chapters, a systematic analysis remains on our to-do list.

What are the boundary conditions for the findings we have provided? That is, under what conditions do they apply, and not? To begin with, we have to acknowledge once more the limitations of what we have done and found. We have examined media coverage (and public opinion) in only a handful of salient policy domains in just one country for a limited period of time. As we have discussed, our analyses were guided by practical concerns – where we could actually measure policy and public opinion – but this also happened to lead us to those areas where the chances of media success probably were greatest. We expect things to work less well in less salient policy domains in the United States. We also expect media to function less well in countries with political and media systems that are less open, not that the United States is perfect by any means. And even within salient domains in the United States, changes taking place in the media environment may matter in substantial ways.

We have shown that mass media content has been critical to informing the public about government actions over the last four decades. There is reason to think that this role has declined over time, given the decline of newspapers and increasing media choice. People can opt out of political news and those who consume it increasingly choose what they get, which may have consequences for the quality of information they receive (see Stroud 2011; Arceneaux and Johnson 2013; Levendusky 2013). Analyses in Chapter 7 nevertheless offer only limited support for this conjecture. This may surprise some readers, given the growth of more partisan television outlets, but recall the tendency (in Chapter 5) for television news across both broadcast and cable outlets to reflect the course of spending policy over time. Although some do better than others, they all roughly capture the ebb and flow. There may well be additional heterogeneity in media effects at the individual level, especially when individuals are matched to specific (more or less accurate) media outlets. This variation nevertheless appears to cancel out at least to some degree when analyzing aggregates of the public, as we have done here.

There is little denying that the role of legacy media (e.g., newspapers and television) has decreased over time, however, which raises the question: What explains the apparently enduring impact of a newspaper-based media policy signal? We regard the relationship as a product of the fact that various news outlets cover some of the basic trends in media coverage. Watching ABC News or CNN may get you at least some of the same policy information that you would receive reading the *New York Times* or the *Houston Chronicle*, and the same may be true for online platforms. Similarities across outlets will partly be driven by the use of wire services and "pool reporting," especially in the case of regional newspapers and/or media conglomerates. News aggregators may also provide a reasonable sample of policy-related content from traditional news sources, as may social media. There are in sum a number of reasons why coverage of policy across *all* media, legacy and otherwise, may look a lot like our newspaper- or television-based policy signals.

The degree to which a newspaper-based policy signal will continue to reflect media coverage more broadly is admittedly unclear, of course. It may well be that in an increasingly "hybrid" media system (see Chadwick 2017), the same information is not simply repeated across different platforms. Digital media news may continue to be a replication and extension of legacy media content, but the capacities of different media platforms and the interests of different media audiences may lead to increasing differences. Perhaps information about budgets continues to be covered by print and online newspapers but disappears elsewhere; or this relatively prosaic information ends up being distributed only online where the "news hole" is effectively infinite. As the media ecology shifts, so too may the frequency and placement of policy information. Public responsiveness may change as a result.

Hints of difference in partisans' responsiveness to policy change also highlight the potential significance of a media ecology in which more media are catering to increasingly partisan audiences. The rise of partisan cable news networks Fox News and MSNBC is well known, but the Trump presidency saw an increase in the number of outlets willing to explicitly support and oppose the administration. CNN and the *Washington Post* became increasing clear about their opposition to Trump, for instance, while a perceived lack of sufficiently strong support from Fox News helped fuel the rise of new right-wing cable networks One America News Network (OANN) and Newsmax. News on legacy media may well be more explicitly partisan in the future, and the degree to which this is the case could make a difference for both our measurement of the media policy signal and public responsiveness.[3]

Concerns about heterogeneity in legacy media pale by comparison with concerns about digital media, of course, and especially social media. Perhaps most importantly, the circulation of a given story in social media is defined not (just) by news outlets but by an unknown (and large) number of social media users and algorithms. Following a given news source does not mean that all their articles will appear on your Facebook stream, after all – that is defined by a combination of your own "engagements" with posts and sources, alongside the engagements of

---

[3] There already is evidence of partisan polarization, and partisan news content, in some domains, including environmental policy (Chinn et al. 2020) and the COVID-19 pandemic (e.g., Hart et al. 2020; Stecula and Pickup 2021). These domains illustrate the ways in which a more partisan media system may confuse both media policy signals and public responsiveness.

your social media contacts and the constantly shifting social media algorithms.

Taking this change in information flows into account is critical to understanding how our findings do or do not apply to the future of information in representative democracy. Our results demonstrate that media have played an important role in producing an informed citizenry. What does introducing citizen-gatekeeping do to the media signal that reaches the voting public? This is observable, at least in part, in our Facebook data. Recall that the data we rely on (produced by Dan Hiaeshutter-Rice) begins in 2008, roughly the beginning of Facebook; but posts by media companies aren't really frequent until 2010. These data then end in 2017, so we have complete fiscal-year data only for FY 2010 through FY 2017.[4]

We have introduced but scarcely considered the Facebook data thus far. This is due to the limited time span during which we have access to Facebook content. There is not enough data for good time-series estimates of the connections between media coverage, public opinion, and policy. But they can give us a general sense for the correspondence between Facebook content and spending, and thus of the impact that social sharing might have on the media policy signal.

TABLE 8.1 *Facebook signals and spending change*

	Defense	Welfare	Health	Education	Environment
Correlation between the weighted and unweighted Facebook signal	0.75	0.57	0.62	0.38	0.32
Multiple R for the *unweighted* Facebook signal and spending change (at $t-1$, t, $t+1$)	0.93	0.64	0.68	0.81	0.71
Multiple *R* for the *weighted* Facebook signal and spending change (at $t-1$, t, $t+1$)	0.95	0.26	0.14	0.37	0.65

---

[4] Social media usage grew tremendously, reaching nearly 50 percent of the US population in 2010 and 69 percent in 2018 (Pew 2018a).

Table 8.1 offers one such analysis. The first row shows correlations between the "unweighted" Facebook signal and the "weighted" Facebook signal. The former is a signal based on exactly the same method used earlier for the newspaper and television signals: every sentence on spending policy from all available Facebook news sources categorized as upward spending (+1), downward spending (–1), or no change in spending (0), summed by fiscal year. The latter signal takes a similar approach, but before summing the sentences by fiscal year, each sentence is weighted by the number of shares it received. Those that are widely shared thus receive a much greater weight than the sentences that are barely shared. This weighted signal represents one possible view of what the media signal looks like once filtered through social media.

Note that neither signal used in Table 8.1 quite reflects what any one Facebook user would see in their feedback. Our feeds are all slightly different, defined by who we follow, who our followers follow, what gets recirculated by friends and followers, and so on.[5] The unweighted signal used in Table 8.1 is nevertheless one possible version, capturing the information that some set of users would receive if their feeds contained the policy information in posts by the major current affairs content providers discussed in Chapter 3. And the weighted signal is another possible version, where information is weighted by the number of shares it received. We see these signals as limited but also useful opportunities to consider both (a) the accuracy of policy content in social media and (b) the differences that sharing may make to the accuracy of the social media signal.

Results in the first row of Table 8.1 suggest that sharing can make a big difference to the media signal. For defense, the correlation between the weighted and unweighted signals is a relatively high 0.75, and for health and welfare it is only somewhat lower (0.57 and 0.62) – there clearly are similarities between the two signals but a good deal of difference as well. In education and the environment, the correlations, while statistically significant, are lower still. In these domains, the weighted signal is more different than it is similar to the unweighted measure.

The second and third rows of Table 8.1 show the coefficient of multiple correlation, R, based on OLS models regressing each Facebook signal on

---

[5] Moreover, news stories that can appear in any user's feed are not necessarily viewed, and even "digital trace data" are generally limited to the content we interact with, not all content that we may learn from as we flip past it on our phones.

spending change.[6] Chapter 5 makes clear that media coverage reflects some combination of past, current, and future spending change, so we include spending at $t - 1$, t, and $t + 1$; and R captures the correlation between the Facebook signal and a linear combination of these three spending variables. The second row shows multiple Rs for the unweighted Facebook signal; the third row shows multiple Rs for the weighted Facebook signal.

Consider first the correlations between spending and the unweighted Facebook signal, in the second row. In defense, the coefficient of multiple correlation is very high 0.93. In this instance, it appears that a hypothetical Facebook user who receives all (or a sufficient random sample of) posts from the top public affairs content producers on Facebook gets a pretty accurate signal about policy. In the domestic domains, the connection between the unweighted Facebook signal and spending change is lower, ranging from 0.64 in welfare to 0.81 in education. Even so, there *is* a connection between the unweighted Facebook signal and policy change.

Weighting sentences by Facebook shares has a rather dramatic effect on the accuracy of the signal, however. In the third row of Table 8.1, only in defense and the environment does the weighted Facebook signal continue to represent policy change to a high degree. In the other domains, correlations drop considerably. Clearly, sharing can produce fundamental changes to the media signal, and the impact mostly is to reduce the degree to which the signal reflects spending. That said, we need to keep in mind that we are working here with a handful of cases, and so results are very fragile, at best only suggestive about Facebook coverage, whether weighted or not.

Facebook obviously is only part of the social media revolution. Political discussion and news dissemination are prevalent on Twitter, Instagram, Snapchat, and a range of other platforms. Among these, Twitter has been around the longest and is currently the most widely used. While it is not in our analysis, some scholars have begun to explore policy content on Twitter, and early returns suggest Twitter coverage looks much like what we see on Facebook and in the traditional news outlets, at least on basic policy facts (Dun 2020).[7] These early returns, focused on defense

---

[6] R captures the correlation between the dependent variable and a linear combination of the predictors. It is of course also the square root of R-squared.

[7] We do not examine Twitter here because at the time of writing access to all Twitter data, that is, the "firehose," is not available going back more than a year. As a consequence, we

spending, are of real significance, but there is much more work to do to more fully understand the frequency and accuracy of policy content on social media platforms – Facebook, Twitter, and otherwise.

There are of course other extensions of our work that would add to our understanding of the role that media play in representative democracy. Where policy domains are concerned, there is a need to examine spending beyond the set of domains we have considered here. The five domains explored here are among the largest and most important, which is part of the reason we chose them; but there is spending in other areas, and (numerous) taxes in which media coverage will matter for public responsiveness and policy too. There also are a host of US national policies that are not explicitly fiscal.[8] We cannot know from our analyses how media coverage works in these areas. We do, however, have some expectations based in part on previous research regarding public opinion and voting behavior that guided our own decisions.

Perhaps most importantly, we know that issues vary in their importance for the public. COVID-19 obviously stands out as we finalize the book (in February 2021), but a broad range of issues can emerge in importance over time and have, including immigration, crime, abortion, policing, and gun control. When these issues are important to the public, there is reason for the media to pay attention to both the problems themselves and government action addressing them. Other factors matter to media attention as well, including editorial judgments, which in turn can impact public concern itself. Such shifts in attentiveness are the focus of a considerable literature on media, the public, and policy agenda-setting (e.g., McCombs and Shaw 1972; Baumgartner and Jones 1993; Soroka 2002; Boydstun 2013). While there is evidence that the media can influence public concern, it also appears that the latter influence the former, seemingly for good reason given that audiences matter to both commercial and public media in the United States and elsewhere.[9]

Effective mediation requires an accurate media signal, of course, and this may be difficult to produce in some policy domains regardless of their importance. Here, it may prove useful to borrow from Carmines and

---

are not able to scrape the time series of Twitter data for relevant sentences. (There are some historical databases available, but they contain only subsets of Twitter data, and the representativeness of those subsets is unclear.)

[8] Of course, for many of these areas spending is important, just not the defining feature, including a host of regulations.

[9] As noted earlier, this helps explain news organizations historical involvement in and reliance on public opinion polling.

Stimson's (1980) research distinguishing between "easy" and "hard" issues, where some are just simpler for voters and others more difficult, requiring greater sophistication. In that now-classic work, the authors compared the easy issue of race and the hard issue of withdrawing troops from Vietnam, although there certainly are other examples of each. The difference between easy and hard issues may influence not only voters, where easy issues matter more than hard ones and for a broader group, but media coverage as well. Government action on easy issues may be simpler to communicate to a large audience. Of course, it may be that the public and the media both can and do simplify hard issues, such as economic and foreign policy as well as regulation, so the characteristics of issues may not be entirely exogenous. These are subjects for future research.

There not only are other policies to consider, there are other governments as well. We cannot know based on what we have done there exactly how things work in other countries, but we do expect that media play an important role in facilitating or impeding public responsiveness and accountability in countries around the world. Our own recent work has highlighted the role that media openness has on public responsiveness to policy across dozens of countries (Hiaeshutter-Rice et al. 2021). Other institutions will matter for the ease with which media coverage and publics can respond to policy change as well.

There also are other levels of government, and we already discussed in the context of our results relating to education. Previous research shows that the mixing of governments in policy areas reduces effective public responsiveness at any particular level of government because it complicates assignment of responsibility (Soroka and Wlezien 2010).[10] Where a single government is involved, by contrast, responsibility is clearer. The involvement of different governments varies considerably across countries: although some countries are about as fiscally decentralized as the United States, for example, Australia, some, like Canada, are even more so, and others are highly centralized, including Great Britain, Israel, and Poland. This has consequences for public responsiveness, which is more evident in the latter than the former (Wlezien and Soroka 2012), and this

---

[10] Under such circumstances, when spending in a policy area goes up, it is unclear whether it is the responsibility of the national government, the states, or the localities, and so public preferences for, say, national spending are more likely to be misinformed, where people underreact to spending taken at that level or else overreact to spending taken at other levels. Also see Wlezien and Soroka (2011).

presumably reflects media coverage. Federalism does not vary only across countries, of course – it varies across policy domains, and within the United States as well. Again, the point is not that the media are necessarily at fault, but that they may communicate spending decisions regardless of where they are happening and this matters for the public; where there is but one government involved, it is easier to keep straight than when there are many. Put in Carmines and Stimson's terms, federalism may produce more "hard" issues. That said, there has been to our knowledge little consideration of the complications that federalism may pose for media coverage of policy.

User-curated social media content, policy complexities stemming from the nature of the domain as well as the nature of governing institutions, and limitations on media freedoms – these are all reasons to expect media to play a far more varied role in public responsiveness and accountability than can been illustrated in the five US policy domains examined here. That said, our objective has not been to capture all of the possible variation in media accuracy and public responsiveness. Rather, our aim has been to assess whether media can and do – in some domains at least – provide the raw material that citizens need to hold governments accountable and respond to policy change. This is of real importance: informed public opinion is a necessary condition for effective representation, after all, and media coverage that helps produce informed opinion is as well. At a minimum, the preceding results demonstrate the potential for media. The task moving forward is to better understand the conditions under which media provide an accurate view of policy change. Doing so may offer a sense for not just when media work but when representative democracy does as well.

References

Achen, Christopher and Larry Bartels. 2016. *Democracy for Realists*. Princeton: Princeton University Press.

Adams, James, Samuel Merrill III, and Bernard Grofman. 2005. *A Unified Theory of Party Competition*. Cambridge: Cambridge University Press.

Allcott, Hunt and Matthew Gentzkow. 2017. "Social Media and Fake News in the 2016 Election." *Journal of Economic Perspectives* 31(2): 211–236.

Althaus, Scott. 2003. *Collective Preferences in Democratic Politics*. Cambridge: Cambridge University Press.

Altheide, David L. 1997. "The News Media, the Problem Frame, and the Production of Fear." *Sociological Quarterly* 38(4): 647–668.

Andrews, Richard N. L. 2018. "American Environmental Policy since 1964." In *Oxford Research Encyclopedia of American History*. Oxford: Oxford University Press.

Arceneaux, Kevin and Martin Johnson. 2013. *Changing Minds or Changing Channels?* Chicago: University of Chicago Press.

Barabas, Jason. 2011. "Review of Degrees of Democracy: Politics, Public Opinion and Policy." *Public Opinion Quarterly* 75(1): 192–195.

Barabas, Jason and Jennifer Jerit. 2009. "Estimating the Causal Effects of Media Coverage on Policy Specific Knowledge." *American Journal of Political Science* 53(1): 73–89.

Barabas, J., J. Jerit, W. Pollock, and C. Rainey. 2014. "The Question(s) of Political Knowledge." *American Political Science Review* 108(4): 840–855.

Bartels, L. M. 2005. "Homer Gets a Tax Cut: Inequality and Public Policy in the American Mind." *Perspectives on Politics* 3(1): 15–31.

Bartels, Larry. 2002. "Beyond the Running Tally: Partisan Bias in Political Perceptions." *Political Behavior* 24(2): 117–150.

  1991. "Constituency Opinion and Congressional Policy Making: The Reagan Defense Build Up." *American Political Science Review* 85(2): 457–474.

Bartle, John, Sebastian Dellepiane-Avellaneda, and Anthony McGann. 2019. "Policy Accommodation versus Electoral Turnover: Policy Representation in Britain, 1945–2015." *Journal of Public Policy* 39(2): 235–265.

Bartle, John, Sebastian Dellepiane-Avellaneda, and James Stimson. 2011. "The Moving Centre: Preferences for Government Activity in Britain, 1950–2005." *British Journal of Political Science* 41(2): 259–285.

Baumgartner, Frank R. and Bryan D. Jones. 2005. *The Politics of Attention: How Government Prioritizes Problems*. Chicago: University of Chicago Press.

1993. *Agendas and Instability in American Politics*. Chicago: University of Chicago Press.

Behr, Roy L. and Shanto Iyengar. 1985. "Television News, Real-World Cues, and Changes in the Public Agenda." *Public Opinion Quarterly* 49(1): 38–57.

Beland, Daniel. 2010. "Reconsidering Policy Feedback: How Policies Affect Politics." *Administration and Society* 42(5): 568–590.

Beland, Daniel and Edella Schlager. 2019. "Varieties of Policy Feedback: Looking Backward and Moving Forward." *Policy Studies Journal* 47(2): 184–205.

Béland, Daniel, Philip Rocco, and Alex Waddan. 2019. "Policy Feedback and the Politics of the Affordable Care Act." *Policy Studies Journal* 47(2): 395–422.

Belanger, Eric and Stuart Soroka. 2012. "Campaigns and the Prediction of Election Outcomes: Can Historical and Campaign-Period Prediction Models Be Combined?" *Electoral Studies* 31: 702–714.

Bennett, Stephen. 1988. "'Know-Nothings' Revisited: The Meaning of Political Ignorance Today." *Social Science Quarterly* 69: 476–490.

Bennett, W. Lance. 1990. "Toward a Theory of Press-State Relations in the United States." *Journal of Communication* 40(2): 103–127.

2016. *News: The Politics of Illusion*, 10th ed. Chicago: University of Chicago Press.

Bennet, W. Lance and Steven Livingston. 2020. *The Disinformation Age*. Cambridge: Cambridge University Press.

2018. "The Disinformation Order: Disruptive Communication and the Decline of Democratic Institutions." *European Journal of Communication* 33(2): 122–139.

Benoit, Kenneth, Kohei Watanabe, Haiyan Wang, Paul Nulty, Adam Obeng, Stefan Müller, and Akitaka Matsuo. 2018. "Quanteda: An R Package for the Quantitative Analysis of Textual Data." *Journal of Open Source Software* 3(30): 774. https://doi.org/10.21105/joss.00774.

Berelson, Bernard R., Paul F. Lazarsfeld, and William N. McPhee. 1954. *Voting*. Chicago: University of Chicago Press.

Bode, Leticia and Emily Vraga. 2015. "In Related News, That Was Wrong: The Correction of Misinformation through Related Stories Functionality in Social Media." *Journal of Communication* 65(4): 619–638.

Bolstad, Jorgen. 2012. "Thermostatic Voting: Presidential Elections in Light of New Policy Data." *PS: Political Science and Politics* 45(1): 44–50.

Bonazzo, John. March 13, 2018. "The State of Real News on Facebook Isn't as Bad as You Think." *The Observer*. Retrieved online October 2020 at https://observer.com/2018/03/facebook-most-shared-news-sites-fake-news/.

Boydstun, Amber. 2013. *Making the News*. Chicago: University of Chicago Press.

Brady, Henry and Paul M. Sniderman. 1985. "Attitude Attribution: A Group Basis for Political Reasoning." *American Political Science Review* 79(4): 1061–1078.

Branham, J. Alexander. 2018. "Partisan Feedback: Heterogeneity in Opinion Responsiveness." *Public Opinion Quarterly* 82(4): 625–640.

Breiman, Leo. 2001. "Random Forests." *Machine Learning* 45(1): 5–32.

Brody, Richard. 1991. *Assessing the President*. Stanford: Stanford University Press.

Buchanan, Ross. 2020. "Dynamic Responsiveness of Invisible Policy: The Importance of Outcomes." Unpublished manuscript.

Campbell, Andrea. 2012. "Policy Makes Mass Politics." *Annual Review of Political Science* 15: 333–351.

2003. *How Politics Makes Citizens*. Princeton: Princeton University Press.

Campbell, Angus, Philip E. Converse, Warren E. Miller, and Donald E. Stokes. 1960. *The American Voter*. New York: John Wiley.

Cappella, Joseph N. and Kathleen H. Jamieson. 1997. *Spiral of Cynicism: The Press and Public Good*. New York: Oxford University Press.

Card, Dallas, Amber E. Boydstun, Justin H. Gross, Philip Resnik, and Noah A. Smith. 2015. "The Media Frames Corpus: Annotations of Frames across Issues." Proceedings of the 53rd Annual Meeting of the Association for Computational Linguistics and the 7th International Joint Conference on Natural Language Processing (Short Papers), 438–444, Beijing, China, July 26–31, 2015.

Carmines, Edward G. and James A. Stimson. 1980. "The Two Faces of Issue Voting." *The American Political Science Review* 74(1): 78–91.

Carpenter, Daniel. 2002. "Groups, the Media, Waiting Costs, and FDA Drug Approval." *American Journal of Political Science* 46: 490–505.

Chadwick, Andrew. 2017. *The Hybrid Media System: Politics and Power*. 2nd ed. Oxford University Press.

Chinn, Sedona, Sol Hart, and Stuart Soroka. 2020. "Politicization and Polarization in Climate Change News Content, 1985–2017." *Science Communication* 42(1): 12–129.

Chomsky, Noam and Edward Edwards. 1988. *Manufacturing Consent*. New York: Pantheon.

Conover, Pamela. 1984. "The Influence of Group Identification on Political Perceptions and Evaluations." *Journal of Politics* 46(3): 760–785.

Converse, Philip E. 1964. "The Nature of Belief Systems in Mass Publics." In David Apter (ed.), *Ideology and Discontent*. New York: Free Press.

Cuzan, Alfred. 2015. "Five Laws of Politics." *PS: Political Science and Politics* 48: 415–419.

De Boef, Suzanna and Luke Keele. 2008. "Taking Time Seriously." *American Journal of Political Science* 52(1): 184–200.

De Boef, Suzanna and Paul Kellstedt. 2004. "The Political (and Economic) Origins of Consumer Confidence." *American Journal of Political Science* 48(4): 633–649.

Del Vicario, Michela, Alessandro Bessi, Fabiana Zollo, Fabio Petroni, Antonio Scala, Guido Caldarelli, H. Eugene Stanley, and Walter Quattrociocchi. 2016. "The

Spreading of Misinformation Online." *Proceedings of the National Academy of Sciences* 124(3): 554–559.

De Vreese, Claes and Peter Neijens. 2016. "Measuring Media Exposure in a Changing Communications Environment." *Communication Methods and Measures* 10(2–3): 69–80.

Delli Carpini, Michael. 2005. "An Overview of the State of Citizens' Knowledge about Politics." In M. S. McKinney, L. L. Kaid, D. G. Bystrom, and D. B. Carlin (eds.), *Communicating Politics: Engaging the Public in Democratic Life*. New York: Peter Lang.

Delli Carpini, Michael and Scott Keeter. 1996. *What American Know about Politics and Why It Matters*. New Haven: Yale University Press.

Deutsch, K. W. 1963. *The Nerves of Government: Models of Political Communication and Control*. New York: Free Press.

Dixon, Travis L., Cristina L. Azocar, and Michael Casas. 2003. "The Portrayal of Race and Crime on Television Network News." *Journal of Broadcasting & Electronic Media* 47(4): 498–523.

Downs, Anthony. 1957. "An Economic Theory of Political Action in a Democracy." *Journal of Political Economy* 65(2): 135–150.

Druckman, James N. 2005a. "Media Matter: How Newspapers and Television News Cover Campaigns and Influence Voters." *Political Communication* 22(4): 463–481.

2005b. "Does Political Information Matter?" *Political Communication* 22(4): 515–519.

Druckman, James N. and Toby Bolsen. 2011. "Framing, Motivated Reasoning, and Opinion about Emergent Technologies." *Journal of Communication* 61(4): 659–688.

Druckman, James N., Erik Peterson, and Rune Slothuus. 2013. "How Elite Partisan Polarization Affects Public Opinion Formation." *American Political Science Review* 107(1): 57–79.

Dun, Lindsay. 2020. "The Twitter Policy Signal: Comparing Twitter and Mainstream Media Coverage of Defense Spending." Unpublished manuscript.

Dun, Lindsay, Stuart Soroka, and Christopher Wlezien. 2021. "Dictionaries, Supervised Learning, and Media Coverage of Public Policy." *Political Communication* 38(1–2): 140–158.

Dunaway, Johanna. 2011. "Institutional Influences on the Quality of Campaign News Coverage." *Journalism Studies* 12(1): 27–44.

Durr, Robert H. 1993. "What Moves Policy Sentiment?" *American Political Science Review* 87: 158–170.

Easton, David. 1965. *A Framework for Political Analysis*. Englewood Cliffs: Prentice-Hall.

1953. *The Political System: An Inquiry into the State of Political Science*. New York: Alfred A. Knopf.

Eichenberg, Richard and Richard Stoll. 2003. "Representing Defence: Democratic Control of the Defence Budget in the United States and Western Europe." *Journal of Conflict Resolution* 47: 399–423.

Ellis, Christopher and Christopher Faricy. 2011. "Social Policy and Public Opinion: How the Ideological Direction of Spending Influences Public Mood." *The Journal of Politics* 73(4): 1095–1110.

Enelow, James and Melvin Hinich. 1984. *The Spatial Theory of Voting: An Introduction*. Cambridge: Cambridge University Press.

Enns, Peter K. 2016. *Incarceration Nation*. Cambridge University Press.

Enns, Peter K. and Paul M. Kellstedt. 2008. "Policy Mood and Political Sophistication: Why Everybody Moves Mood." *British Journal of Political Science* 38(3): 433–454.

Enns, Peter K., Carolina Moehlecke, and Christopher Wlezien. forthcoming. "Detecting True Relationships in Time Series Data with Different Orders of Integration." *Political Science Research and Methods*.

Enns, Peter K. and Christopher Wlezien. 2017. "Understanding Equation Balance in Time Series Regression." *The Political Methodologist* 24(2): 2–12.

Enns, Peter K. and Christopher Wlezien. 2011. *Who Gets Represented?* New York: Russell Sage Foundation.

Entman, Robert M. 2003. "Cascading Activation: Contesting the White House's Frame after 9/11." *Political Communication* 20(4): 415–432.

   1993. "Framing: Toward the Clarification of a Fractured Paradigm." *Journal of Communication* 43(4): 51–58.

Erikson, Robert S., Michael B. MacKuen, and James A. Stimson. 2002. *The Macro Polity*. Cambridge: Cambridge University Press.

Evans, Geoffrey and Robert Andersen. 2006. "The Political Conditioning of Economic Perceptions." *Journal of Politics* 68(1): 194–207.

Eveland Jr, W. P. 2002. "News Information Processing as Mediator of the Relationship between Motivations and Political Knowledge." *Journalism & Mass Communication Quarterly* 79(1): 26–40.

   2001. "The Cognitive Mediation Model of Learning from the News: Evidence from Nonelection, Off-Year Election, and Presidential Election Contexts." *Communication Research* 28(5): 571–601.

Fenno, Richard. 1991. *The Emergence of a Senate Leader: Pete Domenici and the Reagan Budget*. Washington, DC: Congressional Quarterly Press.

Fiorina, Morris. 1981. *Retrospective Voting in American Elections*. New Haven: Yale University Press.

Flaxman, Seth, Sharad Goel, and Justin M. Rao. 2016. "Filter Bubbles, Echo Chambers, and Online News Consumption." *Public Opinion Quarterly* 80: 298–320.

Fleming, Nic. 2020. "Fighting Coronavirus Misinformation." *Nature* 583(7814): 155–156.

Flynn, D. J., Brendan Nyhan, and Jason Reifler. 2017. "The Nature and Origins of Misperceptions: Understanding False and Unsupported Beliefs about Politics." *Political Psychology* 38(S1): 127–150.

Fording, Richard and Dana J. Patton. 2019. "Medicaid Expansion and the Political Fate of the Governors Who Support It." *Policy Studies Journal* 47(2): 274–299.

Fowler, Erika Franklin, Laura M. Baum, Colleen L. Barry, Jeff Niederdeppe, and Sarah Gollust. 2017. "Media Messages and Perceptions of the Affordable Care Act During the Early Phase of Implementation." *Journal of Health Politics, Policy and Law* 42(1): 167–195.

Fowler, Anthony and Andrew Hall. 2018. "Do Shark Attacks Influence Presidential Elections? Reassessing a Prominent Finding on Voter Competence." *Journal of Politics* 80(4): 1423–1437.

Friedman, Sharon H., Sharon Dunwoody, and Carol L. Rogers, eds. 1999. *Communicating Uncertainty: Media Coverage of New and Controversial Science*. New York: Routledge.

Galeotti, Marzio, Silvia Salini, and Elena Verdolini. 2020. "Measuring Environmental Policy Stringency: Approaches, Validity, and Impact on Environmental Innovation and Energy Efficiency." *Energy Policy* 136: 111052.

Garrett, R. Kelly. 2009. "Echo Chambers Online? Political Motivated Selective Exposure among Internet News Users." *Journal of Computer-Mediated Communication* 14(2): 265–285.

Garrett, R. Kelly, Brian E. Weeks, and Rachel L. Neo. 2016. "Driving a Wedge between Evidence and Beliefs: How Online Ideological News Exposure Promotes Political Mispercetions." *Journal of Computer-Mediated Communication* 21(5): 331–348.

Gilens, Martin. 1999. *Why Americans Hate Welfare: Race, Media, and the Politics of Antipoverty Policy*. Chicago: University of Chicago Press. http://books.google.ca/books?id=QORW1i6XDKgC.

Goidel, Kirby and Ronald Langley. 1995. "Media Coverage of the Economy and Aggregate Economic Evaluations." *Political Research Quarterly* 48(1): 313–328.

Gollust, Sarah E., Erika Franklin Fowler, and Jeff Niederdeppe. 2019. "Television News Coverage of Public Health Issues and Implications for Public Health Policy and Practice." *Annual Review of Public Health* 40: 167–185.

Grimmer, Justin and Brandon M. Stewart. 2013. "Text as Data: The Promise and Pitfalls of Automatic Content Analysis for Political Texts." *Political Analysis* 21(3): 267–297.

Gurin, Patricia, Arthur H. Miller, and Gerald Gurin. 1980. "Stratum Identification and Consciousness." *Social Psychology Quarterly* 43(1): 30–47.

Hänggli, R. and H. Kriesi. 2010. "Political Framing Strategies and Their Impact on Media Framing in a Swiss Direct-Democratic Campaign." *Political Communication* 27(2): 141–157.

Hakhverdian, A. 2012. "The Causal Flow between Public Opinion and Policy: Government Responsiveness, Leadership, or Counter Movement?" *West European Politics* 35(6): 1386–1406.

Hansen, John Mark. 1998. "Individuals, Institutions, and Public Preferences over Public Finance." *American Political Science Review* 92(3): 513–531.

Hart, Sol, Sedona Chinn, and Stuart Soroka. 2020. "Politicization and Polarization in COVID-19 News Coverage." *Science Communication* 42(5): 679–697.

Hiaeshutter-Rice, Dan. N.d. Political Platforms: Technology, User Affordances and Campaign Communications. Unpublished manuscript.

Hiaeshutter-Rice, Dan, Stuart Soroka, and Christopher Wlezien. 2021. "Freedom of the Press and Public Responsiveness." *Perspectives on Politics* 19(2): 479–491.

Hiaeshutter-Rice, Dan and Brian Weeks. N.d. "The Nature of Facebook News." Unpublished manuscript.

Hicks, Raymond and Dustin Tingley. 2012. "Causal Mediation Analysis." *Stata Journal* 11(4): 605–619.

Hopkins, Daniel J., Eunji Kim, and Soojong Kim. 2017. "Does Newspaper Coverage Influence or Reflect Public Perceptions of the Economy?" *Research and Politics* (October–December): 1–17.

Huddy, Leonie. 2018. "The Group Foundations of Democratic Political Behavior." *Critical Review* 30: 71–86.

Hyman, Herbert and Eleanor Singer. 1968. *Reading in Reference Group Theory and Research*. New York: Free Press.

Iversen, Torben. 1994. "The Logics of Electoral Politics: Spatial, Directional, and Mobilizational Effects." *American Political Science Review* 76: 753–766.

Iyengar, Shanto. 1991. *Is Anyone Responsible? How Television Frames Political Issues*. Chicago: University of Chicago Press.

Jacobs, Alan and R. Kent Weaver. 2014. "When Policies undo Themselves: Self-Undermining Feedback as a Source of Policy Change." *Governance* 28(4): 441–457.

Jennings, Will. 2009. "The Public Thermostat, Political Responsiveness and Error Correction: Border Control and Asylum in Britain, 1994–2007." *British Journal of Political Science* 39: 847–870.

Jennings, Will and Christopher Wlezien. 2015. "Preferences, Problems, and Representation." *Political Science Research and Methods* 3(3): 659–681.

  2011. "Distinguishing between Important Problems and Issues?" *Public Opinion Quarterly* 75(3): 545–555.

Jerit, Jennifer, Jason Barabas, and Toby Bolsen. 2006. "Citizens, Knowledge, and the Information Environment." *American Journal of Political Science* 50(2): 266–282.

Jessee, Stephen. 2012. *Ideology and Spatial Voting in American Elections*. Cambridge: Cambridge University Press.

Jones, Bryan D. 2001. *Politics and the Architecture of Choice*. Chicago: University of Chicago Press.

Jurka, Timothy P., Loren Collingwood, Amber Boydstun, Emiliano Grossman, and Wouter van Atteveldt. 2012. RTextTools: Automatic Text Classification via Supervised Learning. http://cran.r-project.org/web/packages/RTextTools/index.html.

Kahneman, Daniel. 2003. "A Perspective on Judgment and Choice: Mapping Bounded Rationality." *American Psychologist* 58(9): 697–720.

Kelly, Nathan and Peter Enns. 2011. "Inequality and the Dynamics of Public Opinion: The Self-Reinforcing Link between Economic Inequality and Mass Preferences." *American Journal of Political Science* 54(4): 855–870.

Koch, Jeffrey. 1993. "Is Group Membership a Prerequisite for Group Identification?" *Political Behavior* 15(1): 49–60.

Krippendorff, Klaus. 2004. *Content Analysis: An Introduction*. Thousand Oaks: Sage.

Lacy, Stephen, Brendan R. Watson, Daniel Riffe, and Jennette Lovejoy. 2015. "Issues and Best Practices in Content Analysis." *Journalism & Mass Communication Quarterly* 92(4): 791–811.

Lamberson, P. J. and Stuart Soroka. 2018. "A Model of Attentiveness to Outlying News." *Journal of Communication* 68(5): 942–964.

Lau, Richard R. 1989. "Individual and Contextual Influences on Group Identification." *Social Psychology Quarterly* 52(September): 220–231.

Lawrence, Regina G. 2000. "Game-Framing the Issues: Tracking the Strategy Frame in Public Policy News." *Political Communication* 17(2): 93–114.

Lazer, David M. J., Matthew A. Baum, Yochai Benkler, Adam J. Berinsky, Kelly M. Greenhill, Filippo Menczer, Miriam J. Metzger, Brendan Nyhan, Gordon Pennycook, David Rothschild, Michael Schudson, Steven A. Sloman, Cass R. Sunstein, Emily A. Thorson, Duncan J. Watts, and Jonathan L. Zittrain. 2018. "The Science of Fake News." *Science* 6380 (359): 1094–1096.

Lee, Nam-Jin, Douglas M. McLeod, and Dhavan V. Shah. 2008. "Framing Policy Debates: Issue Dualism, Journalistic Frames, and Opinions on Controversial Policy Issues." *Communication Research* 35(5): 695–718.

Lenz, Gabriel. 2012. *Follow the Leader*. Chicago: University of Chicago Press.

Levendusky, Matthew. 2013. *How Partisan Media Polarize America*. Chicago: University of Chicago Press.

Lichter, S. Robert and Richard Noyes. 1995. *Good Intentions Make Bad News*. Lanham: Rowman and Littlefield.

Lippmann, Walter. 1925. *The Phantom Public*. Piscataway: Transaction.
   1922. *Public Opinion*. New York: Harcourt, Brace.

Lovett, Matt, Saleh Bajaba, Myra Lovett, and Marcia J. Simmering. 2018. "Data Quality from Crowdsourced Surveys: A Mixed Method Inquiry into Perceptions of Amazon's Mechanical Turk Masters." *Applied Psychology* 67(2): 339–366.

Lupia, Arthur. 1994. "Shortcuts Versus Encyclopedias: Information and Voting Behavior in California Insurance Reform Elections." *The American Political Science Review* 88(1): 63–76.

Lupia, Arthur and Mathew D. McCubbins. 1998. *The Democratic Dilemma: Can Citizens Learn What They Need to Know?* Cambridge: Cambridge University Press.

Luskin, Robert. 1990. "Explaining Political Sophistication." *Political Behavior* 12(4): 331–361.

MacDonald, Stuart Elaine, Ola Listhaug, and George Rabinowitz. 1991. "Issues and Support in Multiparty Systems." *American Political Science Review* 85: 1107–1131.

Mackie, Gerry. 2003. *Democracy Defended*. Cambridge: Cambridge University Press.

Maier, Scott. 2010. "All the News Fit to Post? Comparing News Content on the Web to Newspapers, Television, and Radio." *Journalism and Mass Communication Quarterly* 87(3–4): 548–562.

Maioni, Antonia. 2009. "Health Care Reform in the 2008 US Presidential Election." *International Journal* 64(1): 135–144.

Mansbridge, Jane. 2003. "Rethinking Representation." *American Political Science Review* 97(4): 515–528.

McCombs, Maxwell W. and Donald L. Shaw. 1972. "The Agenda-Setting Function of Mass Media." *Public Opinion Quarterly* 36(2): 176–187.

Mettler, Suzanne. 2018. *The Government-Citizen Disconnect*. New York: Russell Sage.

    2005. *Soldiers to Citizens: The G.I. Bill and the Making of the Greatest Generation*. New York: Oxford University Press.

Mettler, Suzanne and Joe Soss. 2004. "The Consequences of Public Policy for Democratic Citizenship: Bridging Policy Studies and Mass Politics." *Perspectives on Politics* 2(1): 55–73.

Miller, Arthur, Christopher Wlezien, and Anne Hildreth. 1991. "A Reference Group Theory of Partisan Coalitions." *Journal of Politics* 53: 1134–1149.

Monroe, Alan D. 1998. "Public Opinion and Public Policy, 1980–1993." *The Public Opinion Quarterly* 62(1): 6–28.

Montgomery, Jacob M. and Santiago Olivella. 2018. "Tree-Based Models for Political Science Data." *American Journal of Political Science* 62(3): 729–744.

Morgan, Stephen L. and Minhyoung Kang. 2015. "A New Conservative Cold Front? Democrat and Republican Responsiveness to the Passage of the Affordable Care Act. *Sociological Science* 2: 502–526.

Motta, Matt, Dominik Stecula, and Christina Farhart. 2020. "How Right-Leaning Media Coverage of COVID-19 Facilitated the Spread of Misinformation in the Early Stages of the Pandemic in the U.S." *Canadian Journal of Political Science/Revue canadienne de science politique* 53(2): 335–342.

Mullinix, Kevin J. 2015. "Presidential Debates, Partisan Motivations and Political Interest." *Presidential Studies Quarterly* 45(2): 270–288.

Nannestad, P. and M. Paldam. 2002. "The Cost of Ruling: A Foundation Stone for Two Theories." In H. Dorussen and M. Taylor (eds.), *Economic Voting*. London: Routledge.

Naurin, Elin. 2011. *Election Promises, Party Behaviour, and Voter Perceptions*. New York: Springer.

Neuman, W. Russell, Marion R. Just, and Ann N. Crigler. 1992. *Common Knowledge: News and the Construction of Meaning*. Chicago: University of Chicago Press.

Neuner, Fabian, Stuart Soroka, and Christopher Wlezien. 2019. "Mass Media as a Source of Public Responsiveness to Policy." *International Journal of Press/Politics* 24(3): 269–292.

Nyhan, Brendan and Jason Reifler. 2010. "When Corrections Fail: The Persistence of Political Misperceptions." *Political Behavior* 32(2): 303–330.

Page, Benjamin I. and Robert Y. Shapiro. 1992. *The Rational Public: Fifty Years of Trends in Americans' Policy Preferences.* Chicago: University of Chicago Press.

Paldam, M. 1986. "The Distribution of Election Results and Two Explanations for the Cost of Ruling." *European Journal of Political Economy* 2: 5–24.

Pasek, Josh, Gaurav Sood, and Jon Krosnick. 2015. "Misinformed about the Affordable Care Act? Leveraging Certainty to Assess the Prevalence of Misperceptions." *Journal of Communication* 65(4): 660–673.

Patterson, Thomas. 1994. *Out of Order.* New York: Vintage.

Pew Research Center. 2019a. Key Findings about the Online News Landscape in America. Retrieved online October 2020 at www.pewresearch.org/fact-tank /2019/09/11/key-findings-about-the-online-news-landscape-in-america/.

 2019b. Social Media Fact Sheet. Retrieved online October 2020 at www .pewresearch.org/internet/fact-sheet/social-media/.

 2019c. Newspaper Fact Sheet. Retrieved online January 2021 at www .journalism.org/fact-sheet/newspapers/.

 2018a. Internet, Social Media Use and Device Ownership in U.S. Have Plateaued after Years of Growth. Retrieved online October 2020 at www .pewresearch.org/fact-tank/2018/09/28/internet-social-media-use-and-device-ownership-in-u-s-have-plateaued-after-years-of-growth/.

 2018b. Americans Still Prefer Watching to Reading the News – and Mostly Still Through Television. Retrieved online October 2020 at www.journalism.org/ 2018/12/03/americans-still-prefer-watching-to-reading-the-news-and-mostly-still-through-television/.

 2014. How Social Media Is Reshaping News. Retrieved online October 2020 at www.pewresearch.org/fact-tank/2014/09/24/how-social-media-is-reshaping -news/.

 May 2011. The Top 25. Retrieved online October 2020 at www.journalism.org /2011/05/09/top-25/.

Popkin, Samuel. 1994. *The Reasoning Voter: Communication and Persuasion in Presidential Campaigns.* Chicago: University of Chicago Press.

Popkin, Samuel and Michael Dimock. 1999. "Political Knowledge and Citizen Competence." In Stephen Elkin and Karol Salton (eds.), *Citizen Competence and Democratic Institutions.* University Park: Pennsylvania State University.

Prior, Markus. 2009. "The Immensely Inflated News Audience: Assessing Bias in Self-Reported News Exposure." *Public Opinion Quarterly* 73(1): 130–143.

 2007. *Post-Broadcast Democracy.* Cambridge: Cambridge University Press.

Rabinowitz, George and Stuart Elaine MacDonald. 1989. "A Directional Theory of Issue Voting." *American Political Science Review* 83(1): 93–121.

Ranney, Austin. 1951. "Toward a More Responsible Two-Party System: A Commentary." *American Political Science Review* 45(2): 488–499.

Rasinski, Kenneth. 1989. "The Effect of Question Wording on Public Support for Government Spending." *Public Opinion Quarterly* 58(3): 388–394.

Riker, William. 1982. *Liberalism against Populism.* Long Grove: Waveland Press.

Sabato, Larry. 1991. *Feeding Frenzy.* New York: Free Press.

Sacco, Vincent. 1995. "Media Constructions of Crime." *Annals of the American Academy of Political and Social Science* 539: 141–154.

Sanders, David, David Marsh, and Hugh Ward. 1993. "The Electoral Impact of Press Coverage of the British Economy, 1979–1987." *British Journal of Political Science* 23(1): 175–210.

Schattschneider, Elmer Eric. 1960. *Party Government*. Livingston, NJ: Transaction.

Scheufele, Dietram and Nicole Krause. 2019. "Science Audiences, Misinformation, and Fake News." *Proceedings of the National Academy of Sciences* 116(16): 7662–7669.

Schneider, Anne and Helen Ingram. 1993. "Social Construction of Target Populations: Implications for Politics and Policy." *American Political Science Review* 87(2): 334–347.

Schudson, Michael. 2003. *The Sociology of News*. New York: Norton.

Schumpeter, Joseph A. 1954. *Capitalism, Socialism, and Democracy*. London: Allen & Unwin.

Shearer, Erica. 2018. "Social Media Outpaces Newspapers in the US as a News Source." *Pew Research Center*. www.pewresearch.org/fact-tank/2018/12/1 0/social-media-outpaces-print-newspapers-in-the-u-s-as-a-news-source/.

Shoemaker, Pamela J. and Akiba A. Cohen. 2006. *News Around the World: Content, Practitioners and the Public*. New York: Routledge.

Shoemaker, Pamela J., Lucig H. Danielian, and Nancy Brendlinger. 1991. "Deviant Acts, Risky Business and U.S. Interests: The Newsworthiness of World Events." *Journalism & Mass Communication Quarterly* 68(4): 781–795.

Siroky, David S. 2009. "Navigating Random Forests and Related Advances in Algorithmic Modeling." *Statistics Surveys* 3: 147–163.

Slothuus, Rene and Claes de Vreese. 2009. "Political Parties, Motivated Reasoning, and Issue Framing Effects." *Journal of Politics* 72(3): 630–645.

Soroka, Stuart. 2014. *Negativity in Democratic Politics: Cause and Consequences*. Cambridge: Cambridge University Press.

2012. "The Gatekeeping Function: Distributions of Information in Media and the Real World." *Journal of Politics* 74(2): 514–528.

2002. "Issue Attributes and Agenda Setting by Media, the Public and Policymakers in Canada." *International Journal of Public Opinion Research* 14(3): 264–285.

Soroka, Stuart, Dominic Stecula, and Christopher Wlezien. 2015. "It's (Change in) the (Future) Economy, Stupid: Economic Indicators, the Media, and Public Opinion." *American Journal of Political Science* 59(2): 457–474.

Soroka, Stuart N. and Christopher Wlezien. 2019. "Tracking the Coverage of Public Policy in Mass Media." *Policy Studies Journal* 47(1): 471–491.

2010. *Degrees of Democracy: Politics, Public Opinion and Policy*. Cambridge: Cambridge University Press.

2008. "On the Limits to Inequality in Representation." *PS: Political Science and Politics* 41(2): 319–327.

2005. "Opinion-Policy Dynamics: Public Preferences and Public Expenditure in the United Kingdom." *British Journal of Political Science* 35: 665–589.

2004. "Opinion Representation and Policy Representation: Canada in Comparative Perspective." *Canadian Journal of Political Science* 37(3): 531–559.

Soss, Joe and Sanford Schram. 2007. "A Public Transformed? Welfare Reform as Policy Feedback." *American Political Science Review* 101: 111–127.

Southwell, Brian and Emily Thorson. 2015. "The Prevalence, Consequence, and Remedy of Misinformation in Mass Media Systems." *Journal of Communication* 65(4): 589–595.

Stecula, Dominik A. and Mark Pickup. 2021. "How Populism and Conservative Media Fuel Conspiracy Beliefs about COVID-19 and What It Means for COVID-19 Behaviors." *Research & Politics* 8(1): 1–9.

Stevenson, Randolph. 2001. "The Economy and Policy Mood: A Fundamental Dynamic of Democratic Politics?" *American Journal of Political Science* 45 (3): 620–633.

Stimson, James A., Michael B. Mackuen, and Robert S. Erikson. 1995. "Dynamic Representation." *The American Political Science Review* 89(3): 543–565.

Stocking, S. Holly and Lisa W. Holstein. 2009. "Manufacturing Doubt: Journalists' Roles and the Construction of Ignorance in a Scientific Controversy." *Public Understanding of Science* 18(1): 23–42.

Stokes, Donald E. 1963. "Spatial Models of Party Competition." *American Political Science Review* 57: 368–377.

Stokes, Donald E. and Gudmund R. Iverson. 1966. "On the Existence of Forces Restoring Party Competition." In Angus Campbell et al. (eds.), *Elections and the Political Order*. New York: Wiley.

Stroud, Natalie. 2011. *Niche News: The Politics of News Choice*. Oxford: Oxford University Press.

    2010. "Polarization and Partisan Selective Exposure." *Journal of Communication* 60(3): 556–576.

    2008. "Media Use and Political Predispositions: Revisiting the Concept of Selective Exposure." *Political Behavior* 30(3): 341–366.

Taber, Charles and Everett Young. 2013. "Political Information Processing." In Leonie Huddy, David O. Sears, and Jack S. Levy (eds.), *Oxford Handbook of Political Psychology*, 2nd ed. Oxford: Oxford University Press.

Tandoc, Edson C., Zheng Wei Lim, and Richard Ling. 2018. "Defining 'Fake News': A Typology of Scholarly Definitions." *Digital Journalism* 6(2): 137–153.

Thorson, Emily. 2016. "Belief Echoes: The Persistent Effects of Corrected Misinformation." *Political Communication* 33(3): 460–480.

Trussler, Marc. 2020. "Get Information or Get in Formation: The Effects of High Information Environments on Legislative Elections." British Journal of Political Science, forthcoming.

Ura, Joseph Daniel and Christopher R. Ellis. 2012. "Partisan Moods: Polarization and the Dynamics of Mass Party Preferences." *The Journal of Politics* 74(1): 277–291.

Vliegenthart, Rens and Hajo Boomgarden. 2007. "Real-World Indicators and the Coverage of Immigration and the Integration of Minorities in Dutch Newspapers." *European Journal of Communication* 22(3): 293–314.

Vliegenthart, R. and S. Walgrave. 2008. "The Contingency of Intermedia Agenda Setting: A Longitudinal Study in Belgium." *Journalism & Mass Communication Quarterly* 85(4): 860–877.

de Vreese, Claes H. 2005. "News Framing: Theory and Typology." *Information Design Journal & Document Design* 13(1): 51–62.

Walgrave, Stefaan. 2008. "Again, the Almighty Mass Media? The Media's Political Agenda-Setting Power According to Politicians and Journalists in Belgium." *Political Communication* 25(4): 445–459.

2006. "The Contingency of the Mass Media's Political Agenda Setting Power: Toward a Preliminary Theory." *Journal of Communication* 56(1): 88–109.

Walgrave, Stefaan, Julie Sevenans, Kirsten Van Camp, and Peter Loewen. 2018. "What Draws Politicians' Attention? An Experimental Study of Issue Framing and its Effect on Individual Political Elites." *Political Behavior* 40 (3): 547–569.

Walgrave, S. and P. Van Aelst. 2016. "Political Agenda Setting and the Mass Media." In *Oxford Research Encyclopedia, Politics*. Oxford: Oxford University Press.

Weeks, Brian. 2015. "Emotions, Partisanship, and Misperceptions: How Anger and Anxiety Moderate the Effect of Partisan Bias on Susceptibility to Political Information." *Journal of Communication* 65(4): 699–719.

Weissberg, Robert. 1978. "Collective vs. Dyadic Representation in Congress." *American Political Science Review* 72: 535–547.

Williams, Christopher and Martin Schoonvelde. 2018. "It Takes Three: How Mass Media Coverage Conditions Public Responsiveness to Policy Outputs in the United States." *Social Science Quarterly* 99(5): 1627–1636.

Wlezien, Christopher. 2017a. "Policy (Mis) Representation and the Cost of Ruling." *Comparative Political Studies* 50(6): 711–738.

2017b. "Public Opinion and Policy Representation: On Conceptualization, Measurement, and Interpretation." *Policy Studies Journal* 45(4): 561–582.

2005. "On the Salience of Political Issues: The 'Problem' with Most Important Problem." *Electoral Studies* 24(4): 555–579.

2004. "Patterns of Representation: Dynamics of Public Preferences and Policy." *Journal of Politics* 66: 1–24.

1996. "Dynamics of Representation: The Case of US Spending on Defense." *British Journal of Political Science* 26: 81–103.

1995. "The Public as Thermostat: Dynamics of Preferences for Spending." *American Journal of Political Science* 39: 981–1000.

1993. "The Political Economy of Supplemental Appropriations." *Legislative Studies Quarterly* 18(1): 51–76.

Wlezien, Christopher, Mark Franklin, and Daniel Twiggs. 1997. "Economic Perceptions and Vote Choice: Disentangling the Endogeneity." *Political Behavior* 19(1): 7–17.

Wlezien, Christopher and Arthur Miller. 1997. "Social Groups and Political Judgments." *Social Science Quarterly* 78(3): 625–640.

Wlezien, Christopher and Stuart Soroka. 2021. "Trends in Public Support for Welfare Spending: How the Economy Matters." *British Journal of Political Science* 51(1): 163–180.

2019. "Mass Media and Electoral Preferences during the 2017 US Presidential Race." *Political Behavior* 41(4): 945–970.

2012. "Political Institutions and the Opinion-Policy Link." *West European Politics* 35(6): 1407–1432.

2011. "Federalism and Public Responsiveness to Policy." *Publius* 41(1): 31–52.

2003. "Measures and Models of Budgetary Policy." *Policy Studies Journal* 31 (2): 273–286.

Wlezien, Christopher, Stuart Soroka, and Dominik Stecula. 2017. "A Cross-National Analysis of the Causes and Consequences of Economic News." *Social Science Quarterly* 98(3): 1010–1025.

Young, Lori and Stuart Soroka. 2012. "Affective News: The Automated Coding of Sentiment in Political Texts." *Political Communication* 29(2): 205–231.

Zaller, John. 2003. "A New Standard of News Quality: Burglar Alarms for the Monitorial Citizen." *Political Communication* 20: 109–130.

1992. *The Nature and Origins of Mass Opinion*. Cambridge: Cambridge University Press.

Index

Other Books in the Series (*continued from page iii*)

Adam F. Simon, *The Winning Message: Candidate Behavior, Campaign Discourse*

Daniela Stockmann, *Media Commercialization and Authoritarian Rule in China*

Bruce A. Williams and Michael X. Delli Carpini, *After Broadcast News: Media Regimes, Democracy, and the New Information Environment*

Gadi Wolfsfeld, *Media and the Path to Peace*

CPSIA information can be obtained
at www.ICGtesting.com
Printed in the USA
LVHW040852260722
724431LV00004B/276